Center for Basque Studies
Current Research Series, No. 6

Basque Cooperativism

Edited by

Baleren Bakaikoa and Eneka Albizu

Current Research Series No. 6

Center for Basque Studies
University of Nevada, Reno

Published in conjunction with the University of the Basque Country
UPV/EHU

Current Research Series No. 6
Center for Basque Studies
University of Nevada, Reno
Reno, Nevada 89557
http://basque.unr.edu

Library of Congress Cataloging-in-Publication Data

Basque cooperativism / edited by Baleren Bakaikoa and Eneka Albizu.
    p. cm. -- (Current research series no. 6)
"Published in conjunction with the University of the Basque Country,
UPV/EHU"
Summary: "Collection of essays on Basque Cooperativism"--Provided by
publisher.
ISBN 978-1-935709-13-8 (paper back)
1. Cooperative societies--France--Pays Basque 2. Cooperative societies-
-Spain--Pais Vasco. 3. Mondrag?n Corporaci?n Cooperativa--History. 4.
Economics--Sociological aspects. I. Bakaikoa, Baleren. II. Albizu, Eneka.
HD3036.A3P3B27 2011
334.0946'6--dc23
                              2011042133

Contents

Introduction

Baleren Bakaikoa Azurmendi and Eneka Albizu

Translated by Jesús Sepúlveda

Cooperative companies form part of what in Europe is called social economy (a third economic sector beyond the private and public spheres that embraces community, voluntary, and not-for-profit activities). It is the most noticeable among different legal structures that constitute this important sector of the economy. Commercial companies distribute their surpluses in relation to the capital they contribute, while cooperatives do so according to the cooperative activity carried out by their members; in short, in a cooperative framework capital is subordinate to work.

Originally, cooperatives tried to be an alternative to capitalist companies where workers were exploited by capital. In order to overcome this situation the first consumer, credit, small artisanal, and even productive cooperatives emerged. Consequently, the International Co-operative Alliance (ICA) was founded in 1895 as a guide for global cooperative movements, establishing the values and principles by which global cooperatives should be ruled.

The cooperative movement has had to respond to different problems. In the Basque Country during the crisis of the 1980s, cooperatives came to replace capitalist companies; workers took control of businesses and adapted them to the cooperative system, and unemployed people organized their own cooperative companies.

In the 1990s and the 2000s cooperatives became more prominent. Certain countries with well-developed welfare states began to embrace neoliberal doctrines and privatize numerous public services. Faced with these changes, the social economy began to replace many of the services previously provided by the public sector.

Auzo-lan (literally, "neighborhood work") or work in cooperation has been a traditional feature of Basque society. However, modern cooperative companies emerged in a capitalist context, with consumer and housing cooperatives the first such companies in the Basque Country. Later, Alfa (based on workers' self-management) was founded in Eibar in 1920. Such development was paralyzed, however, by a Franco regime mistrustful of such companies.

Nonetheless, the cooperative spirit remained important in Basque society, and in 1956 Fagor was created, eventually becoming the Mondragon cooperative group. This is the largest corporate group in the Basque Country, the seventh largest in Spain, and a global reference point. Mondragon, along with other companies in the social economy (cooperative and employee-owned companies), has become a driving force of development, welfare, innovation, and the creation of stable employment in the Basque Country.

The *ikastola* (a school where instruction is in Euskara, the Basque language) movement began in the 1960s. The purpose of this movement was to recover the Basque language, as well as to establish systems of advanced education. *Ikastolas* gradually became an alternative to public and religious schools. Currently, most *ikastolas* have become first-grade education cooperatives, and they are organized into higher-level cooperative systems (federations) with greater all-round participation in the decision-making process by all agents involved.

When there was already a clear crisis of the welfare state, in the Basque Country cooperatives and other elements of the social economy (employee-owned companies, associations, and foundations) were established to satisfy the demand for services not assumed by the public sector or by the market—such as senior citizen care, nursing homes for the elderly, the integration into society of people with disabilities, addressing issues of people suffering social exclusion, preschool services, and so on.

Cooperatives, moreover, in accordance with ICA principles and values, are *socially responsible* companies. Capitalist companies try to increase their market share by "selling" the idea that they are socially responsible. But in most cases this is just a case of marketing an image, in contrast to cooperatives that do not need to employ any such tactic, because they must comply with requirements regarding respect for the environment, the nonexploitation of children, gender equality, and so on.

Besides the cooperatives mentioned above, there are also credit, agricultural, housing, consumer, and transportation cooperatives in the Basque Country. In sum, the Comunidad Autónoma del País Vasco/ Euskal Autonomia Erkidegoa (CAPV/EAE, Autonomous Community of the Basque Country) had 1,686 cooperatives in 2009 (data taken from Eustat, Basque Statistical Institute), which created 46,569 jobs (2008), representing about 5.2 percent of the employment and 5 percent of the added value of the CAPV/EAE.

This emblematic collective in the economic and social life of the Basque Country is currently facing certain changes and challenges that form the analytical basis of this book. With this in mind, this book is divided into three parts.

The first part aims at analyzing the origin of the cooperative movement in the Basque Country, its values and culture, as well as some of the specific issues resulting from the Basque regulatory framework. The questions that we try to answer in this first section are: How did the cooperative movement in the Basque Country emerge? What conditions existed in the Basque Country to encourage the emergence of this phenomenon? What are the characteristics of these organizations?

This section is composed of four chapters. Chapter 1, by Fernando Molina, and entitled "The Spirituality of Economics: Historical Roots of Mondragon, 1940–1974," presents a historic explanation of the Christian origins of the Mondragon cooperative. It also underlines the importance of social change in the 1960s and the transformation of values fostered by the promoters of the movement of corporate and social development in the 1960s and 1970s.

Chapter 2 by Javier Cerrato Allende, addresses the subject of "Culture and Social Representations of Work among Basques: Implications for Organizational Commitment and Cooperative Attitudes." He proposes and applies a theoretical integrative model to expand the study of cultural, social, and psychological factors that influence cooperative thinking and an organizational commitment, together with other factors of an individual and organizational nature.

Chapter 3 is a study of "Developing Intercooperation in the Social Economy: An Analysis of Grant Recipients in the Basque Country," by Jon Morandeira Arca, Baleren Bakaikoa Azurmendi, and Victoria de

Elizagarate Gutierrez. It discusses the need to provide administrations with a data information and analysis system as a means of support for the decision-making process on elaborating, creating, and carrying out grants for commercial intercooperation in the Basque social economy.

The first section ends with the chapter "Accounting Reform: The Case of Workers' Self-Managed Cooperatives," by Miguel Ángel Zubiaurre Artola. It discusses the characteristics of the cooperative model, which have not always been properly understood and interpreted by accounting standards that are designed for capitalist corporations. The chapter focuses on those aspects of accounting where cooperative societies especially differ from their corporate counterparts, emphasizing that such differences must be known and understood in order to properly interpret the fiscal status.

The second part of the book is devoted to analyzing innovation in and the management system of cooperatives. This section focuses on a factor widely acknowledged as a source of competitive advantage (innovation), as well as other dimensions that have enabled Basque cooperatives to become a model for the global cooperative movement. In this vein, we try to answer questions such as: Are cooperatives innovative? Have they generated differential mechanisms for the implementation of innovations? Are their strategies related to the development of innovative activities? Have cooperatives been managed differently than their capitalist counterparts? What is their position as regards new management tools? Do they use specific management systems in relation to innovation? What are the differentiating factors in their success?

The second section comprises three chapters. The first (chapter 5), by Sara Fernández de Bobadilla Güemez and Eva Velasco Balmaseda, is entitled "Is Innovation Better Managed by Corporations than Social Economy Companies? A Comparative Study of Innovative Basque Companies." This chapter analyzes the key elements of innovation and presents a comparative study on innovation management in a group of innovative companies in the Basque Country, half of which are cooperatives. Chapter 6, "Innovation in the Basque Country: An Examination of the Cooperative Situation" by Antón Borja Alvarez, also addresses innovation. This chapter presents some RDI (research, development, and innovation) indicators for the different territories making up the Basque Country, before going on to examine the case of Mondragon in more detail.

This section ends with the work of Imanol Basterretxea Markaida on "Sources of Competitive Advantage in the Mondragon Cooperative Group." This chapter explores the competitive advantages of Mondragon in regard to its more traditional capitalist competitors. It also summarizes and reviews the main reasons that various senior executives of the Mondragon corporation and researchers outside the cooperative group have given to explain its success. Most of these reasons are linked to the human resources policy of cooperatives and the structure of the corporation.

Finally, the third section focuses on the current financial crisis and globalization. The questions that this section seeks to answer are: How are the cooperatives facing up to the crisis? Are they an advantage or disadvantage when compared with capitalist firms? Are cooperatives more resistant to the crisis, or perhaps more vulnerable than capitalist business? Will they overcome the crisis sooner or later than their capitalist counterparts? How has globalization affected cooperative companies? What strategies are cooperatives following in the face of globalization?

The first chapter in this section, by Itziar Villafáñez Pérez, is entitled "Basque Cooperatives and the Crisis: The Case of Mondragon." Here, the author reviews the strengths of Basque cooperatives, particularly in regards to regulations under the Basque Law on Cooperatives and the application of cooperative principles.

Chapter 9 by Aitziber Lertxundi is titled "Characteristics of Human Resource Management in Basque Cooperatives and their Response to New International Contexts." Here, she first contends that one must know how human resources management practices in Basque cooperatives fit those categorized as "best practices," and if such practices are more or less common when compared to other noncooperative companies. Moreover, this study also attempts to establish what the general behavior in the design of such practices is in cooperatives' new overseas plants, when faced with new national contexts where these plants are located. This chapter thus seeks to elaborate a comparative analysis in relation to other companies.

Finally, "Globalization and Knowledge Management in the Industrial Cooperatives of the Mondragon Corporation," by Antxon Mendizábal, concludes the book. It addresses the recent changes implemented by the Basque industrial cooperatives of the Mondragon Corporation in work organization, flexibility, ownership, management systems, customer focus, innovation, the production system, new values, and internationalization processes.

We hope that this book will help readers to identify the main issues in understanding the emergence and contemporary development of cooperatives in the Basque Country.

1

The Spirituality of Economics: Historical Roots of Mondragon, 1940–1974

FERNANDO MOLINA

Traslated by Jennifer Ottman

In 1967 the magazine of the Baiona (Bayonne) Chamber of Commerce introduced French audiences to a group of Basque cooperatives, located in the town of Arrasate-Mondragón, that appeared to represent the progressive Europeanization of a Spain still subject to an authoritarian Catholic dictatorship. A subsequent monograph accompanied by an influential article in the flagship journal of French cooperativism generated the first academic interest in the Mondragon group, opening the way for a number of pioneer doctoral theses (García 1970, 7–21).[1]

In 1972, thanks to these pioneering French monographs, the economist Robert Oakeshott introduced this cooperative experiment to the English-speaking public. After visiting these cooperatives, he published a celebrated article in which he described Mondragon as "a Spanish oasis of democracy," the fruit of a singular "alliance between Church and technology" (Oakeshott 1973, 1976). Many others followed him in those years, culminating in a BBC documentary, *The Mondragon Experiment*, in 1980.

---

1. "L'Espagne franchit les Pyrénées" (1967); "De l'artisanat au complexe industriel: Une importante réalisation coopérative et communautaire" (1967); Aldabaldetrecu and Grey (1967); Desroche (1966, 1970a, 1970b).

Mondragon thus traveled from the old continent to the British Isles and the United States with the multiplication of academic research projects dedicated to studying this business phenomenon, as well as its capacity to handle economic crises, especially the industrial crisis of the early 1980s. This research sought to locate Mondragon within new models of business management, the organization of work, and the social economy. Its object was to evaluate the extent to which Mondragon was a unique phenomenon or one that could be exported to other geographical areas (Vanek 1975; Oakeshott 1978a, 1978b, and 1987; Thomas and Logan 1982; Bradley and Gelb 1983; Whyte and Whyte 1988; Morrison 1991; Greenwood and González 1992; Kasmir 1996; MacLeod 1998; Cheney 1999; Hindmoor 1999).

Many of these studies fell into erroneous commonplaces, especially when addressing the cultural component of this phenomenon, underlining the importance of factors such as ethnicity or Basque nationalism among its constituents. These studies undervalued or were unaware of the transformation of the cooperatives' foundational culture, a product of the time when they emerged (Molina and Miguez 2008).

This research was unable to enrich itself by drawing on work produced by the cooperatives themselves. Despite a dynamic academic and technological structure, Mondragon has given scant encouragement to internal social-scientific analyses. Except for very concrete aspects of its business side, such as technological innovation or management, internal studies of its social dimension have had little substance. There does not even exist a compilation or catalog of research on Mondragon's own business movement, not to mention collections of documents, oral histories, or visual materials. The purpose of the humble social-scientific research promoted by this corporation has been to reinforce the new business identity it has taken on, resituating its cooperative tradition in a globalized and multicultural world, with assistance from Basque nationalism, environmental awareness, and the social economy.[2]

Since the death of its founder, José María Arizmendiarrieta, in 1976, Mondragon's cooperativism has undergone a major change in its business culture. What was, according to French academic opinion of the

---

2. A brief account of Mondragon's new identity can be found in Azkarraga (2006). I am currently preparing a critical evaluation of research on Mondragon in the areas of organization of work, business culture, and collective identity. This work in progress, like the work presented in this chapter, is part of the activities of a UPV/EHU research group IT-286-07.

1960s, a unique model of its kind of industrially and financially oriented Catholic cooperativism, both in Spain and in Western Europe, began to lose the religious cultural foundation of its successful business culture in the second half of the 1970s. This "cooperative secularization" ran parallel to the traumatic secularization underway in Basque society. The gap left by religion, omnipresent in Basque society until then, was filled by a new Basque nationalism that would convert this business phenomenon into a symbol of Basque identity (Elzo 1994; Zulaika 1988). In the 1990s, influences from the European left also came to play a role, especially influences from the intellectual movements reacting to globalization, as well as from modern theories of management centered on ethical values, "self-help," and corporate social responsibility. In a time of crisis for the cooperative ideal, all this facilitated a certain cultural banalization of the once-powerful "Mondragon experiment" (Molina and Walton 2011).

This study aims to explain the origins of this cooperative movement and highlight the impact that social change and modernization in 1960s Spain had on its success. First, I will explain its origins, bound up with the figure of José María Arizmendiarrieta. Subsequently, I will discuss the interaction of these firms with the Spanish market of the 1960s and their social philosophy. Finally, I will demonstrate the historical paradox of a business initiative that served the cause of economic modernization at the same time that it sought to provide an alternative to the social changes this modernization introduced. The study ends at a time—the workers' strike of 1974—when social change was beginning to become a reality within Mondragon's culture. It also opened a caesura that, between then and Arizmendiarrieta's death in1976, marked the close of a historical era and the most original period in the history of this cooperative movement: the era in which the humanist values and principles were established that, duly secularized, still define the cultural order of the cooperative firms known as Mondragon today.

Arizmendiarrieta, the Founder of Mondragon

Getting to know the Mondragon cooperative movement—a name recently adopted by this conglomerate of firms—means first getting to know its founder. José María Arizmendiarrieta, born in Markina (Bizkaia) in 1915, studied for the priesthood at the Vitoria-Gasteiz seminary, which he entered in 1931. The encyclical *Rerum Novarum* (1891), the *Social Code* of the University of Malines (1920), and the encyclical *Quadragessimo Anno*

(1931) formed the theoretical corpus of the Church's social teaching familiar to Arizmendiarrieta.

This Catholic social education was oriented around the ideal of "social priesthood," formulated by Joaquín Azpiazu, among others. This Jesuit and theorist of Catholic corporatism was one of the great promoters of Catholic social reform in the years of the Second Republic (1931–39), a time when Spain experienced intense social conflict fanned by the expectations generated by this laicist and reforming regime among the worker and peasant classes. This ideal advocated careful management by priests of the lay Catholic movements grouped under the heading of Catholic Action, for the purpose of promoting workers' Catholic education (Azpiazu 1934).

The model of social priesthood in which the young Arizmendiarrieta was trained was not new. The spirituality that guided him, on the other hand, was. The young man participated in a singular spiritual movement that arose in the Vitoria-Gasteiz seminary in 1926. This French-influenced movement had as its central axis a conception of the priest as redeemer of the Christian community through his sacrificial dedication to public activity (Goicoecheaundía 1994).

During the Spanish Civil War (which lasted from 1936 to 1937 in the Basque Country), Arizmendiarrieta, a sympathizer of the Basque Nationalist Party, was active on the republican side, working in the Basque government's propaganda service. His political activity was brief. The fratricidal nature of that war, including the course of events on Basque soil, and the final result of the conflict, which ran contrary to the cause of Basque autonomy, led him to a loss of political faith and a reaffirmation of his priestly vocation. Under the direction of Rufino Aldabalde, the spiritual director of the Vitoria-Gasteiz seminary in 1938, Arizmendiarrieta deepened his focus on profiles of social leadership that appealed to Gospel values such as sacrifice, selflessness, hope, self-discipline, responsibility, and work. The social activism in which he was taught to engage had the purpose of restoring the Christian spirit among the working masses through the use of modern means of persuasion, an objective put forward by encyclicals such as *Divini illius Magistri*, for the youth apostolate, and *Casti connubii*, for the family apostolate, as well as the previously noted *Quadragessimo Anno* for the labor apostolate. In 1941, the bishop of Vitoria-Gasteiz charged him with the task of putting this "re-Catholicization" project into practice in Arrasate-Mondragón, a conflict-ridden industrial town in Gipuzkoa.

Arrasate-Mondragón in Postwar Spain

Industrialization in Gipuzkoa had followed a different model than that of Bizkaia. It was less geographically concentrated, more diversified in its sources of investment and capital, and more focused on local workers, who remained culturally linked to a rural environment, since this moderate social change took place in small towns. The firms were smaller than the steel-making giants of Bilbao and were oriented toward the production of paper, textiles, arms, and locks, requiring a high proportion of skilled workers. The Unión Cerrajera (Locksmithing Union) of Arrasate-Mondragón, dedicated to the production of screws, locks, hardware, metal furniture, and wrought iron, arose from the merger of several of these firms. This enterprise was an economic microcommunity with its own canteens, company stores, mutual insurance funds, and even a technical school. These and other dependent enterprises employed two-thirds of the population of Arrasate-Mondragón, which had 8,645 inhabitants in 1940 (González 2005, 11–17, 36–65).

Postwar Arrasate-Mondragón was a society fractured into multiple communities. In the labor sphere, the town was divided between residents who lived under the Cerrajera's protective umbrella and those outside it. This division was accompanied by another in the political arena. The Spanish Civil War had affected this industrial town, taking the lives of dozens of residents who sympathized with the two belligerent parties: the Catholic rebels, backed by supporters of Catholic traditionalism, and the republicans, backed by the leftist republican parties and the Basque nationalists. The division between winners and losers was an identifying mark of the military dictatorship, which sought to purge the defeated from all areas of political, social, and cultural life (Cazorla 2010, 17–49).

The articulating institution of the new society was the Church. As a consequence of the institutional and propaganda support it gave to the rebels during the Civil War, the Church came to perform the tasks of group formation and social control, inserting Catholic morality into all areas of public and private life, including work. Priests had a great deal of power in a society like that of Gipuzkoa, which had not abandoned its strong attachment to the Church. Indeed, religion was the backbone of social habits and public life there. During the Second Republic, this had led to mystical experiences such as the famed visions of the Virgin in Ezkioga, twenty kilometers from Arrasate-Mondragón (Christian Jr. 1996).

Priests had a great deal of freedom in using this immense social and symbolic power. The majority of those in Arrasate-Mondragón chose (whether out of affinity with the regime or in order to "whitewash" their sympathies for Basque nationalism) to follow the bishop's guidelines both in the topics for preaching—intended to legitimize the dictatorship and its official doctrine, National Catholicism—and in facilitating the enrollment of the residents in a Catholic associational life directed toward the same end. Arizmendiarrieta, on the other hand, opted to use this charismatic power to take action in regard to social problems. He decided to do so because social conflict had not been resolved by the regime's fascist- and Catholic-inspired legislation but simply silenced, as would be reflected in the 1947 mobilizations in the industrial conglomerate of Bilbao (Ysas 1991, 195–96).

Arizmendiarrieta thus launched a labor apostolate, aimed at young workers who participated in the discussion groups and doctrinal instruction offered by Catholic Action. He gradually put together a group of "disciples" who were to lead social activities directed toward taking action in regard to the needs of the local community. So it was that he intervened in the promotion of associations and events of all kinds, from a soccer club to theater and mountain-hiking activities and public collections on behalf of the most disadvantaged families.

He inculcated the values of the Church's social teaching in the hundreds of young people who took part in Catholic Action over the years, and he turned the social reality of Arrasate-Mondragón into a laboratory in which to put into practice a Catholic commitment to the world of work. In a letter sent to the president of the Unión Cerrajera, he described his work in this way: "The general objective we have set for ourselves . . . is to *mobilize* the mass of young people in our town. Without neglecting the formation and preservation of the nucleus we have established with the best, we are going to act on the mass."[3]

"Mobilization" is a term that recurs insistently in the memories of those days retained by the priest's young collaborators. Each was educated to be conscious that he had a unique role to play in life: "we believe that we are anonymous, and we are not," he used to tell them. They all considered

---

3. Archivo de José María Arizmendiarrieta, Centro de Estudios Cooperativos de Otalora, Aretxabaleta, folder 18, draft of a letter to Don Ricardo Oreja, August 1942 (citations are according to the catalog dated August 2004). This archive may be partially consulted at www.euskomedia.org/fondo?idi=en&op=8&fclick=1&fl=Arizmendiarrieta.

him "a half spiritual and half organizational leader, who was qualified to try to reestablish social justice and fairness among men," one of the pioneers of cooperativism recalled (Ormaechea 1998, 36). The dual character of his contemplative and mobilizing leadership, and the fact that it was based on a demanding ascetic spirituality, conferred great charisma on him among these young people. In his own later account, he described his leadership as "a process of mobilization, of consciousness-raising and training, of theory and practice, of self-government and self-management, in which young people, faced with the serious problem of financing, organized raffles, pools, and other public events . . . that also gave them the opportunity . . . to acquire a high degree of practical experience. . . . These were the young people who would later on be the protagonists of the cooperative experiment."[4]

In his role as a mobilizing leader, one of his fundamental tasks was to ensure the flow of information about his social work among the residents of Arrasate-Mondragón for whom it was intended. The channel for this was printed matter of all kinds (pamphlets, little magazines that were distributed or posted on walls, leaflets, and posters) together with skilled use of the period's chief means of communication: the pulpit. It was all part of a strategy to affect local opinion in order to engage its support for his social action. In a document from the time, he emphasized, "A properly channeled current of public opinion is so powerful and effective that none or very few resist it, but for that to be the case, it is necessary to create it at the appropriate time . . . and to mobilize it using the same means, once it has been created."[5]

At the same time, moreover, he sought support from the local business community for this involvement by young people and residents. This collaboration was to prepare the way for the firms' internal transformation, through the incorporation of workers into their management, as proposed by the Catholic corporative ideal. Thus, when he founded the Juventud Deportiva (Youth Sports League) of Arrasate-Mondragón in 1942, an association to promote youth sports, he succeeded in getting it financed by businesses and residents through subscriptions. Likewise,

---

4. Archivo de José María Arizmendiarrieta, folder 41, "Experiencias sobre una forma cooperativa: Mondragón," lecture by José María Arizmendiarrieta at the Fomento de Actividades Culturales, Económicas y Sociales [Promotion of Cultural, Economic, and Social Activities] association, January 21, 1965.

5. Archivo Jose María Arizmendiarrieta (Otalora, Aretxabaleta), folder 12, "Irradiación parroquial," talk 1, "Observaciones generales," undated.

when he came up with the idea of a trade school in 1943, he sought to have it financed by all concerned: workers, business owners, and residents.

In fact, professional training became the central axis of his social project. The "redemption of the worker" could not take place except by way of access to modern technical education. Thus, in August 1943, under a heterodox philosophical motto ("socializing knowledge to democratize power"), he launched the Arrasate-Mondragón Professional School. Young people from humble backgrounds would have the opportunity to invest their personal efforts in improving their education, since, as he indicated in talks and sermons, "the proletariat's chief weapon, the primary element in its fighting equipment, has to be culture."[6]

Despite this support, his activities naturally aroused suspicion. His social practice, in which he appealed to terms such as democracy, justice, and equality, was transgressive in a Catholic dictatorship like that of General Franco. The Civil Guard (the Spanish military-status police force) placed obstacles in the way of his youth pilgrimages, while the provincial Catholic Action administration protested the distancing of its Arrasate-Mondragón division with regard to National Catholic doctrine. The Falange, the sole state party, likewise complained of competition from Arrasate-Mondragón Catholic Action in attracting young people, and members of the congregation who were more sympathetic to the regime expressed their irritation with the "Red" (leftist) tone of some of his Sunday sermons.

His pastoral and social work thus fell into dissident categories from the dictatorship's perspective, yet this dissidence was not based on Basque nationalist or Marxist resistance practices. Instead, it relied on a deconstruction of the political culture of Franco's Spain and its Catholic and conservative myths and principles. Arizmendiarrieta reoriented Catholic principles toward social and progressive terrain, as well as on confrontation with the regime's articulating institutions, such as the Falange and Catholic Action, all in defense of a social involvement of the individual founded on values of equality, freedom, and democracy. In 1943, he went so far as to set up polling places in the street to elect the directors of the trade school he had founded. All registered members of the parents' association had the right to vote, and the votes were counted rigorously. This political side of his apostolate, and his personal involvement in all his social

---

6. Archivo Jose María Arizmendiarrieta, folder 103, drafts of "Voy," "Emancipación ... o liberación," undated, circa 1944.

initiatives, differentiated his social work from other "re-Catholicization" experiments of the period that were obsessed with stamping out the laicist and working class culture of the industrial areas (Alfonsi 1999).

Cooperation before Cooperatives

Arizmendiarrieta put his Catholic social ideals into practice in the new trade school and the local Catholic Action headquarters. These ideals incorporated, in addition to papal encyclicals and the writings of Catholic philosophers, new inspirations such as the British Labour Party. In his address marking the end of the trade school's 1945–46 academic year, he assimilated the economic policies of the British Labour Party to the proposals of social Catholicism, scandalizing many (Molina and Miguez 2008, 292–94). Social assistance, housing, and education were areas in which he aspired to bring together private and public initiative, inspired by Labour policies in Great Britain. A consequence of this line of thinking was his promotion of a tuberculosis treatment center and an association to promote social housing in order to combat the overcrowded conditions in which workers lived.

He read the authors who inspired postwar social democracy in Europe and the reformist bishops of Franco's Spain. He also took an interest in the new Spanish Catholic intellectuals and especially in French personalist philosophers such as Jacques Maritain, Jacques Leclerq, and Emmanuel Mounier, who helped him to strengthen his conception of man as a communitarian being who found in work and education the path to restoring the dignity lost to industrialization and secularization. At the base of this personalist philosophy, moreover, lay the spirituality he had learned in Vitoria-Gasteiz, which he further elaborated with the aid of humanist thinkers such as Pierre Teilhard de Chardin. Arizmendiarrieta read these authors and encouraged the young people with whom he worked to read them, in order to develop their own social thinking (Molina 2005, 282–86).

His social projects took advantage of the window of opportunity opened by Franco's regime as a regime of political families that included the Church. In this way, although some of his local initiatives did not enjoy the sympathy of his ecclesiastical superiors, the need to protect the Church's sphere of power forced them to intercede with the regime in his defense. Indeed, his movement of local cooperation among young workers, residents, and business owners benefited greatly from this (Molina and Miguez 2008, 290–91, 297–98).

In 1946, his most select group of young disciples completed their local studies of skilled industrial trades, but this education, in their mentor's opinion, was insufficient for those destined to be "redeemers" of their class. He therefore arranged their admission to the Industrial Engineering School (Escuela de Ingenieros Industriales) in Zaragoza. These upper-level university studies were reserved for the moneyed classes, and only a tiny minority of young people in Arrasate-Mondragón could aspire to them. In one of his pamphlets, addressed to them and to their companions who would follow them in subsequent classes, he had written, "To live is to struggle, whether we wish it or not. . . . The first law of life is the law of effort. The first law of Christian life is the law of sacrifice."[7] The purpose of his initiatives was to create a self-aware, professionally trained proletariat imbued with Christian ideals and determined to create a new social order in which labor had primacy over capital. He believed that without liberating workers from their condition as an exploited class, it was impossible to aim at their Christianization (Molina and Miguez 2008, 294–95).

After obtaining their new professional degrees, his Zaragoza disciples moved up the professional ladder. Three of them found positions with the Unión Cerrajera as heads of workshops (José María Ormaechea, Luis Usatorre, and Alfonso Gorroñogoitia), three of the seven that the firm had among its staff of thirteen hundred workers. For these three individuals and Arizmendiarrieta, reform from within was possible and in the event of success could be extended to other firms in the province and beyond. The Unión Cerrajera was the most important firm in Gipuzkoa and enjoyed the support of a protective state. Its prosperity enabled it to engage in extensive social work in the form of schools, company stores, workers' mutual associations, and so on.

Arizmendiarrieta wished to move beyond this philosophy of business donation to an authentic system of social justice, by way of the possibility of worker participation in the firm's capital and management. In 1954, two of his disciples proposed to management, on the occasion of an expansion of the firm's capital, that workers could subscribe part of the funds as workers' shares. Management's refusal put an end to the hope that reform

---

7. Archivo José María Arizmendiarrieta, folder 20, Aleluya, no. 15, December 1945.

could be achieved from within. Arizmendiarrieta proposed to his three disciples at the Cerrajera (Ormaechea, Gorroñogoitia, and Usatorre) that they leave the firm and create a new one, together with two other former disciples employed elsewhere (Javier Ortubay and Jesús Larrañaga) (Jose Maria Arizmendiarrieta in Escuela de Gerentes Cooperativos 1973).

The social work promoted by Arizmendiarrieta had always involved the people of Arrasate-Mondragón. When he moved from seeking business reform from within to founding a new enterprise, many residents contributed loans intended to finance it. The purpose of this new public fundraising campaign was to accumulate as much capital as possible for the investment that would be necessary. The day came when in September 1955 a resident advised the young men to purchase a firm in Vitoria-Gasteiz dedicated to the manufacture of domestic stoves, a type of production with which they were familiar. The firm was baptized with the name of Ulgor, and its commercial brand was Fagor, by which it would come to be known later (Molina 2006, 35–40).

The rigid culture of work implanted in the new enterprise was Spartan: ten- to twelve-hour days with a forty-minute break for lunch, Monday through Saturday, and ten days of vacation in August. This work rhythm did not reduce the influx of worker-shareholders, who went from ten in August 1956 to 143 in 1959. The pioneer managers met every Sunday in Arizmendiarrieta's office at the trade school. Everything was decided at those meetings, from the incorporation of new shareholders to the design of every building, not omitting the progressive definition of the entity's bylaws. This first managing body, made up of four of the five entrepreneurs of 1955 (one, Ortubay, abandoned the adventure in its first months), was joined as shareholders who were former students of the trade school and, above all, workers who left firms such as Unión Cerrajera. They all knew the four young entrepreneurs, whether from having worked under their supervision or from having collaborated with them on Arizmendiarrieta's social projects. The charismatic ties between the priest and the four pioneers were thus replicated between the latter and the first group of Fagor workers (Molina 2006, 42–43).

The entrepreneurial trail blazed by Fagor was followed by many other enterprises: Talleres Arrasate, born in 1957 as a firm dedicated to the manufacture of machine tools; Copreci, in 1962, destined to manufacture the machined parts needed by Fagor for assembling heaters and washing machines; Comet S.C.I., in 1963, which would soon take the name of Ederlan, dedicated to metallurgy; and dozens of other industrial, agricul-

tural, and consumer cooperatives throughout the 1960s. All these cooperatives relied on financial support from the credit cooperative founded by
Fagor's management in 1959: Caja Laboral, a cooperative bank intended
to provide financial and managerial backing for the new firms.

At the same time, Arizmendiarrieta planned the reorganization of
the trade school as a technical university that would supply the skilled
workers needed by these enterprises, without having to resort to Zaragoza. Financing was the responsibility of the Social Work Fund (Fondo de
Obras Sociales) of the new industrial cooperatives. This measure made it
possible to finance not only this Polytechnic School (Escuela Politécnica)
but also a Children's Home (Hogar Infantil), which would be followed
years later by a hospital. Thus, when the polytechnic school was inau-
gurated in May 1964, the three institutional pillars of Mondragon, each
symbolizing its cultural counterpart, were formally in place: labor, represented by Fagor; financial capital, provided by Caja Laboral; and education or human capital, the responsibility of the polytechnic school.

The Culture of Mondragon Cooperativism

On February 25, 1957, Francisco Franco named the fifth government of
his dictatorship, which designed the 1959 Stabilization Plan, subsequently
continued by the three development plans. The so-called "technocratic
phase" of the dictatorship had begun. The American aid obtained thanks to
the regime's fierce anticommunism, the credit facilities granted by France,
Great Britain, and Belgium, and the slow growth of tourism generated a
significant flowering of economic development. It was the beginning of
the end of economic autarky and the start of economic liberalization, the
relaxation of interventionist controls, financial and budgetary orthodoxy,
openness to international markets, and the modernization of industrial
production. The result of all this was growth in Spanish per-capita income
and an exodus of day laborers and peasants as emigrants to Europe or large
Spanish cities and industrial regions. The population's material well-being
and consumption levels increased, as reflected, for example, in improvements in household furnishings and appliances, precisely the sector tar-
geted by Fagor's production (Townson 2007; Babiano 2009).

Visits to France, Germany, and Italy by Fagor's managers consolidated the firm's orientation toward household appliances, electronics,
and wrought iron. The negotiating model of their production contracts,
based on the import of new technology, allowed them to comprehend the

immensity of the gap between Spain and Western Europe, both in infrastructure and in raw materials and energy sources, communications, and the culture of work (Ormaechea 1998, 63–67, 86–88).

"Either . . . we join Europe or, isolated, our future fate will be the sad one of the underdeveloped countries." These are the words of Fagor's president, Alfonso Gorroñogoitia, speaking to the 1959 shareholders' assembly, where he stressed the road to be followed: "We have to modernize, better equip our industries, train ourselves for an export mentality."[8] Mondragon's young businessmen thus became true entrepreneurs. The first Fagor stoves using butane gas, a new source of energy in Spain, were introduced in 1959. They were followed two years later by refrigerators and washing machines. This production line was joined by another oriented toward the manufacture of selenium plates, destined for another household appliance for which the managers foresaw a growing demand: the television (Molina 2006, 51).

Ulgor's managers included accounts of their travels in Europe in the magazine founded by Arizmendiarrieta to educate workers at Fagor's daughter firms in his idea of cooperativism, a magazine which he named *Cooperación* [Cooperation] (later renamed T.U., meaning Trabajo y Unión or Work and Union). Indeed, the panorama of European development was meant to serve as an example of work-related values and behavior. For that reason, the Germans and the French were points of reference for the Mondragon cooperativists even on questions such as consumption and savings.[9]

Household appliances, a key component in Mondragon's industrial success, became a point of reference for Spanish modernization in the 1960s. Washing machines, gas stoves, and refrigerators became goods that conferred social status (Moreno 2008, 89–90). It was not by chance that Fagor's first stove model took its aesthetic inspiration from a television. Both in Arizmendiarrieta and in the managers of his firms, there was a will to join the world of Western marketing and consumer culture: a will to join modernity.

The Mondragon firms obtained legal cooperative status starting in 1959. That status had been unofficially acquired with the first of them,

---

8. Archivo de Fagor Electrodomésticos, "Memoria que presenta la Junta Rectora y Provisional de Talleres Ulgor ...," April 26, 1959.

9. Archivo de Jose María Arizmendiarrieta, transfer folder 1, "España, país con grandes perspectivas de desarrollo," Cooperación 13, September 1961.

Fagor, in 1955, on the basis of the principle of subordination of capital to labor on which it was founded, but it was not publicly legalized until four years later. The reason was what it cost Arizmendiarrieta and his disciples to create a set of bylaws different from the cooperative model of the Act of 1942, anchored in fascist criteria. When Fagor's bylaws were approved by the Labor Ministry on April 3, 1959, they became the organizational model for the other cooperatives that were set up.

Mondragon's founders embraced the cooperative model as a social channel for seeking Christian reconciliation between capital and labor: "We believed that the firm should be a human community of activities and interests, based on private property and initiative . . . in order to provide society with a necessary or useful production service, in exchange for which it receives economic compensation . . . that is distributed among its members in a just way" (Ormaechea 1998, 67).

In the business conception of the Mondragon pioneers, the firm was to be established on the basis of solidarity, a value that was understood as innate in the human person and deeply spiritual. This solidarity-oriented reading of work was where Christian morality intervened. At the aforementioned assembly of the Ulgor cooperative in 1959, Gorroñogoitia warned the shareholders, "We have to change many things among us: our mentality directed toward immediate profit . . . our limited ability to save, our lack of austerity, which is expressed in that continuous desire to appear to be more than we are and to gain and spend more than we can."[10]

The business definition of these cooperatives started from the idea of a "community of work," which established the preeminence of labor over capital. Each worker acquired a right of participation in the enterprise as a shareholder, which gave him or her the right to vote in the general assembly and to earn dividends if the firm turned a profit. Dividends were distributed monthly as a function of the contribution made by each worker to the cooperative with his or her work (Ormaechea 2000, 469–70). The community of work was conceived as a community in evolution, since, as Arizmendiarrieta affirmed, "Our cooperativism is an organic process of experiment." For that reason, the term he preferred for describing these firms was that of an "experiment," which implied an attitude of ongoing adaptation to social change. "The sign of vitality is not longevity, but

---

10. Archivo de Fagor Electrodomésticos, "Memoria que presenta la Junta Rectora y Provisional de Talleres Ulgor ...," April 26, 1959.

rather rebirth and adaptation" was another of his maxims (Molina 2005, 371, 428).

In 1966, the cooperatives' magazine set out the instruments that regulated that "experiment": "The rules that we all accept for the regulation of our corporate life in the firm are contained in the Corporate By-laws and the Internal Regulations. By signing these documents . . . we accept them as regulating our rights and obligations. . . . The By-laws contain the principles of governance . . . The Internal Regulations . . . have the function of adding detail to those principles, providing for their concrete application to the realities of any given time."[11]

The bylaws thus played the role of a "cooperative constitution," to which the internal regulations added "amendments" in accordance with ongoing social change. According to both sets of norms, Mondragon's workers contributed the firm's capital, together with their labor, and were joined to one another by a cooperative contract. This union was rooted in four principles: *equality, solidarity, responsibility,* and *democracy.*

Equality was reflected in a system that reduced salary differences between the different ranks of shareholders, from the managerial elite to the assembly-line workers. At this time, a shareholder with managerial responsibilities could earn only three times more than the lowest-paid shareholder-worker. *Solidarity* implied renouncing the ambition for personal gain. This was a concept opposed to the capitalist model characteristic of "Spanish developmentalism," which was contrary to any solidarity-oriented perspective on a firm. This option for solidarity implied the worker's *responsibility* in the face of any neglect of duties such as austerity, thrift, or sacrifice. Finally, the worker was to commit to playing a role in managing the firm through the cooperative *democracy* practiced at the annual general assemblies. This democracy was conceived in a highly demanding form, "as a method and resource for selecting the better men for government and an imperative for spontaneous and rigorous obedience to the orders given by those in authority, who should offer effective management in return." At the general assembly, the shareholders designated their "betters," who would then form the firm's governing council.

A fundamental aspect of these cooperative regulations was the part dealing with social assistance to and social security for the shareholders. This service of social assistance was the responsibility of Caja Laboral,

---

11. "Estatutos sociales y Reglamento de Régimen Interior," *Trabajo y Unión* 68, 1966.

which launched a mutual insurance association named Lagun-Aro for this purpose in 1966. All Mondragon shareholders were to contribute a monthly assessment to this entity for that purpose, reinforcing the regime of community solidarity.

This communitarian mentality established at Mondragon's origins can be observed in the relationship between the Social Work Fund and the Reserve Fund (Fondo de Reserva). The former was used by each cooperative to take action in regard to problems of the social environment, and the latter was used to finance new jobs. In this way, the enterprise reinvested its profits in the local community in which it was located. Hence the preoccupation with thrift. In the cooperative philosophy of Arizmendiarrieta and his pioneers, it was not morally admissible to prioritize individual consumption over community investment, something that once again marked a contrast with the developmentalist society of the same period. This resulted in the paradox that firms that produced consumer goods restricted their workers' ability to acquire them (Molina 2006, 64), while the cult of work as a source of communitarian spirituality underlay the whole: "For us, work will never be a punishment and leisure a blessing from heaven," Arizmendiarrieta warned in his talks (Molina 2005, 370–71).[12]

This cooperative philosophy was spread through the cooperatives' aforementioned internal magazine as well as through talks, adult-education courses, seminars, and the cooperatives' general assemblies themselves. Thus, at the Fagor general assembly in 1961, Gorroñogoitia, the firm's president, warned, "Ulgor expects everyone to fulfill his duties. If anyone, in conscience, believes that he has not fully done his part, let him be his own judge."[13]

As the author of these words has recalled, "something that often surprises people ... was the poetic-philosophical strain we had as businessmen; they were surprised by that humanistic side that we owed to Don Jose María, because we could not disassociate our business attitude from a philosophy, a concept, an ideology, after the contact we'd had with him. ... We viewed the development of these firms as a social struggle" (Molina 2005, 374).

---

12. Archivo de Jose María Arizmendiarrieta, folder 59, "La Cooperación," meeting of Ulgor representatives, May 2, 1961.

13. Archivo de Fagor Electrodomésticos, Memorias del Consejo Rector, March 19, 1961.

Conclusion

Mondragon was born as a new kind of firm intended to foster equality of opportunity at work and the distribution of profits, as well as to guarantee, by means of both of the former characteristics, the social progress of the local community in which it was located. Its purpose was to complement the family as a social cell within a Christian industrial community. In the opinion of one of its founders, Arizmendiarrieta "aimed . . . more than to create firms, to move by way of those firms toward a classless society in which there would be equality of opportunity for all members of the community, who should aspire to an increase in collective wealth and not so much in the wealth that each individual might have the ambition to possess for his own personal enjoyment" (Ormaechea 1998, 537–38).

The paradox of Mondragon's history is that it grew thanks to the success of its products in the new developmentalist society at the same time that it was seeking to construct an alternative to that society's capitalist excesses. Spanish developmentalism of the 1960s promoted a leisure- and consumption-oriented, secularized and materialistic society. This model of society promoted inequality in the distribution of wealth and work (Cazorla 2010, 149–63). Mondragon, on the other hand, which was founded to provide products and services to that developmentalism, pursued the construction of a society centered on values such as solidarity, equality, and thrift—values also asserted by the most progressive sector of the Catholic Church in those years (Álvarez Espinosa and Bernal 2003).

Nevertheless, Mondragon was unable to consolidate its roots in Christian religiosity in a decade, the 1960s, during which the Basque Country was experiencing the most intense process of secularization in its history (Pérez-Agote 1990). In resolving this contradictory situation, Arizmendiarrieta's adaptive conception of cooperativism played a role. It was not in vain that his cooperativism was nourished by humanist values that could be shared by the new, secularized generations. Those new cooperativists could make it a site for new social and political concerns foreign to Mondragon's origins, as in the case of the revolutionary left or Basque nationalism. Those new concerns at times filled the space left by religiosity in the public and private spheres (Elzo 2009).

Mondragon's attraction for these new generations of shareholders, ideologically radicalized and committed to the struggle against the dictatorship, is well described in the memoirs of Mario Onaindía, a future ETA activist and political leader of the "new Basque left" in the 1970s (Onaindía 2001, 198–99). This attraction was confirmed by an incident that most conclusively demonstrates the impact of social change in Mondragon: the 1974 strike by hundreds of workers from several of these industrial cooperatives. It was an unusual kind of strike in that it was led by a group of cooperativist shareholders on lower rungs of the pay scale in opposition to the rest of their fellow shareholders at the same level and others above them in the scale. Specifically, their protest centered on the accusation that the latter had formed a "bourgeoisie" that was exploiting a cooperativist "proletariat." One of the major reasons for this strike was the Marxist politicization of a situation of increasing internal conflict generated by new strategies for the organization of work and by the massification of that work. These were changes generated by the economic success of organizations that had been conceived for no more than two hundred workers (compared to the two thousand Fagor had at the beginning of the 1970s). The conflict, traumatically ventilated with the expulsion of several shareholders, reflected the degree to which new political cultures were occupying nonconformist spaces that had once been Catholic domains (Molina 2006, 112–19). The fact that this occurred soon after Robert Oakeshott's laudatory article in *The Observer* reveals that this internal conflict was part of a wider social change these cooperatives were undergoing and part of the entry of a multitude of new shareholders, many of whom lacked a tradition that would link them to Mondragon's initial culture.

This culture originated in the search for spiritual values that would provide practical guidance for work and its economic returns. Arizmendiarrieta, already suffering from the incurable illness that would cause his death in 1976, insisted on this point in a public lecture that turned out to be a sensational synthesis of his thinking and his social work. Its title was "La espiritualidad de la economía" (The spirituality of the economy). Spirituality—he argued—could not be divorced from economic matters, factors that determined social structures and the structures of power. "No one can have a more elevated idea of work than a Christian. Work cannot mean so much to anyone as it does to the man who wants to *cooperate* with God in the task of perfecting or completing nature" (Molina 2005, 526–27).

References

Aldabaldetrecu, Félix, and Jean Grey. 1967. *De l'artisanat industriel au complexe coopératif.* Paris: Bureau d'Études Coopératives et Communautaires.

Alfonsi, Adela. 1999. "La recatolización de los obreros en Málaga, 1937–1966: El nacional-catolicismo de los obispos Santos Olivera y Herrera Oria." *Historia Social* 35: 119–34.

Álvarez Espinosa, Daniel, and Dario Bernal. 2003. *Cristianos y marxistas contra Franco*. Cádiz: Universidad de Cádiz.

Azkarraga, Joseba. 2006. "Cooperativism and Globalization: The Basque Mondragón Cooperatives in the Face of Changing Times (A Cultural Outlook)." At www.eteo.mondragon.edu/IAFEP/IAFEP2006/Azkarraga.pdf.

Azpiazu, Joaquín. 1934. *La acción social del sacerdote*. Madrid: Fax.

Babiano, José. 2009. *La patria en la maleta: Historia social de la emigración española en Europa*. Madrid: GPS.

Bradley, Keith, and Alan Gelb. 1983. *Cooperation at Work*. London: Heinemann Educational.

Cazorla, Antonio. 2010. *Fear and Progress: Ordinary Lives in Franco's Spain (1939–1975)*. London: Wiley-Blackwell.

Cheney, George. 1999. *Values at Work: Employee Participation Meets Market Pressures at Mondragon*. Ithaca, NY: Cornell University Press.

Christian, William A., Jr. 1996. *Visionaries: The Spanish Republic and the Reign of Christ*. Berkeley and Los Angeles: University of California Press.

"De l'artisanat au complexe industriel: Une importante réalisation coopérative et communautaire." 1967. *Cooperation* 3: 3–9.

Desroche, Henry. 1970a. "En Ulgorie... Mondragon." *Cooperation* 40: 1–8.

———. 1970b. "Mondragon, ensemble intercoopératif non conventionnel." In, Preface to *Les coopératives industrielles de Mondragon*, by Quintón García. Paris: Les Éditions Ouvrières.

———. 1966. "Voyages en Ucoopies." *Esprit* 346: 222–45.

Elzo, Javier. 1994. "Nacionalismo, nacionalidad y religión en Euskalerria." In *Tendencias mundiales de cambio en los valores sociales y políticos*, edited by Juan Díez-Nicolás and Ronald Inglehart. Madrid: Fundesco.

———. 2009. "Prólogo." In *Memoria de Euskadi: La terapia de la verdad, todos lo cuentan todo*, by María Antonia Iglesias. Madrid: Aguilar.

Escuela de Gerentes Cooperativos. 1973. *Documentos de Educación*

Cooperativa: Homenaje a Jose Luis del Arco, nos. 18–20. Zaragoza: Escuela de Gerentes Cooperativos.

"L'Espagne franchit les Pyrénées." 1967. *Activités en Pays Basque* 202: 4–17.

García, Quintín. 1970. *Les coopératives industrielles de Mondragon*. Paris: Les Éditions Ouvrières.

Goicoecheaundía, Joaquín. 1994. *Antecedentes históricos del Movimiento Sacerdotal de Vitoria*. Usurbil: Izarberri.

González, José María. 2005. *La metalurgia guipuzcoana en la primera mitad del siglo XX*. Bilbao: Industri Arrastoak.

Greenwood, Davydd, and Jose Luis González. 1992. *Industrial Democracy as Process: Participatory Action Research in the Fagor Cooperative Group of Mondragon*. Assen-Maastricht: Van Gorcum Publishers.

Hindmoor, Andrew. 1999. "Free Riding Off Capitalism: Entrepreneurship and the Mondragon Experiment." *British Journal of Political Science* 29, no. 1: 217–24.

Kasmir, Sharryn. 1996. *The Myth of Mondragon: Cooperatives, Politics and Working-class Life in a Basque Town*. Albany: State University of New York Press.

MacLeod, Greg. 1998. *From Mondragon to America: Experiments in Community Development*. Sydney: University College of Cape Breton Press.

Molina, Fernando. 2005. *Jose María Arizmendiarrieta (1915–1976)*. Mondragón: Caja Laboral.

———. 2006. *Fagor Electrodomésticos: Historia de una experiencia cooperativa, 1955–2005*. Mondragón: Fagor Electrodomésticos.

Molina, Fernando, and Antonio Miguez. 2008. "The Origins of Mondragon: Catholic Co-operativism and Social Movement in a Basque Valley (1941–59)." *Social History* 33, no. 3: 284–98.

Molina, Fernando, and John K. Walton. 2011. "An Alternative Co-operative Tradition: The Basque Co-operatives of Mondragon." In *The Hidden Alternative: Co-operative Values, Past, Present and Future*, edited by Anthony Webster, Alyson Brown, Linda Shaw, David Steward, and John K. Walton. Manchester: Manchester University Press (forthcoming).

Moreno, Roque. 2008. "Las industrias de consumo." In *Eppure si muove:*

La percepción de los cambios en España (1959–1976), edited by Glicerio Sánchez. Madrid: Biblioteca Nueva.

Morrison, Roy. 1991. *We Build the Road as We Travel: Mondragon, a Cooperative Social System*. Philadelphia: Beech River Books.

Oakeshott, Robert. 1978a. *The Case for Workers' Co-ops*. London: Routledge & Kegan Paul.

———. 1976. "'Grass roots' Enterprises Thrive amid the Basques." *The Financial Times*, July 9.

———. 1973. "Mondragon: Spain's Oasis of Democracy." *The Observer*, January 21.

———. 1978b. *The Prospect and Conditions for Successful Co-operative Production*. London: Cooperative Union Ltd.

———. 1987. *Worker-owners: Mondragon revisited*. London: Anglo-German Foundation.

Onaindía, Mario. 2001. *El precio de la libertad: Memorias (1948–1977)*. Madrid: Espasa.

Ormaechea, José María. 1998. *Orígenes y claves del cooperativismo de Mondragón*. Aretxabaleta: Otalora.

———. 2000. "Jose María Arizmendiarrieta Madariaga (1915–1976)." In *Los 100 empresarios españoles del siglo XX*, edited by Eugenio Torres. Madrid: Lid.

Pérez-Agote, Alfonso. 1990. *Los lugares sociales de la religión: La secularización en la vida del País Vasco*. Madrid: CIS.

Thomas, Henk, and Chris Logan. 1982. *Mondragon: An Economic Analysis*. London: Allen & Unwin.

Townson, Nigel, ed. 2007. *Spain Transformed: The Late Franco Dictatorship, 1959–1975*. London: Palgrave MacMillan.

Vanek, Jaroslav. 1975. *Self-Management: Economic Liberation of Man*. Harmondsworth: Penguin Books.

Whyte, William Foote, and Kathleen King Whyte. 1988. *Making Mondragon: The Growth and Dynamics of the Worker Cooperative Complex*. Ithaca, NY: Cornell University-ILR Press.

Ysas, Pere. 1991. "Huelga laboral y huelga política: España, 1939–1975." *Ayer* 4: 193–211.

Zulaika, Joseba. 1988. *Basque Violence: Metaphor and Sacrament*. Reno: University of Nevada Press.

2

Culture and Social Representations of Work among Basques: Implications for Organizational Commitment and Cooperative Attitudes

Javier Cerrato Allende

Translated by Jennifer Ottman

Any analysis of what we might call the "Basque culture of work"—the total-ity of specific Basque understandings, attitudes, and patterns of behavior in relation to work—must include among its parameters the shift from an *industrial* society, stretching from the third quarter of the nineteenth century to the third quarter of the twentieth, to a *postindustrial* society (Touraine 1974), which began to emerge in the late 1960s and that is the characteristic type of society among the major Western countries today.

The term "culture of work" perhaps refers more appropriately to shared understandings of work in industrial and preindustrial society or in traditional society, in which these understandings were much more homogenous and stable because the same was true of work itself, social relationships, and the ways in which reality was defined. At present, change and heterogeneity constitute the essence of postmodern society, so that in place of a culture of work common to all Basques, it seems more appropriate to talk about the different social representations of work that exist among Basques. These presumably coexist in collective memory alongside certain elements of an older Basque culture of work in which aspects characteristic of the industrial era, of traditional forms of work, and of Basque life outside urban centers are superimposed.

Previous studies that have tried to analyze the existence of a specific Basque culture of work in *traditional* and *urban-industrial* societies have been based on the use of qualitative methods. Some of these studies have focused on analyzing the religious ethic of work and thrift among the Basque bourgeoisie that drove the industrial development of Bizkaia and Gipuzkoa from the seventeenth to the beginning of the twentieth centuries (Azaola 1997; Uriarte 1977; Caro Baroja 1990, 2009).

On the basis of his ethnographic studies, renowned anthropologist Julio Caro Baroja indicates in his monograph *The Basques* (2009, 185) that "a distinct concept of life shaped the great Basque economic activities, continuing to the present from its starting point in the sixteenth century, or at least in the seventeenth." To designate this concept of life, Caro Baroja speaks of a "Catholic utilitarianism rather than the one of Protestant origin" (2009, 185).

As we know, Max Weber in his work *The Protestant Ethic and the Spirit of Capitalism* (1965) defends the thesis that the dedication to work promoted by the Calvinist Puritan doctrine of predestination created a set of socioreligious conditions favoring a concept of life in which thrift, austerity, and work are a source of salvation, thereby favoring the development of economic capitalism. From this thesis, one might deduce a lack of aptitude of Catholic peoples (as compared to Protestants) for industrial and commercial development, as was pointed out by some authors derided as pamphleteers by Caro Baroja himself (e.g., Tawney 1948).

Caro Baroja (2009, 184) relates this utilitarianism to the maritime-industrial development of the Basque Country and links it to the sudden emergence in Basque society of the "*indiano*" (the returnee from the Indies) figure. This figure began to emerge in the sixteenth century and eventually came to form a social class with great local influence that gradually came to replace the representatives of the old courtier and Castilian aristocratic lineages. In the eighteenth century, the influence of this social class increased, this being the sector of Basque society that founded the Compañía de Caracas (Caracas Company) in 1728 and that also promoted the Real Sociedad Vascongada de los Amigos del País (Royal Basque Society of Friends of the Country), which began to function in 1766 and that introduced modern capitalism to Spain, as well as a utilitarian philosophical movement rooted in a scientific and encyclopedic tendency originating in its contacts with other countries (Uriarte 1977, 253).

This haute bourgeoisie gradually took shape with the spiritual support of the Jesuits, who in the Basque Country in the eighteenth century "sang the praise of work rather than the aristocratic concept of life, symbolized by Madrid" (Caro Baroja 2009, 185). This confronts us with the paradox, noted by Caro Baroja with Max Weber's work undoubtedly in mind, that "the Basques, the most practicing Catholics in Spain, were the ones who introduced a large number of the economic systems created in Protestant countries through a social class that was neither the aristocracy nor the rural masses, as happened in Protestant countries" (Caro Baroja 2009, 185).

Certainly, Max Weber himself, in his trip to the Basque Country in 1897, was impressed by its industrial development in the mining and metallurgical sectors, describing in a letter to a relative "the foundations on which the most modern of capitalisms unfolds with unheard-of energy." In his study "El viaje a Vasconia de Max Weber" (Max Weber's trip to the Basque Country) (1997) Jose Miguel Azaola returns to the point made by Caro Baroja about the Jesuits' spiritual support for the emerging bourgeoisie in the Basque Country starting in the seventeenth century. This introduced a type of business activity and a culture of work similar in appearance and results to the Protestant work ethic, and Azaola tries to explain how this support by the Society of Jesus could form the basis of the religious justification of that kind of economic activity. In this regard, he notes how certain prominent moralists of the Society of Jesus were already praising work in the seventeenth and eighteenth centuries and how a portion of the Basque secular clergy preached this morality of work among the urban population even when the Jesuits lost much of their influence among the Bilbao bourgeoisie of the age (Azaola 1997, 212).

The Jesuits' inability to establish the Society in Baiona (Bayonne) and to gain control of the secondary school, due to the resistance of the local bourgeoisie, may have been particularly important in this regard. This was because the *collège,* the chief location for the intellectual and moral formation of the dominant social stratum, was a center of *Jansenism* (or *anti-Jesuitism*)—Jansen was the director of the school between 1611 and 1644 (Azaola 1997, 214).

What is interesting is the fact that, as Azaola indicates, there was a paradoxical resemblance between the rigorous Puritan morality of a good part of Basque society until the early twentieth century, which is explained by Jesuit influence, and the even more rigid and inflexible ethics of the Jansenists, who promoted a spirituality entirely opposed to that of the Jesuits. Azaola calls our attention to the scant importance granted to Jansenism as a religious system in Weber's explanation of capitalism, when the Jansenist doctrine of predestination is so close to that of Calvin, and the austerity of Jansenist ethics falls in no way short of Calvinism's Puritan rigor (Azaola 1997, 214). Likewise, Weber pays insufficient attention to Jesuit ethics and interprets in a restrictive way those aspects of Jesuit morality susceptible of being considered "generators" of the capitalist spirit. Instead, he points out that although it was the Jesuits who decisively and definitively gave a "rational" character to Christian asceticism, it was the Protestant Reformation that brought ascesis and the rules of rational and Christian life out of the monasteries, implanting them in professional life, as if St. Ignatius and his followers had not tried to influence the lay circles that surrounded them before Calvin did (Azaola 1997, 216).

In the last decades of the nineteenth century and the first two decades of the twentieth, the vertiginous industrialization of Bizkaia and Gipuzkoa had already been completed. By that time, the Jesuits had achieved the spiritual conquest of the bourgeoisie that was the driving force of this industrialization, while the anticlericalism of the middling and lower strata of industrial society was ever more pronounced (Azaola 1997, 220).

This religious influence on the Basque work ethic may be behind many business activities in the Basque Country. For example, this spirituality may underpin the humanism that laid the original foundations for the birth of the Mondragon Cooperative. The promoters of Mondragon were "familiar with the idea that business cannot and should not lose any of the benefits of efficiency due to the fact that *human values* enjoy a clear predominance over purely economic or material resources" (Arizmendi 1979, 40). This was a notion of business in which "*interpersonal solidarity,* in virtue of which the cooperative or work community is instituted, is further strengthened with the regulation of *intercommunity* solidarity or the establishment of groups of cooperatives, in accordance with the affinities or complementarities that can be appealed to among their members, with the corresponding provisions for the transfer of both human and economic resources culminating in the rebalancing of profits and losses in the general interest" (Arizmendi 1979, 41); and it was carried out in a context in which "the motto heralding the Mondragon cooperative experiment" was "to act and not to win, to create and not to possess, to progress and not to dominate" (Arizmendi 1979, 38).

From the Traditional Culture of Work to Social Representations

A number of studies exist of the social representations and understandings of work among the Basque and Navarrese populations. We can use their findings to delimit the content of organizational commitment in this specific cultural and sociodemographic context, for the purpose of illustrating the relationship between social representations and organizational commitment in the form I set out above.

On the level of the psychosocial analysis of organizational behavior, one of the indispensable elements for the facilitation of organizational commitment indicated by Turo Virtanen (2000, 342) is awareness and systematic description of the understandings, attitudes, and beliefs held by workers with regard to work in general (focus of commitment), as well as the affinity between their social identity and interests (base of commitment), on the one hand, and the implicit norms of the organizational culture to which they belong, on the other. Equally indispensable is the analysis of the antecedents of the base and focus of commitment in relation to variations in the content of the aforementioned social representations, due to sociodemographic anchoring factors such as age and gender or to organizational factors such as contract type.

Social representations of work refer to the totality of specific, socially and culturally determined understandings, attitudes, and patterns of behavior in relation to work. As such, their analysis should take as its starting point both the traditional culture of work and the shift from this traditional culture to an industrial society, stretching from the third quarter of the nineteenth century to the third quarter of the twentieth; and from the latter to a *postindustrial* society (Touraine 1974), which began to emerge in the late 1960s and is the characteristic type of society among the major Western countries today.

The traditional cultural content about work in the Basque Country and Navarre hence constitutes the sociological substrate on which the hegemonic social representations about work in Basque and Navarrese society as a whole are based. On the foundation of this cultural substrate, different positionings and understandings of work have been generated in today's society, giving rise to specific emancipated and polemical social representations among particular groups (defined by gender, age, social and work status, and so on), which, through their manifestation in organizational culture, will necessarily influence the organizational commitment of individuals in a work context.

Work in Traditional Societies and the Beginning of the Industrial Age

Some studies that have tried to analyze the existence of a specific Basque culture of work in *traditional* and *urban-industrial* societies have focused on the traditional economic behavior of Basque men tied to their family and to village life (Echeberría Monteberría 1986), and linked in turn to *cooperativism* as a form of business organization, and to women's roles in the Basque economy. Others have centered on analyzing the religious ethic of work and thrift among the Basque bourgeoisie that led the industrial development of Bizkaia and Gipuzkoa from the seventeenth century to the beginning of the twentieth (Azaola 1986; Uriarte 1997; Caro Baroja 1990, 2009), drawing an analogy to the link between the economic development of Protestant countries and the Protestant work ethic. These elements are presumed to form part of the shared cultural heritage about work transmitted through the process of socialization; in other words, they form part of the *hegemonic* social representations (Moscovici 1988) about work in this concrete sociocultural context.

Work in Industrial and Postindustrial Societies

Logically, the multiplicity of contemporary forms of work in postindustrial society and their relative role as agents of socialization, now in competition with other dimensions of social life such as the family, leisure, and consumption in general (Cerrato et al. 2003), together with immigration to the Basque Country during the era of industrial developmentalism throughout the Spanish state from the late 1950s to the end of the dictatorship in the mid 1970s (Martín, Martínez Shaw, and Tusell 1998), make it necessary to relativize the Basque culture of work in its two aspects: the religious work ethic among the Basque industrial bourgeoisie and the traditional economic behavior of Basque men.

The transition in the Western world from an industrial society to a postindustrial society, with its concomitant changes in the economic world, the world of work, and individual identity, means that it may be more appropriate today to speak about a plurality of social representations of work among Basques, rather than a single Basque culture of work.

At present, change and heterogeneity constitute the essence of society, whether we wish to describe that society as postmodern (Lyotard 1984, 1992), liquid (Bauman 2005), characterized by multinational capitalism (Jameson 2000), an information society (Castells 1996, 1997, 1998), or in some other way, giving rise to the new paradigm of *globaliza-*

tion (Touraine 2007). Thus, in place of a culture of work common to all individuals in a particular society, it now seems more appropriate to talk about different social representations of work that presumably coexist in collective memory with certain elements of an older culture of work in which aspects characteristic of the industrial era and of traditional forms of work and of preindustrial life are superimposed.

In relation to this contemporary socioeconomic context, I will now try to link the results of three studies of social representations of work and work-related values in the context of the population of the Basque Country and Navarre to the model of organizational commitment proposed by Virtanen (2000). Specifically, these studies are:

- A study of social representations of work among a representative sample of 584 individuals from Bizkaia (Cerrato et al. 2003), with a sampling error of ± 4.3 percent at a confidence level of 95.5 percent.

- The results corresponding to the Basque and Navarrese population for questions addressing work-related values and understandings of work in the third wave of the World Values Survey (Elzo 2002), representative of both populations with a sampling error of ± 5.77 percent for the Navarrese population and ± 3.33 percent for the Basque population, at a confidence level of 95.5 percent.

The results of these studies provide us with information about social representations, understandings, and values related to work in the Basque Country and Navarre, or the sociological substrate (or *hegemonic social representations*) that I have described above. As I have argued, this specific content can be considered as a psychosocial aspect of the focus and base of organizational commitment. From this perspective, age, gender, and the type of connection between the individual and the firm, in their turn, will be criteria for the psychosocial anchoring of social representations of work. Such criteria are, as noted, highly relevant to work-related behavior and can explain how this representational content may vary, so that they act as antecedents that modulate the base and focus of commitment at the psychosocial level. These will be *emancipated* social representations, differing from one group to another and even potentially in conflict with one another, if they reflect incompatible content in relation to different ways of understanding work (*polemical* social representations) within each organization.

These psychosocial aspects of the focus and base of organizational commitment will interact with other aspects related to an organization's immediate antecedents in its environment and to the personal and attitudinal psychological characteristics specific to each worker (Vega Rodríguez and Garrido Martín 1998).

In general, these studies indicate that in postindustrial Basque and Navarrese society, the content of social representations of work is highly complex, and there is a very diffuse or heterogeneous image of what is understood by "work," so that these aspects of the focus and base of organizational commitment will also be highly heterogeneous. Starting from these results and applying Virtanen's model of organizational commitment, we can differentiate certain psychosocial elements that are significant for organizational commitment at the level of content (focus of commitment) and of the latter's significance for the worker's social identity and interests, which may or may not coincide with the organization's normative structure at the level of organizational culture (base of commitment).

The need to promote work commitment, not only for the benefit of organizational efficiency but also for individual welfare, is quite obvious if we take into account the fact that when the importance assigned to work in the Basque Country and Navarre in comparison to other spheres of life is considered, the family appears to be the most important sphere with an average score of 3.84 out of 5, followed by work and friends (3.54 and 3.50 respectively), with leisure (3.39), politics (1.88), and religion (2.31) ranked as significantly less important. This tendency is quite similar to that in the rest of Spain, as well as in the major European countries, and signals a favorable predisposition toward organizational commitment at work, since the latter is one of the chief spheres of an individual's life (Elzo 2002).

Nevertheless, if we analyze the importance of work in relation to its characteristics by comparing the 1999 data with that from 1995, we see that those aspects most closely related to the social consideration of work and its "respectability" have lost force, as have aspects linked to self-realization such as "the opportunity to take initiative" and "a good fit for one's capabilities." At the same time, instrumental aspects such as "good income" or "job security," aspects that enable leisure and free time such as "a good schedule" or "good vacations," and aspects related to autonomy such as "no pressure," "responsibility," "the ability to make decisions," and finally "interesting work," have become important for a greater percentage of those surveyed (table 2.1). Consequently, the promotion of organizational commitment must take its cue from this trend, which indicates that although aspects related to personal self-realization are less important, autonomy at work, the possibility of balancing work with social and family life, and economic and instrumental aspects are more important.

Consequently, for Basques and Navarrese, work is one of the most important parts of their lives and shares that importance with other dimensions of life, such as family and friends. In harmony with this, the value placed on economic and instrumental aspects, recreational and social aspects, and autonomy at work has increased, to the detriment of aspects related to personal growth, self-realization, and social utility (Cerrato et al. 2003). All these aspects are presumed to be elements that, when the work performed by an individual is consistent with them, will increase the worker's organizational commitment.

Table 2.1. The implications of the evolution of valuations for workplace characteristics for organization commitment in the Basque and Navarrese autonomous communities, 1995–1999 (in percentage of subjects)

	% 1995	% 1999	Difference	Trend
Good salary	70.0	87.7	+7.7	Increase
Not undue pressure	26.9	50.0	+23.1	Increase
Job security	56.6	79.1	+22.5	Increase
Respectable work	47.4	39.6	−7.8	Decrease
Good schedule	41.4	70.6	+29.4	Increase
Initiative	47.5	43.5	−4.0	Decrease
Vacations	23.8	46.2	+22.4	Increase
Responsibility	31.7	45.6	+13.9	Increase
Interesting work	55.3	66.4	+11.1	Increase
Adapted to one's skills	68.1	64.4	−3.7	Decrease
High degree of decision-making	37.6	42.3	+4.7	Increase

Source: Elzo (2002).

At the level of the organization of work, and in agreement with the increased importance of autonomy at work, Basques are the Europeans who most strongly support a democratic and participative system of work, giving a very negative evaluation of traditional management systems based exclusively on the observance of rules and hierarchy. In comparison to the rest of Spain and to the major European countries, the Basques have the highest percentage of individuals surveyed who prefer to collaborate with their supervisors rather than to obey them without question, 54.5 percent. Similarly, the percentage of those who prefer to obey their superiors is among the lowest (28.9 percent). For this reason, the organizational structure (aside from the cooperative formula) that can best foster the worker's identification with the firm's objectives and successes is one in which the organization of work is based on autonomous or semi-autonomous work groups (Ayestarán and Cerrato 1996), in which workers, in a meaningful way, have a high degree of autonomy in making decisions, something that will obviously be a condition promoting work commitment.

Psychosocial Anchoring of Social Representations of Work and Psychosocial Antecedents of Organizational Commitment and Cooperation: Age, Gender, and Contract Type

Within these social representations and understandings of work that are common to all Basques, there nevertheless exist specific positionings, the variation of which is subject to the peculiarities of membership in particular social categories that act as specific criteria for psychosocial anchoring and also as antecedents of the focus and base of organizational commitment, and therefore of cooperation at work. Among these, three of the most important are age, gender, and the type of contractual tie with the organization, the contract type (Cerrato et al. 2003).

Age as an antecedent of the base and focus of commitment: Some dimensions of social representations of work include aspects that differ as a function of age and have implications for the promotion of organizational commitment. Cerrato and colleagues (2003) find that individuals over the age of fifty had an image of work that was more closely tied to *personal realization* and to work's *psychosocial functions* than individuals in the eighteen-to-thirty and thirty-one-to-fifty age ranges (table 2.2), who shared an economic and instrumental image of work to a greater extent than those fifty-one years of age or older. These younger age ranges associated work to a greater degree with *money, salary,* and its economic function, but considered self-realization, good pay, and good colleagues ideal aspects of work not present in actuality. Young Basque people consequently have an *economic and instrumental* image of work, with the result that, even if self-realization and the social aspects of work interest them as ideal elements, their fundamental work-related goal is money, something relatively unlikely to foster commitment to an organization.

On the other hand, middle-aged Basques and those over fifty have a *social and identity-oriented* image of work that appears to be due more to their having been socialized in the context of an industrial society—in which the understanding and functions of work were different from those that predominate in today's postindustrial society—than to an improvement in the characteristics of their jobs in comparison to the positions held by younger workers. Be that as it may, older individuals consider work a site for *self-realization* and as having *psychosocial utility*, even without devaluing its economic aspects. Consequently, the implications of age as an antecedent of commitment are quite obvious, as shown by these results.

Table 2.2. Implications for organizational commitment of statistically significant differences (z) in the significance and social representation of work as of a function of age

	18–30	31–50	51+	F	Sig.
Job image: Personal development	−.21	−.15	.25	10.714	.000
Psychosocial function	−.19	−.28	.27	14.101	.000
Ideal work: Permits self-realization	.28	.05	−.28	13.284	.000
Ideal work: Good pay and coworkers	.23	.06	−.32	12.045	.000
Economic function of work	.03	.03	−.21	2.639	.072
Job image: Money and salary	.21	.06	−.29	11.290	.000

Source: Cerrato et al. (2003).

Gender as an antecedent of commitment: From a psychosocial perspective, the role of gender as an antecedent of organizational commitment is determined in part by its role as an anchoring criterion for social representations of work in the Basque Country (Cerrato et al. 2003): although these representations are similar between men and women in certain dimensions of work, some differences nevertheless exist in certain dimensions. The image of work among women places greater emphasis than that among men on *organizational aspects,* as well as the aspects of *independence* and *self-realization,* work's *psychosocial function,* and its *intrinsic and expressive* function, despite a greater association between work and *stress* and lower levels of *work-related satisfaction* (table 2.3). In general, work for men is to a greater extent than for women a context in which satisfaction predominates over commitment, while women show a greater capacity for commitment together with a lower level of satisfaction.

Table 2.3. Implications for organizational commitment of the significant statistical differences (z) in the differential aspects of the meaning and social representation of work as a function of gender in the CAPV/EAE

	Men	Women	F	Sig.
Job image: Organizational aspects	−.08	.07	3.389	.066
Job image: Stress	−.08	.07	3.598	.058
Job image: Independence	−.17	.15	14.986	.000
Ideal work: Self-realization	−.15	.13	11.297	.001
Pyschosocial function	−0.14	.13	10.988	.001
Job goals: Intrinsic and expressive dimension	−.14	.13	11.139	.001
Job satisfaction	.16	.01	3.897	.049

Source: Cerrato et al. (2003).

These results have clear implications for the management of commitment as a function of gender: while for women commitment seems to be a priority in itself (it provides independence, they highlight its expressive function, it is a site of realization, and so on), for men it is likely to be mediated by satisfaction. Consequently, Basque women appear to show a greater tendency toward commitment to a firm, but this would be expected to be the case under conditions of equality with men. In effect, Basque women express an image of work as a self-affirmation of identity, with a high capacity for commitment to a firm, based on the high degree of centrality work has in their lives and on seeking collaboration among colleagues, even without renouncing private and family life. This is not something that comes without a cost, since, as has already been mentioned, women's average stress level appears to be higher than men's, and their work-related satisfaction appears to be lower (Cerrato et al. 2003).

Contract type as an antecedent of commitment: Self-employed, temporary, and permanent workers express different social representations of work, clearly indicating the repercussions of contract type as an antecedent of the base and focus of organizational commitment. In table 2.4 we can observe the differential aspects of these social representations in the Basque Country (Cerrato et al. 2003).

Self-employed Basque workers have an image of work that is closely linked to *personal realization* and to work's *psychosocial functions,* in addition to expressing the highest level of *work-related satisfaction,* as compared to other types of workers. This appears to correlate with the nonexistence of a stable, formally defined, hierarchical organizational structure for the performance of their work. This is another argument in favor of organizational flexibility, cooperative work, and democratic leadership in promoting workers' organizational commitment.

On the other hand, the organizational commitment that can be expected from a worker with a temporary contract is not very high from the perspective of contract type as an antecedent, since the image of work that characterizes workers of this kind is not so linked to *personal development* or *stability,* implying a low level of belief in work as a *right* and a low level of work-related satisfaction, although greater than that of workers without contracts. All this should lead business organizations and society as a whole to reflect on the effect that this kind of work has both on the psychological welfare of individuals and on their motivation and organizational commitment.

Finally, with regard to workers with stable employment contracts, the representational elements that specifically characterize these workers are that they define ideal work in terms of a *good schedule* and *free time* to a greater extent than self-employed workers and workers with temporary contracts and that they have a higher level of work-related satisfaction than temporary workers, although lower than that of self-employed workers. All this indicates that, from the perspective of social representations, their organizational commitment will tend to be greater than that of individuals with temporary contracts, although this seems to depend on the possibility of adequately combining work with free time.

Table 2.4. Implications for organizational commitment of statistically significant differences (z) in the significance and social representation of work as of a function of the type of contract in the CAPV/EAE

	Self-employed	Temporary	Permanent	F	Sig.
Job image: Organizational aspects	−.36	.11	−.14	3.677	.006
Job image: Personal development	.14	−.25	−.02	5.250	.000
Job image: Independent	0.00	−.21	−.10	7.419	.000
Psychosocial function	.47	−.19	.00	4.343	.002
Work as a right	.27	−.15	−.02	3.389	.011
Ideal job: Good schedule	.07	−.20	.22	4.463	.002
Job satisfaction	.57	.35	.02	7.542	.000

Source: Cerrato et al. (2003).

The content of social representations of work and the processes of psychosocial and sociological anchoring of this content in the context of Basque and Navarrese society can be respectively articulated with the (psychosocial) focus of organizational commitment, its base, and its antecedents, influencing the psychosocial aspects of these dimensions, which are also acted upon by other organizational and personal aspects not addressed in this study. Within the content of the social representations common to society as a whole with regard to the definition and understanding of work (hegemonic social representations), we can find images of work characteristic of traditional society, and more obviously, of industrial society, coexisting with much more up-to-date images and understandings characteristic of postindustrial society. At the same time, particular understandings and specific positionings with respect to work (emancipated and polemical social representations) emerge from this generic representational content with respect to work in postindustrial society, as a function of particular criteria of sociological and psychosocial anchoring such as age, gender, or the type of contractual tie. Membership in these different categories should be expected to imply different forms of commitment to the organization, due to the fact that, from this perspective, they also imply different ways of understanding work and ascribing it meaning, affecting the social identity of the organization's members as a function of the mentioned social categories and of the degree to which the organization may be useful in achieving their interests.

Conclusion

The new socio-structural and economic changes brought about by globalization in the contemporary postindustrial age have affected work, giving rise to new work practices and transforming the way in which work is understood. These changes necessarily affect the form acquired by organizational commitment and cooperative attitudes among workers, as well as the mechanisms that regulate them. It is therefore necessary to expand the concept of organizational commitment, incorporating a wider range of cultural and social aspects, as well as other socio-structural and group-oriented psychosocial aspects, based both on the social categories into which the members of the organization fall and on the totality of formal and informal relationships existing within the organization.

Virtanen's multidimensional model of organizational commitment enables this expansion of the concept, thanks to its incorporation of dimensions making reference to the *base, focus,* and *antecedents* of commitment, determined in part by cultural, social, and group-oriented psychosocial aspects. The connection between organizational commitment and these psychosocial aspects is articulated by way of the social representations with regard to work that are shared by members of the organization as members of the same society or culture, hegemonic social representations (Moscovici 1988) of what working means, or different representations that may come into conflict due to the workers' membership in different social categories and their different positions within the organization, giving rise to polemical and emancipated representations. These distinct social categories and positions within the organization are anchoring criteria for social representations and act as specific antecedents of organizational commitment, since by determining differences in representational content, they give rise to different foci and bases of commitment. This will necessarily affect the psychosocial aspects of the content of commitment (focus) and the way in which the organization affects the social identity and structure of interests of its members (base), all of which will be reflected in latent form in its organizational culture.

It does not appear that we can talk about a homogenous and unequivocal culture of work that is characteristic of Basques in the context of today's postindustrial society. Rather, what seems to exist in Basque society is a complex of attitudes and understandings at the collective level, within which it is possible to detect specific positionings in relation to work as a function of parameters such as gender, age, or work experience, and in which certain elements linked to a traditional culture and a work ethic belonging to previous eras present in collective memory may perhaps find expression. Moreover, this heterogeneity has clear implications for cooperative attitudes, since they will vary as a function of the worker's position not only in the structure of the organization, but also in the social structure.

The management and incentivization of cooperative attitudes among Basques must take into account the fact that work continues to be one of the most important parts of an individual's life, but that this importance has been diminishing and must today share its significance as an agent of socialization with other dimensions of people's lives such as leisure, family, and friends. At the same time, the value placed on work's economic and instrumental aspects and its recreational and social aspects is increasing, to the detriment of aspects related to personal growth, self-realization, and social utility, even if the latter continue to be highly important.

References

Arizmendi, Jose María. 1979. "La experiencia cooperativa en Mondragón." *Tribuna Cooperativa* 36–37 (January–June): 38–41.

Ayestarán, Sabino, and Javier Cerrato. 1996. "La creación de equipos de trabajo en las organizaciones." In *El grupo como construcción social*, edited by Sabino Ayestarán. Barcelona: Plural.

Azaola, Jose Miguel. 1997. "El Viaje a Vasconia de Max Weber." *Bidebarrieta* 2: 189–222.

Bauman, Zygmunt. 2005. *Liquid Life*. Cambridge, MA: Polity Press.

Caro Baroja, Julio. 2009. *The Basques*. Translated by Kristin Addis. Introduction by William A. Douglass. Reno: Center for Basque Studies, University of Nevada, Reno.

——. 1990. *Nosotros los vascos: Etnología*. Vol. 3. Bilbao: Lur.

Castells, Manuel. 1996. *The Rise of Network Society: Information Age*. Vol. 1. Malden, MA: Blackwell.

——. 1997. *The Power of Identity: Information Age*. Vol. 2. Malden, MA: Blackwell.

——. 1998. *End of Millennium: Information Age*. Vol. 3. Malden, MA: Blackwell.

Cerrato, Javier, Mikel Villarreal, Itziar Ugarteburu, Eduardo Apodaca, and Eduardo Rubio. 2003. "Nuevas prácticas de trabajo, representaciones sociales del trabajo e identidad social en la sociedad postindustrial." *Revista de Psicología Social Aplicada* 13, no. 2: 79–123.

Echeberría Monteberría, Juan José. 1986. "Reflexiones sobre el hombre vasco y el cambio de modelo económico." *Revista Internacional de Estudos Vascos* 31, no. 3: 1001–18.

Elzo, Javier. 2002. *Los valores de los vascos y navarros ante el nuevo milenio*. Bilbao: Universidad de Deusto.

Jameson, Frederic. 2000. "Globalization and Political Strategy." *New Left Review* 4 (July–August): 49–68.

Lyotard, Jean-François. 1984. *The Postmodern Condition: A Report on Knowledge*. Translated by Geoff Bennington and Brian Massumi. Foreword by Frederic Jameson. Manchester: Manchester University Press.

——. 1992. *The Postmodern Explained to Children: Correspondence, 1982–1985*. Translations edited by Julian Pefanis and Morgan Thomas. London: Turnaround.

Martín, José Luis, Carlos Martínez Shaw, and Javier Tusell. 1998. *Historia de España*. Madrid: Taurus.

Moscovici, Serge. 1988. "Notes Towards a Description of Social Representations." *European Journal of Social Psychology* 18, no. 3: 211–50.

Tawney, Richard Henry. 1948. *Religion and the Rise of Capitalism*. London: Penguin.

Touraine, Alain. 2007. *A New Paradigm for Understanding Today's World*. Translated by Gregory Elliot. Cambridge: Polity Press.

———. 1974. *The Post-industrial Society: Tomorrow's Social History: Classes, Conflicts and Culture in the Programmed Society*. Translated by Leonard F. X. Mayhew. London: Wildwood House.

Uriarte, Pedro. 1977. *Psicosociología de los vizcaínos a través de la historia*. Bilbao: Editorial La Gran Enciclopedia Vasca.

Vega Rodríguez, Teresa, and Eugenio Garrido Martín. 1998. *Psicología de las organizaciones, proceso de socialización y compromiso con la empresa*. Salamanca: Amaru.

Virtanen, Turo. 2000. "Commitment and the Study of Organizational Climate and Culture." In *Handbook of Organizational Culture & Climate*, edited by Neal Ashkanasy, Celeste P.M. Wilderom, and Mark F. Peterson. London: SAGE.

Weber, Max. 1965. *The Protestant Ethic and the Spirit of Capitalism*. Translated by Talcott Parsons. London: Allen & Unwin.

3

Developing Intercooperation in the Social Economy: An Analysis of Grant Recipients in the Basque Country

Jon Morandeira Arca, Baleren Bakaikoa Azurmendi, and Victoria de Elizagarate Gutierrez

Translated By Lauren DeAre

Marketing and Market Orientation in Public Administration

The philosophy of marketing represents a conceptual position or an attitude; it is a way of conceiving the exchange relationship between two or more parties (Santesmases 2004). Applications of marketing have traditionally been in the business and profit-making world, but the marketing staff at Ohio State University (1965, 43) define marketing as "the process in a society by which the demand structure for economic goods and services is anticipated or enlarged and satisfied through the conception, promotion, exchange and physical distribution of such goods and services." Consequently, marketing is considered a social process and not just a combination of business activities (Cervera 1999). Philip Kotler and Sidney J. Levy (1969) propose broadening the notion of marketing further based on the idea that every organization creates some type of product that it

* A previous version published as "El Fomento de la intercooperación empresarial en economía social: Análisis del comportamiento de los beneficiarios de ayudas en el País Vasco," in *Ciriec-España, Revista de Economía Pública, Social y Cooperativa* 67 (May 2010): 157–83.

offers to a group of consumers in one way or another, in order to achieve its acceptance. The same Philip Kotler, along with Gerald Zaltman (1971), defines the field of social marketing as the application of traditional marketing concepts and techniques in order to gain citizen acceptance of certain ideas and/or social causes (Vázquez 2004, 18).

The continuous process of broadening marketing's scope shifted it from the business world into nonprofit organizations. It later came to include nonmonetary exchanges and, finally, was no longer limited to customer, consumer, and user markets. It now has a leading role in all types of exchanges that work toward achieving any of the multiple objectives set forth by various individuals, organizations, or institutions (Vázquez 2004, 18).

This line of thinking has led to a type of nonbusiness marketing that is a specialized area within the discipline. It is comprised of subareas that include nonprofit marketing, public marketing, social marketing, and political and electoral marketing (See, for example, Santesmases 2004, 927).

Marketing represents a philosophy that guides an organization to connect to its customers' knowledge and understanding, in order to satisfy customers' needs. In this philosophy, the adoption of marketing as a concept implies considering the public's needs when creating public projects. Through participation, both the organization and the services offered change and adapt (marketing/market orientation) (Cervera 2001, 119). In this context, Magnus Söderberg (2009) believes that citizen preferences can reveal ideas about the way the public sector operates that traditional models are unable to provide.

For public agencies that seek to satisfy the needs of citizens and provide real value, marketing has become the best platform for planning. Its primary concern is in offering results that are valuable for a target market. In the public sector, marketing's mantra is citizen value and satisfaction (Kotler and Lee 2007).

In this context, the central core of public marketing is managing the exchange relationship between the public administration and the public. The major components in this relationship are the actors and the flow between them. The actors include the administration on one side and the managed party/citizen/user/customer on the other.[1] The flow is

---

1. The concept of citizens as customers should be understood as an expression of greater demand and activism on the part of both parties, and should include not only people or indi-

intangible from the customer to the administration and basically consists of information that, in practice, represents a proposal of needs that the customer wants the administration to satisfy. Flow in the opposite direction is of a tangible nature and usually consists of solutions offered by the administration.

This began in the 1960s when the exchange between two or more parties became marketing's subject of study. Out this idea emerged the current marketing concept that starts with knowledge of consumers or user needs. From this perspective, customer orientation or market orientation has becomes a subject of scientific study. As Jean-Jacques Lambin (1993) explains, organizations that are market-oriented must address the fundamental problem of how to monitor needs in order to anticipate future ones.

John C. Narver and Stanley C. Slater (1990) performed one of the first empirical applications of market orientation in the profit-making sector. In their study, they apply philosophical and behavioral aspects to marketing, including three behavioral components: customer focus, competitor orientation, and cross-functional teams. In turn, Ajay K. Kohli and Bernard J. Jaworski (1990) support market orientation from the behavioral standpoint of information processing. The creation of market-generated information (in order to understand the market's needs), dissemination of that information (to share that understanding), and the response to it (to satisfy the needs of the market) constitute the central core of market orientation, in the profit-making and nonprofit fields, the private sector, and the public sector (Cervera 2004, 58).

Considering this, public administrations and specifically the core bodies involved in public operations that introduce the philosophy of market orientation into management must include provisions for continual instruments that monitor how needs change over time. In this framework, it is essential that the administration have an information gathering and data analysis system that facilitates market-oriented decision-making (Elizagarate 2008, 65).

---

viduals but also groups, associations, and collectives (Subirats 1990–1991). The change in the management model of the European public sector, at both federal and local corporation levels, has translated into the promotion of public services, considering users as customers instead of receivers (Bouinot and Bermils 1995). In Spain, the tendency has been to use the term customer (*cliente*), especially in modernizing the public administration (Chias 1995).

Based on the above, it is also important to create a market information system (MIS) to support market decisions. A decision support system
(DSS) is a group of programs and tools that compile information necessary for decision-making processes, in order to send them to intermediaries and administrations during the decision-making process. An MIS can
be defined as a group of elements, instruments, and procedures used to
obtain, record, and analyze data for the purpose of transforming it into a
marketing or market decision-making "tool" (Santesmases 2004).

In order to design public policy strategies, as in marketing, being
familiar with and understanding the market is a necessity. Knowing the
different segments that comprise the market and what their needs are is
also necessary. To find out this information about the individuals that
form a market, pertinent data must be gathered. However, just compiling
the data is not enough; data alone does not comprise information. The
data must go through a process of development and relevant post-analysis
in order to extract relevant information.

Marketing research makes two contributions to the information system: it functions as a suitable methodology to obtain the necessary data
and it provides the methods and techniques necessary to process and
analyze this same data. Thus, it provides methods and techniques for the
information system that are relevant for obtaining and then rigorously
analyzing data. Finally, once research-based analysis has been employed,
it must then be interpreted, and this interpretation leads to useful conclusions for decision-making.

But the decision to solve a public problem or to prioritize solutions
is not marketing's responsibility, but instead that of the public decision-
maker. Marketing may help advise or support decisions and provide
objective information, but the responsibility always lies with the public
manager (Rivera 2004, 13).

Following Josep Chias's (1995) strategic planning model for public
marketing (Chias 1995), wherein the author defines the different stages of
planning—and taking into account that in public management there are
various levels of decision-making hierarchies and in all of them a marketing methodology can be valuable (Rivera 2004, 16)—this chapter focuses
on the final stages of this process when a competent authority defines the
program and services that will satisfy market needs.

The processes of designing programs and services constitute what is
known as strategic development within the all-encompassing planning

process (Vázquez and Placer 2000, 78). Strategic development includes stating objectives and how to transform them into an offer of products/ services. An all-encompassing planning process involves the operative development of the elements that comprise the services offered by the public administration (Chias 1995, 82).

Implementation is the stage of the strategic planning process when a series of actions and effects derived from the previously defined strategic plan regulatory framework takes place, attempting to implement or bring them into practice, with all of the difficulties that this involves (Vázquez and Placer 2000, 80).

Evaluation is the systematic application of social research procedures in order to evaluate and eventually perfect the conceptualization and the design, its implementation, and the usefulness of the social intervention programs (Ballart 1992). In other words, the evaluation stage within an organization provides feedback that becomes a tool used in decision-making regarding the definition, implementation, and usefulness of the service offered. Here, we focus on this stage in the process by analyzing recipients and their behavior related to services offered by the administration. In doing so, these services can be evaluated and/or improved based on the organization's objectives and the needs of the public sector market.

Moreover, following Chias's (1995) classification of the public sector from a marketing standpoint and administrative services offered, we are especially interested in these services and in particular those that encourage social activity.

Justification of and Interest in Research on the Development of Intercooperation in the Basque Country's Social Economy

Following Rafael Chaves (2008), public policies can be divided into supply-side and demand-side policies. The former are aimed at strengthening the sector through measures that are institutional, regulatory, financial, and subsidized. In turn, demand-side policies motivate the economic activity that they support, facilitating access in the role of a public sector provider.

Additionally, supply-side public social economy development policies have two channels of application (Chaves 2008): toward social economy organizations and toward jobs that could have a specific application for social economy institutions.

Along with this brief description of public policies that promote the social economy, it should be pointed out that the model applied in the Basque Country is based on supply-side policy (Bakaikoa et al. 2009, 70). This chapter will analyze financial measures that are based on supply-side policy.

The Office of Social Economy in the Basque government's Department of Justice, Employment, and Social Security is responsible for creating, managing, and executing programs that foster, develop, and promote the social economy.[2] To do so, the competent authority is the Office of Social Economy, which is dedicated to implementing the financial[3] measures of the social economy promotion policy in the Basque Country. In other words, it is the main public action body that promotes the social economy.

The Basque government, through its Office of Social Economy, offers grants that promote and develop the social economy. These grants are based in several programs (Bakaikoa, Etxezarreta, and Etxezarreta 2007, 133) and include grants for business intercooperation, aimed at creating structures and agreements that create synergy and produce greater added value among different companies. Therefore, the Office of Social Economy has identified the need and utility of promoting business intercooperation among social economy companies, especially for those that are smaller and that demonstrate a need to adopt growth strategies. With ever-increasing intensity, due to the progressively more complex and less local economic reality that these companies are working in, these strategies can help them reach an optimum size to access the resources and capabilities that they will need to survive and also improve their competitiveness.

---

2. This is one of the functions of the Office of Social Economy, according to Decree 315/2005 of October 18, 2005, by which an organic and functional structure of the Department of Justice, Employment, and Social Security is established in Article 19. 1. a) *Boletín Oficial del País Vasco* (BOPV, Official Bulletin of the Basque Country) No. 205, October 27, 2005. Although it is important to point out that currently, according to Decree 4/2009 (BOPV No. 141, June 23, 2009), the Department of Justice, Employment, and Social Security was terminated and the Office of Social Economy became part of the new Department of Employment and Social Matters, under the new name Office of Social Economy, Social Business Responsibility, and Autonomous Work, but that it maintains the functions described in the aforementioned decree, according to Decree 538/2009 of October 6, 2009, by which the organic structure of the Department of Employment and Social Matters was established in Article 20 a) (BOPV No. 196, October13, 2009).

3. No reference is made to registered financial measures or subsidies.

In short, its task is to promote all opportunities within the social economy, in all geographic areas and economic sectors, through an annual competition for grants that promote business intercooperation.[4]

Turning to the classification of the content of these policies directed at the social economy (Chaves 2006), these grants are categorized within the supply-side financial policies that promote the social economy included in public budgets; for example, they comprise a package of economic-financial measures that includes grants and subsidies for the sector.

The timeframe for this research was from 2005 to 2007 (both years inclusive). This time period was chosen because starting with the 2004–5 competition, substantial changes were introduced to several of the grants and more data became available beginning in 2005. There are a total of fifty-two units for analysis or subsidy cases that were granted as of September 19, 2008 and that comprise the population included in this research.

We want to identify the recipients' primary characteristics, based on the reality of the intercooperation grants themselves. In other words, we will identify a profile of the recipients and their behavior, and in so doing, will be able to evaluate and/or improve this service, taking the organization's objectives and market needs into account. An empirical study and field study of the database had not been undertaken from a market orientation perspective.

Research Objectives

The general objective of this chapter is to analyze the recipients of annual grants supporting business intercooperation in the social economy. In other words, we will analyze a specific service that promotes the social economy and that is offered by the competent authority of the Basque Public Administration, the Office of Social Economy.

Based on this primary objective, we propose a further group of objectives that includes the following: analyzing intercooperation grant recipients from a market perspective by applying business or market research practices to a social economy administrative development activity; iden-

---

4. Grants offered for the period of analysis by means of the July 6, 2005, order by the Department of Justice, Employment, and Social Security (BOPV No. 135, July 15, 2005); the July 5, 2006, order by the Department of Justice, Employment, and Social Security (BOPV No. 133, July 13, 2006); the July 4, 2007, order by the Department of Justice, Employment, and Social Security (BOPV No. 141, July 23, 2007) by which the grants that support business intercooperation in the social economy are established.

tifying the dependent relationships that exist between different variables analyzed and their consequences in grant management; and categorizing recipients into groups according to certain behavior (the amount of grant monies received) that serves as variable criteria.

With these goals in mind, we can establish an identification and problem-solving tool. In this case, it pertains to the grants for business intercooperation issued by the Office of Social Economy of the Basque government. In short, statistical techniques have provided rigorous and reliable information, and this study proposes to identify the variables that determine certain behaviors among recipients. Consequently, the Office of Social Economy, in order to obtain the desired response from applicants, could consider introducing these variables as a requirement in the grant competition, or modify those previously used. In this way, we can see the importance of developing a market information system for the core units of public operations, which could improve this service in relation to the desired objectives.

Research Methodology and Results

The purpose of this section is to describe the research process carried out, the statistical techniques used to analyze the data, and the results obtained. This study is a descriptive study that intends to describe the recipients' characteristics, describe their profile, and identify nonindependence between determined variables that may provide a basis for the application of certain public decisions. In addition, this is a transversal study because it is our intent to show a snapshot of the variables of interest and their relationship in a given moment. This study uses secondary information as a source. In other words, it uses data that was already available and that serves as the data for this research. It is also a census study because it takes the target population as a whole into consideration.

These grants are designed to promote or encourage all business opportunities within the social economy in all geographic regions and economic sectors. The grants for business intercooperation include eight types of activities or subsidized actions: (1) intercooperation studies, (2) creation of intercooperative businesses or structures, (3) intercooperation agreements, (4) mergers, (5) incorporating existing intercooperation companies or structures, (6) participation in representative international organizations, (7) creation of international business groups, or (8) combinations of activities.

The grant recipients are legal entities that meet the established requirements set forth in the order the grants/subsidies are announced each year. For our analysis, we have used recipient data taken from the grant applications. The data obtained and extracted from the applications for analysis include the following: type of action performed, grant amount/quantity, recipient's legal status, recipient's activity sector, use of an external consultant in performance of the activity, consultant's legal status, if applicable, number of participants in the activity performed, and Basque province to which the recipient pertains.

The Office of Social Economy's databases were used to begin the quantitative or statistical analysis of the aforementioned data. In brief, an analysis of grants from 2005–7 was performed wherein initially a simple tabulation was used identify a profile of the recipients; then, a two-way tabulation with Pearson's chi-square test was used to identify nonindependence of the variables; and finally, an AID (automatic interaction detection) analysis was performed to separate the recipients into groups, using the Dyane data processor version 4.

First, we applied simple tabulation involving univariate analysis for the purpose of obtaining the frequency of all variables analyzed and in order to establish a specific intercooperation grant recipient profile for said period.

Regarding the types of activities, intercooperation studies predominated, accounting for 38.46 percent of the observations analyzed, followed very distantly by the other activities including: creation of intercooperative businesses or structures (13.46 percent), intercooperative agreements (11.54 percent), mergers (7.69 percent), incorporation of existing intercooperative structures (13.46 percent), participation in representative international organizations (1.92 percent), or a combination of actions (13.46 percent). In addition, two types of legal entities participated in this grant/subsidy: cooperatives, with 57.69 percent, and associations, with 42.31 percent.

Moreover, when observing the activity sector variable, we saw that the service sector is most involved in grant activity, with 76.92 percent. This was followed by the industrial section (19.23 percent) and agriculture (3.85 percent). In regards to the provinces of the CAPV/EAE Araba predominated with 40.38 percent, followed by Bizkaia (34.62 percent) and Gipuzkoa (25 percent).

Upon examination of the use of a consultant in performing relevant activities, we observed that in 46.15 percent of the cases, a consulting entity was used or contracted and in the remaining cases no consultant was used. As we show in table 3.1, the most common legal status among the consulting entities was cooperative, accounting for 26.92 percent of cases (58.33 percent of those that made use of a consulting entity).

Table 3.1. Legal type of consulting entity

Legal type	Frequency	%
Cooperative	14	26.92%
Associations	1	1.92%
*Sociedad limitada (SL)**	6	11.54%
*Sociedad anónima (SA)***	3	5.77%
No consultants used	28	53.85%
Total	52	100.00%

* Literally "limited society," Spanish legal business form similar to the US limited liability corporation (LLC).

** Literally "anonymous society," Spanish legal business form similar to the US corporation.

For the number of participants in the intercooperative activity performed, it is worth noting that in 40.38 percent of cases there were two or less participants.

And finally, we examined the variable figure that represents the grant/subsidy amount or quantity (see figure 3.1) received in order to perform the subsidized action. We observed that the majority of the recipients (61.5 percent) received a less-than-average amount. In other words, the concentration of the amounts was below the average.

In short, it can be concluded that grant recipients met the following average profile: the recipient was a cooperative in Araba in the service sector that performed an intercooperation study with the collaboration of two or less participants, without the help or contracting of any consulting entity in performing the activity and that received, on average, €9,542.62 to perform said activity.

In examining the individualized analysis (a census analysis for each year that is included in an internal working document from the Office of Social Economy and that analyzes the recipient profile for each year),[5] a similar conclusion can be made: the recipient profile remained stable.

---

5. Internal working document from the Office of Social Economy: *Study of Grant Recipients for Developing the Social Economy in the Autonomous Community of the Basque Country*. In this

Figure 3.1: Histogram and polygram of important frequencies

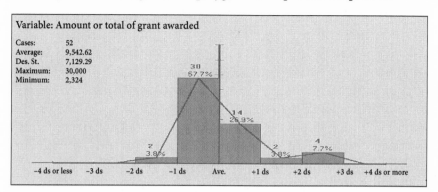

Furthermore, in regards to the grant amount, note that the recipients primarily fell below, but remained very close to, the average (specifically, 57.7 percent). This indicates that the amount dispersed is not very high, with few recipients receiving a grant amount higher or lower than the others. This outcome is an *a priori* consequence of the differing amounts established for different grants in the departmental order, given that the activity of intercooperation study is most typical and the grant limits are lower than others established in the order. Therefore, a possible hypothesis is that the type of activity determined the amount or grant given.

It is also important to point out that, among recipients, we found only two different types of legal status: cooperatives and associations. The most recent report published on social economy statistics states that social economy companies with a higher tendency toward cooperative relationships are cooperatives, representing 34.6 percent of businesses that establish some type of relationship (Dirección de Estudios y Régimen Jurídico 2008). We can see that the grant recipients follow the same tendencies that social economy businesses follow in day-to-day business.

Secondly, an analysis was made using a bivariable model of two-way tabulation for the fifty-two observations obtained from the recipients. With this technique, the level of relationship or association that exists between two variables can be determined. The results of the analysis were as follows, where the contingency tables and graphs show the relationships of variables in which the independence between them has been rejected

---

study, a profile analysis was performed that included all of the grants issued by the Office for 2005, 2006, and 2007.

with a level of confidence equal to or greater than 95 percent (p ≤ 0.05) by using Pearson's chi-squared test.

According to the chi-square value and a significance level of 0.05, the hypothesis of independence between the type of activity and the use of a consulting entity is rejected (see table 3.2), in this case, with a confidence level of 99.96 percent (p = 0.0006). In observing table 3.2 i shows that in the entire sample, intercooperation studies were the most represented activity (38.46 percent), followed by the creation of intercooperative businesses or structures, incorporation into intercooperative businesses or structures, and combinations of activities, each with 13.46 percent. However, this distribution changes as we look at the distribution of activities in terms of the use of a consultancy, where the percentages increase in a significant manner but only for intercooperation studies and combinations of activities. For the other activities, the percentages are higher in value when they did not use a consulting entity.

Table 3.2. Cross tabulation between type of activity and consulting entity

| | Consulting entity | | | | | |
| | Total sample | | Yes | | No | |
Type of activity	Freq.	%	Freq.	%	Freq.	%
Intercooperative study	20	38.46%	14	58.33%	6	21.43%
Creation of intercooperative business or structure	7	13.46%	1	4.17%	6	21.43%
Intercooperative agreement	6	11.54%	0	0.00%	6	21.43%
Merger	4	7.69%	2	8.33%	2	7.14%
Incorporation of intercooperative business or structure	7	13.46%	0	0.00%	7	25.00%
Participation in representative international organization	1	1.92%	0	0.00%	1	3.70%
Combination of activity	7	13.46%	7	29.17%	0	0.00%
Total	52	100%	24	100%	28	100%

Chi squared with 8 degrees of freedom = 27.6272 (p = 0.0006)

According to the chi-square value and a significance level of 0.05, the hypothesis of independence between the type of activity and the Basque province to which the recipient pertains is rejected as is shown in table 3.3. This table shows, with a confidence level of 95.22 percent (p = 0.0478), that in the entire sample, intercooperation studies are the most represented activity (38.46 percent), followed by the creation of intercooperative businesses or structures, incorporation into intercooperative businesses or structures, and combinations of activities, each with 13.46 percent. However, this distribution changes if we look at the distribution of activities in terms of the corresponding Basque province, where the percentages increase significantly for intercooperation studies and mergers in Bizkaia; creation of intercooperative businesses or structures, incorporation into intercooperative businesses or structures, and combinations of activities in Gipuzkoa; and, in Araba, intercooperation agreements, and participation in international representative organizations.

Table 3.3. Cross tabulation between type of activity and province

| | CAPV/EAE province | | | | | | | |
| | Total sample | | Araba | | Bizkaia | | Gipuzkoa | |
Type of activity	Freq.	%	Freq.	%	Freq.	%	Freq.	%
Intercooperative study	20	38.46%	6	28.57%	11	61.11%	3	23.08%
Creation of intercooperative business or structure	7	13.46%	2	9.52%	0	0.00%	5	38.46%
Intercooperative agreement	6	11.54%	6	28.57%	0	0.00%	0	0.00%
Merger	4	7.69%	2	9.52%	2	11.11%	0	0.00%
Incorporation of intercooperative business or structure	7	13.46%	3	14.29%	2	11.11%	2	15.38%
Participation in representative international organization	1	1.92%	1	4.76%	0	0.00%	0	0.00%
Combination of activities	7	13.46%	1	4.76%	3	16.67%	3	23.08%
Total	52	100%	21	100%	18	100%	13	100%

Chi squared with 16 degrees of freedom = 26.4651 (p = 0.0478)

Analyzing the results with two-way tabulation and always keeping the type of subsidized activity as the core element revealed two relationships: Firstly, a relationship existed between the type of activity and the use of a consulting entity in the performance of the activity. Secondly, there was a relationship between the type of activity and the Basque province to which the recipient pertained.

In regards to the former, it is worth noting that the activities in which the percentage increased when using a consulting entity when compared to the total sample are: intercooperation studies, mergers, and combinations of activities. Therefore, it appears that these activities tended to be linked to the participation of a consultant in the performance of the activity and the rest were not. With these results, it is possible to reflect on the need/requirement or lack thereof regarding participation of consultants in the various activities when defining and writing the grants. And, in regards to the latter, the dependent relationship that exists between the two variables may be related to the specific makeup of each province in the social economy.

Thirdly, we performed an AID (automatic interaction detection) analysis. It does not provide a function that determines the existing relationship between the dependent variable and the independent variables, but its primary application is market segmentation (Santesmases 2009). In other words, this implies dividing up a group of individuals or entities according to a certain behavior or activity that serves as a dependent variable. Officially, it constitutes a sequential variance analysis that seeks the explicative variable in each stage and within it; in other words, the division into categories that maximizes the intergroup variance or minimizes intragroup variance. We use the grant amount received for intercooperation as a dependent variable.

The AID analysis was applied in order to separate the recipients according to the amount or quantity of grant allotted, in terms of the characteristics of the type of activity, the recipient's legal status, activity sector, use of a consultant in the performance of the activity, legal status of the consultant, number of participants in the activity, and the Basque province in which the recipient was located.

The dependent variable (response) is the amount of the grant, and the independent variables (explanatory) are activity, legal status, sector, consultant, legal status of consultant, participants, and Basque province. As we see in table 3.4 and figure 3.2, categorization has been performed with the smallest value of segments (2) and with the minimum contribution to variance (1 percent).

The grouping process ends because of an inability to find any more that meet the size and minimum contribution to variance requirements. Altogether, 58.92 percent of the variance in the dependent variable (amount) was explained.

The main conclusion that can be taken from the AID analysis is that the independent variable (explanatory) with the greatest segmentation value in regards to a certain behavior (dependent variable = quantity) was the type of activity, given that it was the causal variable for the first split. This indicates that activities defined in the grant have the capability of seg-

Table 3.4. Description of AID variable analysis

Variable type	Name	Concept
Dependent variable	Amount	Amount of total of grant awarded
Independent variable	Activity	Beneficiary type of activity
	Legal type	Legal type of beneficiary
	Sector	Beneficiary sector of activity
	Consultant	Has obtained assistance of consultant
	Type consult.	Legal type of consultant
	Particip.	Number of participants
	Prov.	Beneficiary province

Minimum segment size: 2
Minimum participation contribution to variant explication: 1%

Figure 3.2. AID analysis

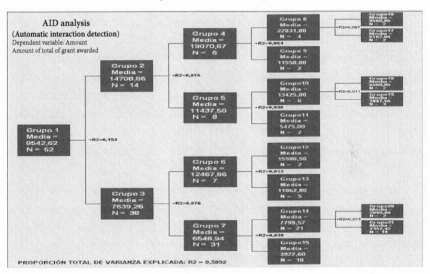

menting and therefore the capability of determining the subsidy amount. In other words, the administrative activity of defining and writing a grant is what determined the amount or best explains the differences in them. This hypothesis was set forth in section one, after simple tabulation.

Another item to take into consideration is that the second split was enacted based on the "legal status of the consulting entity" variable. This is closely related to the dependent relationship analyzed previously, given that "not applicable" was among the options for legal status and was chosen when no consulting entity had been used. Reflection on this second split reveals that, as a variable definition criterion for the amount, the use of a consulting entity could be introduced into the grant process. Legal status of the consultant could also be included, positively differentiating those pertaining to the social economy and, in that way, indirectly promote the social economy.

Lastly, within the AID analysis, it is important to point out the splitting ability of the "number of participants" variable, which served as the fourth split. Therefore, it could be of interest to introduce this variable when setting the quantity or amount of the grant.

Conclusions

In conclusion, we will present the principal findings of this empirical study of grants for business intercooperation in the social economy of the Basque Country.

There was some stability in the recipient profile. It is worth noting that within the variables that defined the profile, in terms of the type of activity, intercooperation studies held strong throughout the period as the primary action performed. This explains the below-average concentration of the amounts or quantities received by the recipients, because with intercooperation studies, the established limits were lower than others. From this, it can be seen that the type of activity determined the amount of grant monies given.

Also, in regards to the legal status of the recipients, cooperatives were the primary recipients of intercooperation grants, which coincides with the fact that 34.6 percent of the cooperatives reported some type of cooperative inter-business or intercooperative business relationship (Dirección de Estudios y Régimen Jurídico 2008). From this, we can conclude that the grant recipients concurred with the business reality of the social economy.

As a result of the relationship between the "type of activity" variable and the use of a consulting entity in the performance of the activity, reflection should be made on the need to introduce consulting entities as a criteria in evaluating applications or as a requirement included in the definition given by the departmental order that establishes grants for intercooperation. This could especially apply to activities that require specific knowledge, including mergers and creation of intercooperative businesses and structures.

The "type of activity" carried out under the grant was the variable with the highest capacity for segmentation in respect to a certain behavior (in this case, the grant amount issued). In short, it is the variable that explains the majority of differences that existed between the grant amounts issued. This outcome indicates that the administrative actions of defining and writing the grant are what determined the amount and not any other factor or variable.

Several variables were identified that had segmentation capability with respect to the amount that the recipient was allotted, and in contrast to the case with the type of activity, they are not incorporated into the grant when the amounts are set. The variables referred to are: the use of a consultant in performing the activity, the consultant's legal status, and the number of participants in the intercooperation activity. As stated, they are the variables that have shown capacity for segmenting the recipients in terms of the amount received, but they are not introduced as criterion variables in determining the amount. As such, their segmentation capability is not under the control of the administration but it could be an issue to explore further.

On the one hand, the use of a consulting entity and its legal status as evaluation criteria in the grant applications should be considered. It could also serve as an incentive, through positive discrimination, for those consulting entities that belong to the social economy, and therefore promote the sector even more.

And on the other hand, including the number of participants in the activity for which the grant monies are requested and given should be considered. In this case, activities where a greater number of entities participate could be given a positive evaluation because it indicates broader scope or coverage for the activity and possibly implies greater effort required for the activity, based on the number of participants.

References

Bakaikoa, Baleren, Aitziber Etxezarreta, and Enekoitz Etxezarreta. 2007. "La economía social y bienes de interés preferente: Estudio sobre las cooperativas de vivienda y de educación en el País Vasco." In *La economía social en las políticas públicas*, edited by Rafael Chaves. Valencia: Ciriec-España.

Bakaikoa, Baleren, Anjel Errasti, Enekoitz Etxezarreta, and Jon Morandeira. 2009. "Gizarte Ekonomiaren sustapenerako politika publikoak

Euskadin." *Revista de Dirección y Administración de Empresas* 16 (December): 65–82.

Ballart, Xavier. 1992. *¿Cómo evaluar los programas y servicios públicas?* Colección Estudios. Madrid: Instituto Nacional de Administración Pública.

Bouinot, Jean, and Bernard Bermils. 1995. *La gestión stratégique des villes.* Paris: A. Colin.

Cervera, Amparo. 1999. *Marketing y orientación al mercado de la administración pública local.* Valencia: Institució Alfons El Magnànim, Diputació de València.

———. 2001. "La gestión del marketing en la administración pública local." *Dirección y Organización: Revista de Dirección, Organización y Administración de Empresas* 26: 113–24.

———. 2004. "Orientación al mercado y administración pública local: Determinación de un modelo teórico y de medición." *Revista Internacional de Marketing Público y No Lucrativo* 1, no. 1: 53–72.

———. 2006. "La economía social en España: Concepto, agentes y políticas públicas." In *La economía social en Iberoamérica: Un acercamiento a su realidad,* edited by José Mª Pérez Uralde. Madrid: Fundación Iberoamericana de la Economía Social (FUNDIBES).

———. 2008. "Public Policies and Social Economy in Spain and Europe." *Ciriec-España, Revista de Economía Pública, Social y Cooperativa* 62 (October): 35–60.

Chias, Josep. 1995. *Marketing público: Por un gobierno y una administración al servicio del público.* Madrid: McGraw-Hill Interamericana de España.

Dirección de Estudios y Régimen Jurídico. 2008. *Estadísticas de la economía social 2006: Informe del bienio 2004–2006.* Vitoria-Gasteiz: Departamento de Justicia, Empleo y Seguridad Social, Viceconsejería de Trabajo y Seguridad Social del Gobierno Vasco.

Elizagarate, Victoria. 2008. *Marketing de ciudades: Estrategias para el desarrollo de ciudades atractivas y competitivas en un mundo global.* 2nd ed. Madrid: Pirámide.

Kohli, Ajay K., and Bernard J. Jaworski. 1990. "Market Orientation: The Construct, Research Propositions and Managerial Implications." *Journal of Marketing* 54, no. 3 (July): 1–18.

Kotler, Philip, and Gerald Zaltman. 1971. "Social Marketing: An Approach to Planned Social Change." *Journal of Marketing* 35, no. 3 (July): 3–12.

Kotler, Philip, and Nancy Lee. *Marketing in the Public Sector: A Roadmap for Improved Performance*. Upper Saddle River, NJ: Wharton School Publishing.

Kotler, Philip, and Sidney J. Levy. 1969. "Broadening the Concept of Marketing." *Journal of Marketing* 33, no.1 (January): 10–15.

Lambin, Jean-Jacques. 1993. *Strategic Marketing: A European Approach*. London and New York: McGraw-Hill.

Marketing Staff of The Ohio State University. 1965. "A Statement of Marketing Philosophy." *Journal of Marketing* 29, no. 1 (January): 43–44.

Narver, John C., and Stanley C. Slater. 1990. "The Effect of a Market Orientation on Business Profitability." *Journal of Marketing* 54, no. 4 (October): 20–35.

Rivera, Luis Miguel. 2004. *Marketing para las administraciones públicas: Gestión de la satisfacción en un servicio público*. Valencia: Universidad Politécnica de Valencia.

Santesmases, Miguel. 2004. *Marketing: Conceptos y estrategias*. 5th ed. Madrid: Ediciones Pirámide.

———. 2009. *DYANE versión 4: Diseño y análisis de encuestas de investigación social y de mercados*. Madrid: Ediciones Pirámide.

Söderberg, Magnus. 2009. "A Broad Performance Benchmark Based on Citizens' Preferences: The Case of Swedish Public Transport." *Annals of Public and Cooperative Economics* 80, no. 4 (December): 579–603.

Subirats, Joan. 1990-1991. "La Administración Pública como Problema: El Análisis de Políticas Públicas como Propuesta." *Documentación Administrativa* (INAP), nos. 224–25: 15–57.

Vázquez, José Luis. 2004. "Pasado, presente y futuro de las dimensiones pública y social en el desarrollo conceptual del marketing." *Revista Internacional de Marketing Público y No Lucrativo* 1, no.1: 9–34.

Vázquez, José Luis, and José Luis Placer. 2000. *Cinco temas de introducción al marketing público*. León: Imprenta Moderna.

4

Accounting Reform: The Case of Workers' Self-Managed Cooperatives

MIGUEL ÁNGEL ZUBIAURRE ARTOLA

Translated by Julie Waddington

The evolution towards increasingly more open economic models in which capital flows between countries with tremendous speed has generated a need for financial information drawn up with homogeneous criteria that facilitate decision-making. Cooperative societies are economic agents that are immersed in this economic reality and that must confront this tendency. However, if this process of seeking common theoretical frameworks to draw up and present financial information is not carried out taking due account of the characteristic features of the issuing agent of the information, the results may be inadequate.

The latest accounting reform carried out in Spain is the result of a decisive step toward the harmonization of the key criteria of returns, wealth, and equity within the European Union. The inclusion of financial information within the new harmonized European model has basically been produced in two stages. Spanish Law 62/2003 on fiscal, administrative, and social measures made it obligatory from the financial year 2005[1] to draw up annual accounts of listed companies according to the International Accounting Standards/International Financial Reporting Standards (IAS/IFRS). This initial change meant that it was obligatory to apply

---

1. 2007 for companies with listed debt instruments.

the entire contents of the international accounting regulations accepted by the European Union to Spanish listed companies. Subsequently, Law 16/2007 adapted and reformed commercial legislation in relation to accounting to make it harmonious at an international level. At the same time, it authorized[2] the government to approve the general accounting plan through a royal decree. Thus, Royal Decree 1514/07 was published in November 2007 in the *Boletín Oficial del Estado* (BOE, Official State Bulletin) approving the General Accounting Plan (GAP) along with Royal Decree 1515/07 that approved the GAP for small- and medium-sized businesses. It was, without doubt, this second reform that involved more companies as it affected the individual annual accounts that are mandatory for all companies according to the commercial code, regardless of the size of the business.

In this second phase, the Spanish accounting model maintains its own autonomy while evolving in order to find a point of convergence with international accounting standards. The Spanish regulator adapts the general accounting plan, which is the basis accounting instrument in Spain, and incorporates the necessary changes to avoid any clash with the criteria contained in international accounting standards. Clearly, its modification did not mean the assumption of the entire content of the IAS/IFRS. Out of the different valuation options accepted by international standards, Spain elected the most appropriate criteria according to its Instituto de Contabilidad y Auditoría de Cuentas (ICAC, Institute for Accountancy and Auditing). In this way, for example, the possibility of applying a fair value basis is limited in this case to financial instruments.

Cooperatives have not been excluded from this process of reform. Most[3] of the country's autonomous communities have assumed an area of responsibility in their statutes of autonomy concerning the legal status of cooperatives and therefore have their own legislation to be applied exclusively in each autonomous community. Nevertheless, it is important to take into account that the Spanish constitution awards the state exclusive powers in relation to commercial matters and, given that accounting standards are found within the area of commercial responsibilities, all cooperatives in the Spanish state, regardless of where they carry out their

---

2. Final Provisions First Clause.

3. Andalusia, Aragon, Catalonia, Euskadi, Extremadura, Galicia, the Community of Madrid, Navarre, La Rioja, Castile and León, Castile-la Mancha, the Community of Valencia, the Balearic Islands, and Murcia.

main business activity and of the autonomous standards to which they are subject, will have to apply the general accounting plan and whatever other accounting legislation applies to them on a mandatory basis.

In this respect, in terms of accounting, the distinguishing features of the cooperative model brought about the need for a specific accounting document that would resolve the question of activities deriving from the specific nature and characteristics of cooperative societies. To this end, since the end of 2003 cooperative businesses have been able to use a legislative development that specifically regulates cooperative accounting matters.

Order Eco/3614/2003, according to which the accounting standards for cooperative societies were passed, meant that, for the first time in the case of Spain, standards for calculating and presenting annual accounts adapted to the particularities of these kinds of entities could be used. Until the aforementioned regulation was passed, there was no specific legislative text on accountancy for cooperatives.

Subsequently, in December 2010, Order EHA/3360/2010, a new legislation covering accounting matters for cooperative societies, was passed. This document signals a new commitment on the part of the national regulator in favor of the need for a set of accounting standards capable of adapting general accounting criteria to the particular features of cooperatives. Thus, after the accounting reform, cooperative accounting will be regulated by both documents: the PGC, and the standards related to cooperative accountancy matters.

On the other hand, and as it used to be before the reform process, cooperative societies that carry out financial activities (basically credit cooperatives and cooperative insurance societies) will have to apply the specific accounting standards[4] established for these kinds of entities that, in turn, have been duly reformed. This means that the accounting aspects of Order EHA/3360/2010 will only be applicable in cases that are not expressly regulated by specific standards.

Characteristics of Cooperative Societies

The distinctive nature of the organizational model of cooperative societies generates activities that are not considered in commercial organizations, or which add nuances that are clearly new in relation to a traditional finan-

---

4. Regulation issued by the Bank of Spain or the General Directorate for Insurance.

cial instrument such as capital. Before discussing accounting matters, and considering the case of the workers' self-managed cooperatives[5] (the economically most important kind of cooperatives in the Basque Country), I would like to briefly highlight some of the most relevant distinguishing features of cooperative societies that have particular repercussions for the accounting model:

- These are open organizations that function under the principle of the free acceptance and voluntary withdrawal of their members.

- In order to become a member, one must contribute a minimum capital requirement that will be returned when the member leaves due to retirement, voluntary withdrawal, or expulsion from the cooperative. Therefore, the capital becomes a more volatile figure than in public or limited companies. In a cooperative of a certain size, there will be movements in terms of new members and departing members on a regular basis in each financial year.

- In a first-level cooperative[6] all members have equal rights to guarantee that its organization, management, and control are democratic. Each member has equal power in terms of decision-making, regardless of the amount of capital they contribute. Each member has one vote that marks a radical difference from the reality of commercial entities in which each share has a vote.

- The capital contributed by the members is remunerated by way of an interest that is determined in the cooperative's statutes.

- The members' stake in the cooperative's profit is independent of the amount of capital. The distribution of the positive or negative results is made in proportion to the functions, services, and activities carried out in the cooperative; work becomes a distribution factor of the income generated.

- They are committed to training, education, and social promotion. Part of the profit must, legally, be directed to the training and

---

5. In workers' self-managed cooperatives, individuals join together who, generally speaking, carry out an economic activity through their work in order to produce goods or services for third parties and to make a financial profit from this. They are different from other cooperatives such as, for example, housing or educational cooperatives in which the social objective aims to deliver a service in the most economical way to their members and therefore they do not pursue profit.

6. In first-level cooperatives, members are individuals. A second-level cooperative is one whose members are other cooperatives.

education of members and workers in cooperative principles, to the promotion of cooperative relations, and to cultural, professional, and healthcare initiatives.

These distinctive features of cooperative societies result in specific functions as regards their activities, or sometimes alter the nature of more traditionally held business concepts; in so doing, cooperatives acquire different features to those of commercial entities, even though the same name or format may be used to describe both. All these aspects require a proper assessment of their economic implications in order to be represented accurately later in financial statements.

Key Points in Cooperative Accounting

Here I will address from an accounting perspective the main distinguishing features of cooperatives that, to a great extent, were resolved by the introduction of specific cooperative accounting standards in 2003. The accounting reform of 2007, however, threw up some doubts concerning the compatibility of these solutions with the new conceptual framework of the GAP, which has since been reinterpreted in the 2010 review of the specific accounting standards for cooperatives.

The Concept of Equity

The liquid assets of equity contain many of the singular accounting features of cooperatives. Although most of the elements that comprise such assets appear on the balance sheets of commercial companies under identical or similar headings, the classification of many of their components is marked with controversy.

The 2003 standards on accounting matters of cooperative societies placed particular emphasis on the delimitation of the concept of equity. Contributions by members or other parties were identified as ongoing sources of equity whose availability is subject to limitations and that guarantee the society against third parties. This proposal meant consolidating cooperative capital and the cooperatives' stocks as items of equity as they had been traditionally presented in the financial statements.

This proposal, however, did not coincide with that of international accounting standards that do not offer any definition of equity. The IAS/IFRS (that inspired the conceptual framework developed in the first part of the 2007 GAP) attempt to define the concept of assets and liabilities, with equity resulting as the residual concept that refers to the difference between the value of assets and liabilities. In fact, in the new configuration of the balance sheet, while the economic structure of a company continues to be called an asset, its financial structure, presented up to that point purely as liability, starts to be identified as equity and liability, emphasizing the significant nuance implied by the consideration of the different types of financing to which the business has had access.

Any economic act that can be defined as a liability and that exceeds the recognition criteria must be identified as such on the balance sheet. According to the conceptual framework, liabilities are current obligations that have emerged from past events and that the company intends to settle by selling off resources that may produce benefits or economic profit in the future. Liabilities will be listed on the balance sheet when it is likely that the obligation to list them exists and when they can be reliably assessed.

The conceptual framework does not establish what the exact features of equity are, either in the original version of the International Accounting Standards Board (IASB) or in its interpretation in the GAP. With regards to the contractual relation implied by any issuing of a financial liability, the company must classify it as either an equity instrument or as a financial liability depending on its characteristics and, therefore—whenever an obligation is derived from it on the part of the issuing company—it must figure as a liability on the balance sheet.

The particular way in which the relation between a cooperative society and its members is configured generates specific features that require a detailed analysis of how the different items of equity fit into the conceptual framework of accounting.

Cooperative Capital

Cooperative capital includes both voluntary and mandatory contributions[7] made by the members to the cooperative. Contributions are credited by way of registered securities that are not considered to be marketable securities, or through registered shareholders accounts or passbooks that

---

7. Law 27/1999 on cooperatives (articles 46 and 47) Mandatory Contributions: the minimum amount necessary to attain membership will be established in the statutes. *Voluntary Contributions*: the general assembly and the governing council, if provided for in the statutes, may accept voluntary contributions from members to the capital. Law 4/1993 on Cooperatives in Euskadi (articles 58 and 59); similar to the Spanish state law in terms of its developments.

record the successive contributions made, as well as (when appropriate) the allocation of the results to the capital.

This implies far greater mobility than in commercial entities given that an upturn or downturn in membership has a direct impact on its value. Contributions can be transferred to the capital through *inter vivos* acts, solely between members, or to those who will become members in the three months following a transfer or through inheritance (*mortis causa*) to the heirs if they are members, and if they are not after their acceptance as such. Nevertheless, in response to the withdrawal of members, the most common option is to recuperate the invested capital directly from the cooperative.

The accounting classification of cooperative capital is the subject of major international debate. There are two features that give rise to ambiguous connotations concerning cooperative capital. On the one hand, its remuneration is not directly related to the size of profit but, rather, is remunerated according to an interest rate that is established in the statutes or by the general assembly. In a similar way to the enforceable liabilities paid, its quantity will be calculated by multiplying the volume of capital by the percentage of interest. Furthermore, although it is true that cooperative legislation conditions remuneration when there are profits, in the case of the law on cooperatives in Euskadi, the existence of free reserves allows for the remuneration of capital even with a negative surplus. It is important to understand that the role of capital in cooperatives is totally diluted with regards to the question of labor. Cooperatives need contributions of capital in order to set up societies in the first place and to exercise their business activities, but with the ultimate aim of establishing good labor relations between members and the cooperative in question. As such, the role of capital is just a necessary step that must be taken, in contrast the greater importance attached to labor relations. The philosophy of workers' self-managed cooperatives recognizes the need to remunerate the capital factor in terms of a fixed percentage, not in terms of fluctuations based on the size of the financial year's profit. The fluctuation in this annual profit thus affects members not as a result of the amount of capital contributed, but rather in terms of their participation in the cooperation's activities.

One of the particularities of the remuneration system of cooperative capital is the obligatory remuneration via interest that makes it especially difficult to quantify it as equity. Order EHA 3360/2010 considers any capital with an entitlement to obligatory remuneration as a liability. It will no doubt be necessary to make adjustments to the statutes of many cooperatives in order to take into account their obligation to pay interest, leaving the question of the payment of annual interest in the hands of the assembly. The obligation to remunerate the returns appears to present less of a problem in this respect.

On the other hand, although the refunding of capital contributions is subject to a series of limitations imposed by the law and the statutes, a cooperative cannot prevent its members from exercising a basic right such as withdrawal of membership. If members decide to leave the cooperative, they are entitled to a reimbursement of the capital they have contributed once the losses that the cooperative has incurred in relation to the part attributed to the members in question have been deducted if and when applicable.

It is this second feature that generates greater problems with regards to the consideration of capital as equity. The IASB issued a document interpreting the standards on financial instruments (IAS 32) specifically for cooperatives called "Members' Shares in Co-operative Entities and Similar Instruments" (IFRIC 2, 2004). The main aim of this was to interpret the content of the IAS 32 in relation to the particular case of financial instruments issued in favor of members of cooperative societies. Among the main agreements adopted, what stands out in particular is the point that members' contributions will be considered as equity if the entity has an unconditional right to reject its recovery (paragraph 7). If it does not have this right, as has traditionally been the situation in the case of cooperatives, this capital should be included on the balance sheet under liabilities. Fernando Polo Garrido (2007) has carried out a comprehensive analysis of this.

In view of the forthcoming incorporation of IASB criteria into Spanish accounting standards, and with the aim of maintaining capital as equity, reform of the legislation on cooperatives was promoted as a means of opening up the possibility of identifying cooperatives' capital as contributions whose refunding—in the case of withdrawal by members—can be unconditionally refused by the governing council. Law 8/2006, which presented a second amendment to the law on cooperatives in Euskadi (article 57.1), was a pioneering initiative in Spain, offering a solution to the conflict that the application of the IAS/IFRS implied at the end of 2007 in the case of the consolidated annual accounts of two leading cooperatives— Eroski and Fagor—that were forced to apply international standards for financial instruments traded on European Union stock markets. This initiative was subsequently incorporated into the law on state cooperatives (article 45) through the fourth additional provision of Law 16/2007. As argued by Sonia Martín Lopez, Gustavo Lejarriaga Pérez de las Vacas, and Javier Iturrioz del Campo Martín (2007, 68), this initiative distorted part of the essence of cooperative societies.

Logically, each cooperative would have to decide whether to reconfigure capital or not under this new option at its assembly. If it agreed to this, the cooperative would continue to identify it is as equity. However, cooperatives that retain members' unconditional right to apply for a refund would have to present capital as a payable liability once the transition period has expired (December 31, 2010) and Order EHA 3360/2010 has come into effect. This may cause serious capitalization problems in many cooperatives by requiring them to reclassify a substantial part of their equity as liability.

In my view, it may have been more prudent to prolong the transition period and to wait for the results of the open debate at the core of the IASB concerning how to calculate the accounts of cooperative capital. The change in accounting standards promoted by Order EHA 3360/2010, which incorporates IFRIC 2 (2004) of the IASB into Spanish regulations, may be too late and may run contrary to the most current approaches of the international accounting regulator.[8]

The main objective of the IASB discussion paper "Financial Instruments with Characteristics of Equity" (2008) is to consider whether the classification of the principles of international standards on financial instruments (IAS 32) adequately distinguishes between financial instruments as equity or liabilities. Among the cases in which the IASB considers the distinction between equity and liability to be inadequate, are those in which the company is left with no equity instruments as a result of having classified all those issued as liabilities. This could be the case with cooperatives whose members do not renounce the right to a full refund.

The project is still in the discussion phase, and the publication of the Exposure Draft is expected in 2011. Some of the provisional decisions taken by the committee that directly affect the interests of cooperative societies are already known. Namely, according to the March 2009 bulletin (IASB Update), a financial instrument that the company is obliged

---

8. Fernando Polo Garrido, Germán López-Espinosa, and John Maddocks (2010), in addition to commenting on IASB standards, consider the perspective of American accounting standards, analyzing the latest standard-setting developments of the Financial Accounting Standards Board in relation to the accounting of cooperatives.

to reimburse only in the case of death or retirement must be classified as an equity instrument. The original term used in the comment is "retirement," which is specifically nuanced in the case of cooperative societies and extended in the final version to "withdraws their membership or ceases to be a member of a cooperative."

The efforts made by different spheres of the European cooperative world in order to raise awareness among international accounting bodies of the reality of their particular organizational model appear to be paying off. Similarly, the impact that the consideration of capital as payable liability could have on the future development of these societies also seems to have been highlighted. The consolidation of this position in terms of future reforms of international standards would mean an about-turn in the accounting classification of cooperative capital, rendering some parts of the changes proposed to this effect in Order EHA 3360/2010 unnecessary.

In my opinion, and in line with other observers (Fernández-Feijóo Souto and Cabaleiro Casal 2007; Cubedo Tortonda 2007), capital is an ongoing source of equity for cooperatives. While it is true that members have the right to a refund of the capital they have invested, when this has not been renounced in view of the latest legislative changes, the essence of the contract signed by members on joining the cooperative is, in the main, of a long-standing nature. The cooperative needs the contribution of capital in order to set up the society in the first place and to exercise its economic activity, and members agree to the contribution of capital in order to establish good labor or user relations. As suggested by Belén Fernández-Feijóo Souto and Mª José Cabaleiro Casal (2007), the debate should be focused on an analysis of the economic scale of the contractual relation implied by the cooperative contribution of capital.

The capital contribution becomes a necessary instrument for establishing membership of the cooperative, after which one attains two of the basic features of the equity instruments: decision-making power and access to profit. In the same way, when the withdrawal or expulsion of a member is accepted, the member in question will lose these two basic rights upon accepting the reimbursement of the capital he or she originally invested. It is well known that the amount of capital loses the right to structure the assignation of these rights but maintains the power to access them.

If we focus on workers' self-managed cooperatives, after an initial phase of being an employee of the cooperative, when the worker becomes a member and agrees to contribute capital, he/she does so on the understanding that they will maintain a long-standing association with the cooperative. By taking this decision, the basic link established by the member is through the working relation with the cooperative, thereby generating links that do not exist with other forms of capital contributions. Nevertheless, contribution to the capital is a necessary step in the assumption of this new status. From this point onwards, the member will be fully entitled to participate in the management of the cooperative, enjoying decision-making power and access to the cooperative's profit.

Even when free and voluntary joining or withdrawal forms an essential part of the contractual relation between the member and the cooperative, I believe that the basis of this relation is a long-lasting link. Therefore, international standards seem to be going in an appropriate direction that, at the same time, simply implies maintaining the accounting classification criteria used in Spain until Order EHA 3360/2010 came into effect.

Reserves

As in any other company, the reserves of a cooperative will be mainly replenished from the retention of accounting profits. The most characteristic reserve account for cooperatives is the mandatory reserve fund. This reserve is similar in nature to the legal reserve of public and limited companies, and is intended to constitute a fund to consolidate, develop, and guarantee the cooperative society.

Cooperatives are obliged to allocate at least the minimum legal quantity to the mandatory reserve fund on an annual basis. Law 4/1993 on cooperatives in Euskadi requires that at least 20 percent of the profit be allocated in all activities with a profit throughout the lifetime of the cooperative, without any attempt being made to free the cooperative from this obligation for having accumulated a specific amount of capital in this fund. It is important to note that in the Basque case, the variable (legal or available profit) upon which the percentage is applied is defined by law and is not the same as the surplus determined by the profit and loss account.

In addition to the mandatory reserve fund, cooperatives tend to strengthen their self-financing by directing their benefits to voluntary reserves. The cooperatives belonging to the Mondragon Corporation are committed to capitalizing surpluses[9] by way of voluntary reserves over and above the legal obligation to allocate funds to the mandatory reserve. Voluntary reserves may be distributable or non-distributable. This nuance takes on particular importance in cooperatives, given that if they are considered non-distributable, members will have lost all rights to a refund of funds capitalized in voluntary and non-distributable reserves.

In that case, members do not have any effective rights over the total net profit of the cooperative. By withdrawing from the cooperative, members may ask for a refund of the capital contributions that they are entitled to, whether these are those previously made by these members or those made by capitalized cooperative returns. However, of the funds capitalized in reserve funds, they will only be able to recuperate the voluntary reserve funds that are distributable. Members are not entitled to a refund of other reserves and in particular the mandatory reserve fund, except in the case of some autonomous legislation.[10]

In a commercial company, from the perspective of its members there is no financial difference in terms of deciding to distribute the surplus as dividends or opting to maintain it as a reserve. In this case, retaining surplus in the reserve will add value to the shares and therefore there is no equity loss for the member compared to the option of being paid a dividend. Nevertheless, in cooperatives the repercussions in terms of members' equity are evident given that the member loses all direct rights over the funds capitalized as reserves. This aspect may, in some cases, generate a sense of frustration for cooperative members who, on retirement, and after a long working career, feel a sense of ownership over the capital that they now abandon, recovering only a part of its value. Some authors, such as the European Foundation for Public Policies-EZAI Fundazioa (n.d.), have called for a review of the system of mandatory reserves in cooperatives. In my view, this signals a clear act of solidarity that is a direct consequence of the philosophy of the cooperative movement. According to this philosophy, the aim of collaboration among people is to carry out an economic activity that allows them to satisfy their economic needs, while guaranteeing and protecting the future of the cooperative as a necessary economic agent for future generations.

---

9. 45 percent of the surplus in obligatory and voluntary reserves.

10. They are partially distributable in Andalusia and Murcia if permitted by the autonomy statutes. For more information see Asociación Española de Contabilidad y Administración de Empresas (Spanish Association for Accounting and Business Administration) (2010).

On the other hand, in addition to retained surpluses, contributions carried out directly by members are also collected in reserve accounts. On becoming a member, the cooperative can request the contribution of an entry fee in addition to the minimum mandatory capital contribution established in the statutes. The legal limit of this entry fee is 25 percent of the minimum mandatory capital contribution and is paid directly into the mandatory reserve fund. This represents a nonrefundable contribution that is carried out to strengthen the cooperatives' resources over which the members lose any possible claim in the future. For this reason, the entry fee cannot be compared to the issue premium of commercial companies. By contributing the mandatory minimum capital, the new member benefits from being included in a consolidated cooperative business with a share in the profits of the cooperative that is proportionally similar to that of longer-standing members, given that this is determined on the basis of the work carried out and not on the amount of capital contributed. Once again, this represents a basic principle of cooperative ideology whereby work and not capital is the governing factor in terms of distributing the wealth generated.

After approval of Order EHA 3360/2010, the distributable reserve funds that the cooperative society has the right to reject unconditionally should be classified as a liability. In the case of the Basque Country, where the mandatory reserve fund is legally nondistributable, this will be mainly limited to the distributable voluntary reserves where the cooperative does not have the option to unconditionally reject their distribution.

Education, Training, and the Promotional Fund

In accordance with the fifth[11] basic principle of the International Cooperative Alliance, cooperative societies are legally obliged to direct part of their profits[12] to an education, training, and promotional fund. Here, we come face-to-face once more with a distinctive feature of cooperatives that is rooted in the different nature of these organizations that dedicate part of the profit made to ends that are quite distinct from those emerging from the needs of the business itself.

---

11. Fifth Principle (ACI): Education, Training, and Information.

12. Law 27/1999 for Cooperatives: 5 percent of total. Law 4/1993 for Cooperatives: 10 percent of available profit. Nevertheless, if the mandatory reserve fund does not come to an amount equal to 50 percent of the social capital, the minimum contribution established for the fund may be reduced to 5 percent.

The monies directed to the education, training, and promotional fund should be employed for different activities that benefit members, workers, and, when appropriate, the community in general. Thus, article 68 of the cooperative law of Euskadi establishes that the educational and promotional fund should be directed, in accordance with the basic guidelines set down in the general assembly statutes, to some of the following areas of public interest:

- The cultural, professional, and cooperative promotion of the local environment and of the community in general, as well as the improvement in quality of life and of community-based development and environmental development activities.
- The training and education of its members and workers in cooperativism, cooperative activities, and other matters not related to their actual posts.
- The promotion of inter-cooperative relations.
- The promotion of education, cultural formation, training, and healthcare.
- The promotion of new cooperative businesses.

The different regulations that develop the legal aspects of cooperative societies consider the distribution of surpluses (whether as contributions to this fund or the reserve fund) to be mandatory. In fact, the quantity that cooperatives must allocate to these funds is a percentage of the profit, whose precise detail may vary according to the legislation applied.

In accountancy terms, from 2004 on, contributions to the educational fund were considered to be an expense of the cooperative, even when this meant that its calculation was carried out by taking the very result of the exercise as a base. These are funds that the cooperative is obliged to allocate to activities that are different from those of the cooperative's social aim and that, even when the internal bodies of the cooperatives themselves decide where the funds should be allocated, should still be considered as enforceable funds for the cooperative. The nature of the obligation emerging from the educational fund is clear within the theoretical accounting framework; therefore, the amount paid will result in an expense that, based on Order EHA 3360/2010, will be reflected in a particular part of the operating results.

In terms of the "Education, Training, and Promotion Fund," this will be presented[13] as current or noncurrent liabilities in a new balance sheet subtotal that cooperative societies should identify to such effect.

Equity and liabilities (GAP 2007)

A) Net equity

A-1) Equity

A-2) Adjustments for changes in value

A-3) Grants, gifts, and bequests

B) Noncurrent liabilities

Cooperative Education and Promotional Fund

C) Current liabilities

Cooperative Education and Promotional Fund

On the other hand, in cases where the cooperative receives grants, gifts, or other aid, or funds derived from imposing sanctions on members that are linked to the fund in accordance with the law, such items will be recorded as revenue for the cooperative.

The Cooperative's Profit

With the approval of Order EHA 3350/2010, the structure of the profit and loss account is the same as that which any other commercial business would have to present, which after the process of reform will include operating results, financial results, results before taxes, and the financial year profits.

The typical structure of the profit and loss account will be adjusted to incorporate specific functions of cooperative societies such as transactions with their members, the acquisition of goods, purchases of raw materials, or the acquisition of employment services and contributions to the education fund. More precisely, contributions to the education fund will be presented in a specific section along with the different parts of the operating results.

Another section to which we should pay particular attention is the remuneration of interests to capital. International accounting standards (IAS 32) only consider remunerations to capital that have been classified as enforceable as expenditure. This can be interpreted from valua-

---

13. BOICAC 76 December 2008, Consultation 3 and Order 3360/2010

tion rule 9ᵃ, section 4 of the PGC where it highlights that any transaction carried out by the company with its own instruments will be recorded in the equity as a change to the funds owned, but that this result cannot be recorded in the profit and loss account.

In accordance with international standards, after the implementation of Order EHA 3360/2010, the remuneration of capital will be regarded as expenditure only when it is presented as a current liability on the balance sheet, in which case its remuneration will have an additional entry in the company's financial expenditure. For other cases, remunerations to capital that are presented on the balance sheet within equity will be regarded as a distribution or application of the profit.

In order to carry out an accurate evaluation of the profits, analysts should take into account the implications that the remuneration to capital or contributions to the education fund may have on the profit variables. Two organizations with similar profitability results may end up presenting very different details depending on whether an unconditional right to refuse reimbursement exists or not—a right that, in my opinion, does not bring about a radically different basis to the current financial model of cooperatives. Contributions to the education fund that are considered as another part of the operating expenses may, at the same time, hinder a comparative analysis of economic efficiency with other commercial companies in which there is no such legal obligation.

Expenditure for Tax on Profits

As in other organizations, the profit generated by the cooperative must be able to withstand the direct taxation chargeable on the society's income. It should be noted that in the case of the Basque Country,[14] the taxation of cooperatives presents some important advantages in comparison to public or limited companies.

According to current tax legislation, cooperatives can apply a special regime that will result in a lower level of taxation. Among the main advantages of this, the following are worth highlighting:

- For cooperatives with tax protection, the taxation rate is 20 percent, which is reduced to 18 percent for cooperatives that fulfill the SME status. With regards to the types of levy that are gener-

---

14. Araba, Bizkaia, and Gipuzkoa have their own legislation for company taxation.

ally applied, there is a fiscal advantage of eight points for large companies and six for small enterprises.

- The following can be deducted when calculating the tax base:
  - The interest of capital contributions or other equity. From a fiscal point of view, and regardless of its accounting status, a deductable expenditure with the maximum legal interest rate plus two points.
  - Half of the contribution to the obligatory reserve fund. Cooperatives, being subject to greater legal self-financing requirements, are entitled to a tax deduction of 50 percent of their contributions.
  - 100 percent of the annual contribution to the education fund.
- Cooperatives considered to be especially protected according to taxation laws—which include the workers' self-managed cooperatives that are subject to certain limits and conditions—will be entitled to a bonus of 50 percent of their tax liability. This is a bonus that is generally applied with cooperatives that, in practice, reduces the real tax rate of the cooperative by 50 percent.

The advantages are, therefore, three dimensional: more deductible expenditures when calculating the tax base, lower tax rates, and better bonuses. The result of these three effects is that the accounting expenditure for tax purposes on the profit and loss account will be markedly less than other noncooperative entities. This point should be considered, at the same time, when proposing a comparative analysis between cooperative societies and other commercial businesses, with it being fairer to consider this by using profit variables before taxation to avoid the effect of differences in the fiscal levy applicable.

On the other hand, in the case of the Comunidad Autónoma del País Vasco/Euskal Autonomia Erkidegoa (CAPV/EAE, Autonomous Community of the Basque Country), the calculation of cooperatives' expenditure for tax purposes presents a difficulty in terms of how to quantify the permanent differences that arise from contributions to funds that are compulsory by law. The difficulty emerges from the fact that the law on cooperatives in Euskadi means that contributions to obligatory funds have to be made as a percentage of a variable after tax: the available profit. This means that calculations of the accrued expenditure for tax purposes have to be made when the definition of the permanent differences needed to determine it base their calculation on variables after taxation. The solution lies in considering an equation where tax itself should be declared as still unknown.

Conclusion

In order to interpret the financial information presented in the annual accounts of cooperative societies accurately, it is important to take into account the particular aspects of these organizations. The presentation of information on the basis of annual accounting models similar to other organizations does not exempt the user from the need to understand the fundamental repercussions of the distinguishing features of the cooperative model in order to take appropriate decisions.

The role of cooperative capital is in fact instrumental with regards to the leading role of employment relations. The philosophy of workers' self-managed cooperatives recognizes the need to remunerate the capital factor in terms of a fixed percentage, without fluctuations in terms of the size of the financial year profit. When there are profits, members will be remunerated not on the basis of the size of their capital contribution, but instead depending on their involvement in the cooperative's activities.

Members do not have any effective rights over the total net profit of the cooperative. In the case of the Basque Country, on withdrawing from the cooperative, members may demand a refund of the capital contributions that they are entitled to. However, they have no right to a refund of the rest of the reserve and, in particular, of the obligatory reserve fund.

From the financial year 2011 on, cooperatives that retain the right for members to unconditionally request a refund will have to present capital as a payable liability. The reclassification of a substantial amount of equity as liability may cause capitalization problems in many cooperatives.

There is still considerable debate about how to consider cooperative capital in accountancy terms in the main international regulatory accounting bodies. The efforts made from different spheres of the cooperative world to raise awareness of the distinct case of the cooperative model in these bodies may, in the future, see results and produce a change in the current international accounting regulatory framework to strengthen the role of capital as equity.

The solution to the debate about how to consider cooperative capital in accountancy terms lies in considering an analysis of the economic basis of the contractual relation implied by the contribution of cooperative capital. The reality and nature of cooperatives is diverse and requires detailed analysis of the specific cases of cooperative membership.

I believe capital is an ongoing source of equity for cooperatives. The essence of the contract signed by the member upon joining the cooperative is of a permanently binding nature. The capital contribution becomes a necessary instrument for establishing membership of the cooperative, which is essential in order to attain two of the basis features of the equity instruments: decision-making power and access to profit. It is well known that the amount of capital loses the right to structure the assignation of these rights but maintains the power to access them.

In my view, it may have been more prudent to prolong the transition period and to wait to see the results of the open debate at the core of IASB concerning how to calculate the accounts of cooperative capital. The change in accounting standards promoted by Order EHA 3360/2010, including regulation IFRIC 2 (2004) of the IASB, may be too late and may run contrary to the most current approaches of the international accounting regulator.

From the annual accounts of the financial year 2011, cooperatives will present their accounts in a similar way to other commercial organizations in terms of how the results are structured. In order to carry out an accurate evaluation of the profits, the analyst should take into account the implications that issues such as the remuneration to capital or contributions to the education fund may have on profit variables.

The process of international harmonization of the preparation and issuing of financial information is focused on the most conventional structures of economic agents without taking into account current specific cases such as those of cooperative societies. The indiscriminate application of common standards to a wide range of agents involved in economic relations may generate undesirable effects that make it difficult to present a true picture of financial information.

References

Asociación Española de Contabilidad y Administración De Empresas (AECA). 2010. "Fondos Propios de las Cooperativas." *Documento nº 1. Serie Contabilidad de Cooperativas.*

Cubedo Tortonda, Manuel. 2007. "El régimen económico de las sociedades cooperativas: Situación actual y apuntes para una futura reforma." *CIEREC-España* 58 (August): 161–87.

European Foundation for Public Policies (EZAI). N.d. "Reserve Funds in European Cooperative Societies." Position Paper. Arrasate: EZAI.

Fernández-Feijoo Souto, Belén, and Mª José Cabaleiro Casal. 2007. "Clasificación del capital social de la cooperativa: Una visión crítica." *CIEREC-España* 58 (August): 7–29.

———. 2004. "IFRIC 2 Members' Shares in Co-operative Entities and Similar Instruments." At www.icaew.com/en/technical/financial-reporting/ ifrs/ifrs-standards/ifric-2-members-shares-in-co-operative-entities- and-similar-instruments#Version.

———. 2008. "Financial Instruments with Characteristics of Equity." Discussion Paper (February). At www.ifrs.org/NR/rdonlyres/ AE2FC463-BB40-4835-8805-13E44BBFE96F/0/dp_financial_ instrumentsfeb2008_186.pdf.

Martín Lopez, Sonia, Gustavo Lejarriaga Pérez de las Vacas, and Javier Iturrioz del Campo. 2007. "La naturaleza del capital social como aspecto diferenciador entre las cooperativas y las sociedades labo- rales." *CIEREC-España* 58 (August): 59–82.

Polo Garrido, Fernando. 2007. "Impactos de las normas internacionales de información financiera en el régimen económico de las sociedades cooperativas." *CIEREC-España* 58 (August): 83–108.

Polo Garrido, Fernando, Germán López-Espinosa, and John Maddocks. 2010. "The International Diversity of Co-operative: Concerns for Accounting Standards Setters." Paper presented at the European Accounting Association 33rd Annual Congress, May 19–21, Istan- bul, Turkey.

Legislation

Law 4/1993 of June 24, on cooperatives in the Basque Country, *Boletín Oficial del País Vasco* (BOPV, Official Gazette of the Basque Coun- try), July 19.

Law 27/1999 of July 16, on cooperatives, *Boletín Oficial del Estado* (BOE, Official State Gazette) no. 170, July 17.

Order ECO/3614/2003 of December 16, BOE no. 310, December 27.

Decree 58/2005 of March 29 by which legislation on the law on coopera- tives was passed, BOPV no. 73, April 19.

Royal Decree 1514/2007 of November 16, by which the general account- ing plan was passed, BOE no. 278, November 20.

Order EHA/3360/2010 of December 21, BOE no. 316, December 29.

5

Is Innovation Better Managed by Corporations than Social Economy Companies? A Comparative Study of Innovative Basque Companies

Sara Fernández de Bobadilla Güemez
and Eva Velasco Balmaseda

Translated by Jesús Sepúlveda

Innovation and Social Economy in the Twenty-First Century

Innovation and the innovation process are not linked solely to profit-making enterprises (with their market and customers, competitors, and exclusively economic or monetary values). It is imperative, in our view, to take and drive the need for innovation in the nonprofit sector and more specifically in the nonprofit business sector.

Under the umbrella of the third sector, the nonprofit sector is a macrosystem with varied profiles and different approaches according to its limits, composed of different entities with different legal forms and ways of acting in relation to its surroundings. Thus, when defining the field in which this sector functions, one must turn to social economy and the nonprofit approaches, which have increasingly come to share many similarities and connections. Moreover, this same space is occupied by

* A previous version of this chapter was published as Sara Fernández de Bobadilla and Eva Velasco. 2008. "¿Gestionan mejor la innovación las empresas de economía social que las sociedades anónimas?: Estudio comparativo de empresas innovadoras vascas." *CIRIEC-España* 63: 5–37.

both entities that are rooted in and operate within the market (the business sector) and others that are more philanthropic in nature, which do not consider themselves producers in the private market and that form part of the nonbusiness sector (Barea and Monzón 1992; Chaves and Monzón 2001; Montserrat 2004; Pinar 2005).

While innovation—as the driving impulse of growth and survival—is important for the entire nonprofit sector, it is clear that the commercial subsector needs to implement more innovation management (IM) models because of its market exposure. Like the profit-making sector, this is subject to threats and opportunities of various kinds with the addition and the need for its own social objectives and values.

In order to implement such models, it is necessary to import, adapt, and redefine ways and concepts used in both areas, exchanging, for example, the term "market" for "value space"—in such a way that concepts like "satisfaction" and "values" are embraced, and a place created for agents, who think and influence but do not consume and are non-clients.

On the other hand, and especially in the Basque Country, the nonprofit business sector is widely studied from a social economy approach. This approach includes four main groups: cooperatives, mutuals, associations, and foundations (July 2004, 10). It is important, however, "to avoid an overly rigid interpretation of the forms and statutes of the social economy and always perceive them in relation to the objectives of the social economy" (Jeantet 1999, 64). In other words, although specific legal forms influence market performance and certain internal and external processes, what determines the configuration of an entity in this space is to be a company and have a specific philosophy (people before capital, democratic management, the distribution of income not linked to capital or participation, cohesion and social ethics, being in private sector but public interest, and so on). It is also true that most of the entities that make up the social economy are equipped with organizational structures that facilitate the necessary systematization process for proper IM, so it is natural that these are at the forefront when innovative processes are implemented.

Current interest revolves around whether there is a system of innovation (Freeman 1987; Lunddvall 1992) specifically for the social economy, or if existing innovation systems and theories about them sufficiently consider companies in this sector, taking into account that the origin and evolution of the sector constitute a real innovation in themselves (as regards, organizational and management skills, rather than technology).

In line with this, in its report *The Social Economy in the European Union* (International Center of Research and Information on the Public, Social and Cooperative Economy 2007, 30–31), the European Economic and Social Committee (EESC) describes the ability of innovation in the social economy, especially in non-technological innovation.

Therefore, we believe there is an innovation system for the social economy itself because of the following reasons:

- There is a delimited and visible space, which consists of subsectors with common features and objectives.
- There are cultural, legal, relational, and organizational elements, as well as its own agents, that interact within the system.
- It has developed its own networks that make the system and its agents grow, improve, and evolve.
- A space of self-worth and a specific way to function in environments and markets have been created.
- It has its own systemic elements, such as the treatment of benefits, social responsibility, the concept of value provided to society, relational dynamics, the human dimension of growth, and so on.

In short, in this particular system companies coexist with their own defined characteristics, specific research and training networks, ad hoc funding methods, their own legal and fiscal norms, observatories, and groups of agents in supra-business structures, together with the important role of and recognition by the public administration, universities, their own surroundings, and civil society. The goal now and in the near future is to improve our understanding of this system—in other words, how it is articulated and the elements that make it up.

However, at the company level (as elsewhere) there is a need to systematize innovation activities. The creation of an internal innovation system is a guarantee of success, and in our view there is no difference here, with a few small exceptions, between nonprofit and profit-making bodies. In fact, as discussed in the comparative study below, such differences are not as significant as a whole and the methodology of the processes is similar. Ultimately, innovation is a very democratic process and transcends just technological research and development, which requires in itself specific and substantial resources.

The Challenge of IM: Its Constituent Elements

While most companies emphasize the tremendous complexity involved in IM, they recognize that it can and should be managed (Jonash and Sommerlatte 1999, 135). Although there is no one simple answer to the challenge of IM, there is increasing agreement on a number of issues, stemming from different research and experiences of organizations trying to manage innovation. The result is a growing body of knowledge and models about what and how we can better manage innovation.

The main conclusion from the analysis of IM models is that it is essential to adopt an approach that includes, in addition to the innovation process itself, another set of elements (Velasco 2010). Thus, although the innovation process should be designed specifically according to the particularities of the company, this cannot be considered an isolated activity. The innovation process is, then, one more element within an overall framework and comprehensive management of innovation (Velasco and Zamanillo 2008).

In this way, companies must have a clear innovation strategy to guide the efforts of their members in the right direction and to focus on the use of limited resources. Moreover, company leaders must show their commitment to innovation, defining innovation objectives, leading innovation in an integrated manner, and promoting initiatives and the creation of new ideas among members of the organization. Thus, an ability to cope with uncertainty, assume risk-taking, and encourage creativity, collaboration, and exchange of knowledge must be the foundation of any organizational culture. Innovative culture must be fully reflected in the values, mission, and vision of the company and involve linking goals to rewards.

On the other hand, the company must also establish a suitable organization, enabling it to achieve the set objectives of innovation. The organizational structure should facilitate the flow of information as well as communication and cooperation among its members and between them and external agents. By connecting employees at all levels, leaders encourage personal interactions and cross-fertilization that fosters innovation.

People are the source of innovation, and nothing takes place without them. If people are dissatisfied with their basic working conditions, their desire to innovate, cooperate, and put ideas forward will be limited. Likewise, leaders of organizations and the prevailing culture in the company play a fundamental role in people's behavior. The company must have the financial resources to enable people to implement their ideas and innovation projects. Companies should allocate funds for the proper development of plans for long-term innovation.

In order to successfully innovate, companies should provide the tools their employees need and the necessary training to use them (innovation management tools or IMTs). Information and communication technologies (ICTs) accelerate the exchange of information among company members and allow fluid communication with partners, forming an alliance for the development of innovation.

For its part, the basic process of innovation should be integrated by the concept or idea creation, product development, process innovation, and innovation in marketing processes. Technology management—which involves the formulation of a technology strategy, or the selection, creation, and supply of technology, and intellectual property management—should strongly underpin the innovation process. Knowledge management should also frame this process. Indeed, both technology management and knowledge management are closely related to IM.

The innovation process must be customer oriented; in other words, the customer must be the focus of innovation. Therefore, we need to know, listen to, and respond to his or her requirements. In addition, innovation is stimulated by various external actors and sources of innovation resources such as universities, technology centers, customers, suppliers, competitors, financial institutions, business associations, concentrations of like-minded enterprises, patent offices, regional development agencies, and so forth. Together they make up what are termed (national or regional) innovation systems. Innovation system agents contribute significantly to companies' innovative capacities. Networking (or partnerships and alliances with third parties) involves building and maintaining effective external ties, so as to exploit the knowledge, resources, and intelligence of this whole set of agents outside the boundaries of the organization.

A closely related element to networking is the monitoring or study of a company's environment. A company is an open system that is influenced by an environment, and this environment is a survival resource as well as a source of opportunity for either future success or threats. Monitoring this environment involves analyzing and searching for potential signals of innovation, threats, and opportunities for change within a company's surroundings.

Finally, the company must capture the improvements that the competitive advantage has achieved. Numerous IM models underscore the fact that measurement and monitoring are imperative for continuous improvement. Meanwhile, organizational learning implies reviewing experiences of success and failure in order to learn how to improve IM and capture the relevant knowledge that can be extracted from those experiences.

We will now analyze the importance and application of each of these elements in social economy companies (cooperatives) in the Basque Country, comparing them with capitalist companies. Underpinning these elements there is a set of processes, routines, and practices that enable the effective management of innovation. The extent to which companies are more systematic in applying these elements will affect their chances of success in innovation.

IM in Industrial Cooperatives and Joint-Stock Companies in the Basque Country

The objective of this study was to obtain a sample of known firms, so that we could analyze IM practices in detail in a set of innovative organizations. These were not just technologically innovative organizations, but innovative organizations in the broadest sense of the term.[1] For this purpose, the top one hundred fifty companies to receive funding from the Basque government's 2006 "Intek" call for public funding of technological innovation projects were selected. Next, we checked which of these companies were among the eighty-three selected by the knowledge cluster for its "advanced management enterprises" analysis.[2] As a result, we obtained a total of twenty-two companies for the focus of our study.

When assessing what kind of companies these were, we found them to be evenly divided between cooperatives and joint-stock companies. Here,

---

1. The OECD (2005, 46) considers innovation to be "the implementation of a new or significantly improved product (good or service), or process, a new marketing method, or a new organisational method in business practices, workplace organisation or external relations."

2. A list of cluster companies was used because it fulfilled the basic criteria of the study: it incorporated companies that were innovative in some form of management that, moreover, mostly belonged to the industrial sector. Using this list guaranteed that the companies we questioned were not just technologically innovative, but instead incorporated a wider definition of the term "innovation."

then, our aim is to compare IM in both groups of companies. In order to carry out this comparative study, we chose to employ the nonparametric Mann-Whitney U statistical test. This test both suited the sample sizes with which we were working ($n1 = 11$ and $n2 = 11$, both of them independent) and allowed us to state whether the two groups had statistically significant different behaviors.[3]

Finally, the sources used to conduct this research were primarily collected through a questionnaire designed specifically for this purpose. The questionnaire contained eighty-five questions in total, which allowed us to obtain a personal assessment of the heads of the twenty-two organizations. This assessment addressed two aspects: how important the subjects of the questions were for their organizations; and to what extent the topics raised in the questions had been implemented in their companies. When the interviewees valued the importance of routines and processes in their company, 0 indicated not relevant, 1 slightly relevant, 2 indifferent, 3 important, and 4 essential. In assessing the degree to which the topics mentioned had been implemented in their organization, 0 indicated never, 1 rarely, 2 sometimes, 3 with some regularity, and 4 always.

Study Results

Below are the results of the survey operation for the cooperative societies and joint-stock companies as well as the values obtained through the Man-Whitney U statistical test. First, we analyze the average importance that both types of companies give to the integral elements of IM, with the corresponding ranking of these elements. This is followed by a study of the degree to which these elements have been implemented. And finally, we analyze the gaps[4] that mark the differences between both types of organization by comparing the results of one group with the other.

Importance of the Integral Elements of IM

One of the first conclusions to be drawn from the comparative analysis is that both groups of companies have some overlap in their assessment of the elements of the IM. In general, cooperatives assign great importance

---

3. Specifically, a unilateral analysis was undertaken for a significance $\alpha = 0.1$, with the group variable being the legal status of the company.

4. The gaps indicate the differences in values between the average importance accorded an element and the degree of implementation within companies.

to all elements, except for leadership, knowledge management, measurement, and monitoring.

Moreover, both groups of companies consider customer orientation as the fundamental element of IM and learning as less important. Similarly, both include among the most important elements product development, strategy, and the innovation process.[5] Both groups also coincide in considering among the less important elements innovation in marketing process, IMTs, and concept creation.

Thus, as shown by the results of Man-Whitney U contrast, one can conclude that, regardless of the legal status of the companies analyzed, they display similar behavior in their assessment of how important the integral elements of IM are. Both groups have very similar views on the crucial role played by technology management and financial resources. Both groups also coincide on considering learning, IMTs, and IM less important.

The findings show that the only element in which there is a notable divergence between the two groups is in the case of knowledge management. Specifically, capitalist enterprises generally considered it more important for the company to organize knowledge, so it could be classified, accessed, and used in a simple way within the company (using knowledge databases, records of experiences of new projects, records of corrective and preventive actions for quality, and so on). Moreover, they were more concerned that information be distributed within the company (to facilitate people's access to knowledge they are looking for and encouraging use of this knowledge), and that employees share knowledge within the company with their peers, who might also benefit from it.

Degree of Implementation of the Component Elements of IM

Initially, the results confirm that regardless of the companies' legal status, they have all incorporated many of the processes and routines that facilitate development of an innovative capacity. Therefore, the average score achieved in implementing the integral elements of IM was 2.7 out of a total of 4, with 77.3 percent of the companies analyzed being located

---

5. The innovation process is an element composed of two aspects: On the one hand, if the innovation process forms part of a company's critical processes, and it is identified and managed in a systematic way (objectives have been established and indicators defined); on the other, the innovation process is regularly (for example, annually) revised in such a way to assure it is not static and can be periodically improved.

between 2 (sometimes) and 3 (with some regularity). This analysis concerned implementing processes, routines, and practices that allow innovation capability to flourish.

In addition, five companies were at levels close to excellence in IM, regularly implementing elements considered essential for good IM. Three of these were joint-stock companies (corporations) and two were cooperatives (see figure 5.1). However, the next six companies that were closest to the excellence mark were all cooperatives. Consequently, among the eleven most systematic companies in applying IM elements, the top three were capitalist corporations and the remaining eight were cooperative companies. Furthermore, among the latter, only one was not part of the Mondragon Cooperative Corporation (MCC) group.

Figure 5.1. Results obtained by cooperatives (coop) and corporations (S.A.) in innovation management

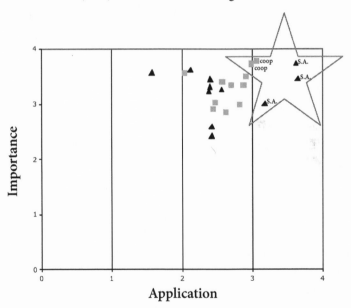

As regards implementing the various components of IM, both groups of companies focus on organization, financial resources, product development, customer orientation, and innovation in production processes. However, the application of elements such as concept creation, innovation in commercial processes, and learning is less systematic, especially in the case of joint-stock companies.

On the other hand, if we look at the results of the Mann-Whitney U contrast, it is once more a case of innovative companies that behave very similarly in regard to implementing the IM elements. This consistency is striking as regards establishing an organization capable of encouraging innovation, promoting cooperation with outside agents (networking), and technology management. There is a similar convergence as regards concept creation, although in this case, it is due to the fact that this element is implemented less across the board in all the companies studied.

Where cooperatives and joint-stock companies differ is on innovation in the marketing process. As we have already seen, both groups of companies do not have the processes and routines in place to carry out innovations in the field of marketing processes. However, according to the survey, joint-stock companies lag far behind cooperatives when it comes to implementing mechanisms to analyze and measure the best practices for business management in relation to competing firms as well as commercial global standards. Furthermore, and in a more significant way than in cooperatives, new forms of marketing and marketing strategies aiming to raise prices are rarely considered in the joint-stock companies. Thus, among the latter the creation of new concepts almost always starts from a fixed commercialization process. Therefore, the precise definition of what distribution channel to use and method of sale and after-sales service does not usually take place during the product development process, exposing the whole process to complete revision at any moment.

Comparative Analysis of the Importance and Application of Elements

After analyzing the importance of these elements to the companies under consideration and the degree to which they were employed and systematically applied, while the companies evinced great consistency in implementing some elements, they were much less coherent in the implementation of others.

In the case of cooperatives, companies were broadly consistent in three areas: organization, financial resources, and the innovation process. These are among the most important elements for IM, so it is not surprising that they had a high implementation rate in these fields.

There was also a small gap between the importance attributed to the elements and everyday practice in enterprises (see table 5.1) when we analyzed the innovation in production process and measurement and monitoring. In this case, although cooperatives did not include these elements as among the most important for IM, they were applied quite regularly. As we can see in table 5.1, all items discussed so far have values in the interval from the first quartile.

However, in the group made up of human resources and culture, the gap between the importance attached to these elements and their implementation in the company was very high. Innovative cooperatives were not consistent in the deployment of these elements, so that even if they gave enough importance to them when it came to implementation, their degree of effort was relatively low.

Consequently, as it is clear from the survey, it appears that human resource policies in cooperatives do not conform entirely to those typically deployed by innovative organizations. There are selection policies that support innovation through the search of personnel with different experience and knowledge in these organizations. There are also staff development policies that promote the acquisition of innovation tools (technical expertise, creative skills, teamwork, conflict resolution problems, decision analysis, risk/opportunity analysis, project management, and so on). And there are assessment policies that encourage a favorable attitude toward carrying out employee initiatives and contributions, as well as recognition and reward schemes that promote innovation (original ideas, entrepreneurship, information sharing, and so on are rewarded).

Meanwhile, learning, concept creation, and knowledge management are among the lowest rated items of IM. Therefore, cooperatives do not make a great effort in their application. However, as table 5.1 shows, the gap between the importance accorded to these elements and their implementation is wider than would be desirable.

In comparison to cooperatives, joint-stock companies were less coherent in implementing the various elements of IM.

On the one hand, three of the elements that these companies give more importance to—customer orientation, product development, and leadership—were also among those they most regularly applied. However, and contrary to what one might expect, the gap between the importance given to and the implementation of these elements was not among the smallest companies (as table 5.1 shows, none of these elements have a gap within the smallest 25 percent group of companies or first quartile).

On the other hand, we find very small gaps between the value that these companies attach to innovation in the production process, financial resources, and organization, and their implementation (see table 5.1). Thus, while joint-stock companies do not consider these to be the most important elements for IM, their implementation is relatively formalized.

Table 5.1. Gaps between cooperatives and corporations (difference between importance and application of the elements)

Component	Coop.	Ranking	Corp.	Ranking
Strategy	0.527	14th	0.764	7th
Leadership	0.615	8th	0.515	11th
Culture	0.826	4th	0.561	10th
Organization	0.327	20th	0.200	20th
Human resources	0.970	1st	0.712	9th
Financial resources	0.379	18th	0.212	19th
HGI	0.636	7th	0.367	17th
ICTs	0.568	11th	0.432	15th
Innovation processes	0.455	16th	0.955	4th
Concept generation	0.911	3rd	0.818	6th
Product development	0.562	13th	0.460	13th
Production processes innovation	0.364	19th	0.341	18th
Commercialization process innovation	0.591	10th	1.121	3rd
Technology management	0.564	12th	0.400	16th
Knowledge management	0.788	5th	0.818	5th
Client orientation	0.697	6th	0.515	12th
Networking	0.600	9th	0.436	14th
Environment security	0.477	15th	0.727	8th
Measurement and follow up	0.409	17th	1.136	2nd
Learning	0.970	2nd	1.227	1st
First quartile	0.472		0.424	
Third quartile	0.720		0.818	
Average	0.612		0.636	

Note: The lighter gray rows show the smallest gaps between the groups. The darker gray rows show the largest.

Joint-stock companies have not yet fully taken on board measurement and monitoring, the innovation process, and knowledge management. Even though these elements are considered to be very important in

IM, these companies implement them in a less systematic way than would be desirable.

Finally, learning, innovation in the marketing process, and concept creation received the lowest evaluations among joint-stock companies. Consequently, these companies do not focus on their implementation, leading to them being among the least implemented elements. However, the gap between the importance given to and the implementation of these elements was still higher than expected.

Conclusions

Organizations within the business sector of the social economy, whatever their mission in society or legal status, are affected like any industry by issues such as competition; globalization; technological, social, fiscal, and regulatory changes; market trends; and so on.

This set of organizations with their specific characteristics constitutes an emerging innovation system. This system is a reference point in social and organizational innovations and it is strongest in non-technological innovation. However, the systematization of internal processes to define a system of IM is, in many cases, embryonic, especially at the micro level (as is the case with companies in other sectors). The future challenge for cooperatives is to define and consolidate their own innovation systems and confront, at a company level, the challenge of innovation itself. In order to do so, they must bear in mind that an innovative organization must be able to solve problems creatively and turn ideas into value for the customer, the company, and society as a whole.

Here we have presented the results of a research carried out among twenty-two leaders in innovation in the Basque Country. Significantly, half of them turned out to be joint-stock companies and the other half cooperatives, of which all but one belongs to the Mondragon group. We were therefore able to conduct a study of IM in a group of companies belonging to the social economy, comparing these cooperatives with capitalist corporations.

The first thing we noted was that the Basque companies analyzed have incorporated many of the processes and routines that encourage development of an innovative capacity. Indeed, the average score achieved in the deployment of the constituent parts of IM listed was of 2.7 out of 4. And of the eleven companies that have a more systematic IM, eight were cooperatives. This provides an idea of the excellent level of this group of companies in relation to IM.

On the other hand, the statistical Man-Whitney U contrast employed allows us to conclude that cooperatives and joint-stock companies do not show significantly different approaches to IM practices. Some of the most striking coincidences between the the two groups were based on the large gap they both had between the importance and the implementation of learning and concept creation. Although these components are not among the most important for IM in the opinion of both groups, their practical implementation in Basque companies remains far from what might be considered desirable values. In fact, as the Mann-Whitney U contrast reveals, these companies do not have any significant differences in the gap (or gaps) regarding these elements (see table 5.1). Specifically, it is striking how practices that enable organizational learning are not very widespread. Although every innovation is new, elementary tasks are repeated over time, so the innovation development process of innovation does not occur normally in a completely unpredictable way. It therefore seems essential to incorporate a learning phase into IM. Learning involves the internalization of knowledge, so it would seem prudent to carry out a learning process that is both ex-ante as well as ex-post internalizing knowledge. Ex-ante learning clarifies ideas and externalizes tacit knowledge, while ex-post learning favors identifying the sources of problems, ways to solve them, and the best practices to learn from them (Scozzi, Garavelli, and Crowston 2005, 129). One of the requirements of learning is the desire of the organization to learn from its own experience, yet this phenomenon does not seem so widespread as yet among the analyzed innovative companies.

In the case of knowledge management, the gap between the assessment of this element and its implementation is high in both groups. However, in the case of cooperatives this phenomenon is not as striking as it is in joint-stock companies. For the latter, this is among the most important elements for an effective IM. Apart from this slight difference, both groups of companies offer a similar pattern in their knowledge management practices, showing a high gap in this element. Basque innovative companies, whatever their legal status, should be more active in organizing knowledge. It should be classified, accessed, and used in a simple way within the company (using a knowledge database, a record of experiences in new projects, a record of corrective and preventive actions for quality, and so on). A better distribution of knowledge within the company, facilitating easy access to the knowledge that people are looking for and encouraging its use, would also appear to be necessary. It is likewise important that employees share knowledge within the company with other employees to whom this knowledge can be helpful.

Another set of IM elements in the companies we studied are similar in their approach to productive innovation processes, organization, and financial resources (the levels of unilateral significance were 0.2312, 0.2646, and 0.1687 respectively). Here, both groups showed a small gap in the productive innovation process. This was because these companies—although they do not believe this is a fundamental element in IM—implement it with a relatively high regularity. With regard to organization and financial resources, both cooperatives and joint-stock companies again had small gaps. As regards these elements, however, one must acknowledge a slight difference in the approach of both groups. The reduction of the gap in cooperatives is explained by the general consistency maintained by this group of companies, which gave great importance to these elements. Meanwhile, in the case of joint-stock companies, these gaps were reduced because of efforts to deploy these elements—although this did not reflect on the importance this group of companies assigned both elements.

Among the most outstanding differences between the two groups were those related to implementing IMTs as well as measurement and monitoring (the levels of significance were 0.0714 and 0.0463 respectively).

Regarding IMTs, the surveys confirm that the use of such tools in cooperatives—which do not consider these tools the most essential element for IM—was below desirable levels (even below the levels of joint-stock companies, which do not even grant them the same degree of importance). Cooperatives should be more proactive in the use of tools for creating new concepts and ideas. They should also make a more substantial and sustained use of the tools for the development of products: for example, computer-aided design, computer-aided manufacturing, and computer aided engineering (CAD-CAM-CAE), quality function development (QFD), value engineering (VE), and virtual prototyping. Cooperatives should also be more proactive in the application of advanced tools for redefining and controlling the production process, which should also be more widespread: for example, failure mode and effects analysis (FMEA), statistical process control (SPC), process simulation, controlled pilot experiences, and total productive maintenance (TPM).

As regards measurement and monitoring, the gap of these elements was relatively small among the cooperatives because, although they are not considered very important, they are applied fairly regularly in their implementation. However, the opposite is the case in joint-stock companies. Here, both elements have very large gaps related to their importance and implementation because joint-stock companies are inconsistent in their approach. Thus, implementation of measurement and monitoring is far from what is considered desirable by capitalist corporations that consider these the second most essential elements of IM. Therefore, measurement and monitoring become a major issue for joint-stock companies and, in light of the importance attributed to these elements by these companies, urgent action is needed in this area.

An analysis of the results indicates that both cooperatives and joint-stock companies face the challenge of IM in a similar way. However, we also discovered that cooperatives were more systematic in deploying innovative practices and routines (with a 2.7 average application of the elements, compared to 2.6). Cooperatives were also more consistent in implementing the elements of IM (as table 5.1 shows, the average gap of elements is 0.61 against 0.64).

We should also emphasize that the results of this study were conditioned by the particularity of the Basque social economy and the specific importance of the MCC group within this economy. MCC is the largest Basque industrial group and has a very structured innovation network (Bakaikoa et al. 2004). Indeed, the set of cooperatives that makes it up demonstrates far superior results to noncooperative companies in areas such as quality management (Charterina, Albizu, and Landeta 2007). There is both internal and external innovation within the Mondragon group. Internal innovation is a feature of any company that wishes to remain competitive in the global economy (innovation in process, products, and management). External innovation is specific to cooperatives, which are responsible for regional economic development. Such development includes creating mixed technology centers, structures for involving young people in business enterprises, and elements of inter-business cooperation (Irizar and MacLeod 2008, 43).

At the time of the field study, ten out of the eleven cooperatives analyzed belonged to the MCC group. Consequently, although the cooperatives were independent of each other, they also shared certain values, management models, and resources. It would therefore be interesting to repeat a similar study among other (non-MCC) cooperatives in the Basque Country or other regions to see if they show the degree of IM development.

References

Bakaikoa, Baleren, Agurtzane Begiristain, Anjel Errasti, and Gorka Goikoetxea. 2004. "Redes e innovación cooperativa." *CIRIEC-España* 49: 263–94.

Barea, José, and José Luis Monzón. 1992. *Libro blanco de la economía social*. Madrid: Centro de Publicaciones del Ministerio de Trabajo y Seguridad Social.

Charterina, Jon, Eneka Albizu, and Jon Landeta. 2007. "The Quality of Management in Basque Companies: Differences Existing between Cooperative and Non-cooperative Companies." In *Cooperative Firms in Global Markets: Incidence, Viability and Economic Performance*, edited by Sonja Novkovic and Vania Sena. Vol. 10 of *Advances in Economic Analysis of Participatory and Labor-Managed Firms*. London and Amsterdam: Elsevier JAI.

Chaves, Rafael, and José Luis Monzón. 2001. "Economía social y sector no lucrativo: Actualidad científica y perspectivas." *CIRIEC-España* 37: 7–33.

Freeman, Christopher. 1987. *Technology Policy and Economic Performance: Lessons from Japan*. London: Pinter.

International Centre of Research and Information on the Public, Social and Cooperative Economy (CIRIEC). 2007. *The Social Economy in the European Union*. Brussels: European Economic and Social Committee.

Irizar, Iñazio, and Greg MacLeod. 2008. "Innovación emprendedora en el Grupo Mondragón: El caso de sus centros tecnológicos." *CIRIEC-España* 60: 41–72.

Jeantet, Thierry. 1999. *La economía social Europea o la tentación de la democracia en todas las cosas*. Translated by Raquel Boix and Maria José Miquel. Valencia: CIRIEC-España.

Jonash, Ronald S., and Tom Sommerlatte. 1999. *The Innovation Premium: How Next-generation Companies are Achieving Peak Performance and Profitability.* Reading, MA: Perseus Books.

Juliá, Juan Francisco. 2004. "La economía social y el cooperativismo, la democracia en la economía: A modo de introducción." In *Economía social: La actividad económica al servicio de las personas,* edited by Juan Francisco Juliá. Almería: Editorial Caja Rural Intermediterranea, Cajamar.

Lundvall, Bengt-Åke. 1992. *National Systems of Innovation: Towards a Theory of Innovation and Interactive Learning.* London and New York: Pinter.

Montserrat, Júlia. 2004. *La fiscalidad de las fundaciones y asociaciones.* Barcelona: Gestión.

Organisation for Economic Co-operation and Development (OECD). 2005. *Oslo Manual: Guidelines for Collecting and Interpreting Innovation Data.* 3rd ed. Paris: OECD and Eurostat.

Piñar, José Luis. 2005. "Tercer sector, sector público y fundaciones." *Revista Española del Tercer Sector* 1: 1–13.

Scozzi, Barbara, Claudio Garavelli, and Kevin Crowston. 2005. "Methods for Modeling and Supporting Innovation Processes in SMEs." *European Journal of Innovation Management* 8, no. 1: 120–37.

Velasco, Eva. 2010. *La gestión de la innovación: Elementos integrantes y su aplicación en empresas innovadoras del País Vasco.* Serie Economía y Empresa. Leioa: UPV/EHU.

Velasco, Eva, and Ibon Zamanillo. 2008. "Evolución de las propuestas sobre el proceso de innovación ¿Qué se puede concluir de su estudio?" *Investigaciones Europeas de Dirección y Economía de la Empresa* 14, no. 2: 127–38.

6

Innovation in the Basque Country: An Examination of the Cooperative Situation

ANTÓN BORJA ALVAREZ

Translated by Lauren DeAre

This chapter begins with a description of how RDI (research, development, and innovation) spending has evolved in Navarre, Iparralde (the Northern Basque Country), and the Comunidad Autónoma del País Vasco/Euskal Autonomia Erkidegoa (CAPV/EAE, Autonomous Community of the Basque Country). Next, I address in more detail the CAPV/EAE, both in terms of its industrial network and the dynamic of resources allocated to RDI. Specifically, I discuss the 2010 Science and Technology Plan, an important institutional step to renew and advance research and development in the CAPV/EAE.

In the second part of this chapter, I focus on the dynamic of cooperatives, and particularly Mondragon Group, and examine the importance of R&D spending in Mondragon's 2005–2008 Science and Technology Plan. Finally, I assess the evolution of the Basque industrial network, its scientific and technological development and the challenges it faces, and reflect more generally on the MCC (Mondragon Cooperative Corporation) dynamic.

* Published in a previous form as Antón Borja and Antón Mendizábal. 2009. "Innovación en Euskal Herria: Aproximación a la situación de las cooperativas," *Gezki* 5: 89–108.

Navarre

In Navarre, industrial wealth represents 31 percent of the total and 28 percent of overall employment. It should be noted that although 95 percent of the companies in Navarre are small and medium enterprises (SMEs), there are also large companies (twenty of them are majority owned by foreign capital and account for 25 percent of actual industrial employment). Furthermore, multinational companies have a strong presence in Navarre (112 companies in 2005). Important manufacturing sectors include: metal industries, food products, and transportation equipment. Low- and medium-tech industries and those with average demand are also numerous.

In terms of innovation policy, important changes have occurred in recent years, with 1.67 percent of the Navarrese GDP gross domestic product (GDP) in 2006 devoted to R&D funding (higher than the equivalent expenditures in the CAPV/EAE). The three existing technology plans demonstrate the importance given to the technology sector. The first and second technology plans (2000–2003 and 2004–2007, respectively) signaled progress and provided important funding in the field of technological R&D. A further €228.9 million were allocated to the third technology plan (2008–2011), based on four central elements: innovation, cooperation, eduction, and internationalization.

Note that the amount devoted to RDI is significant. However, a free-market approach continues to dominate given the reduced influence of the public sector and an increased importance of companies that are the major engines of technological change. The technology plan also fails to determine a group of systemic actions that would invigorate the region as a whole. It encourages technological innovation (motivation for technology-based companies) but barely mentions organizational innovations that companies need.

There is little support for SMEs and low- and medium-tech companies, although they represent the vast majority of the companies in Navarre. It is significant that in Navarre, technological monitoring and economic intelligence services are not reaching SMEs effectively. Continuous training or vocational education is not in any way included as a strategic component of the technology plan. In order to strengthen the economy through knowledge, continuous training must be a strategic focus for technicians, management teams, and labor collectives as a whole.

Moreover, the lack of coordination between the current technology plan and the concomitant science plan in Navarre constitutes a fairly significant error. The technology plan also lacks any reference or connection to the Navarrese territorial strategy plan, demonstrating a lack of overall vision and absence of essential coordination. Finally, I would also point to a lack of consensus (or any attempt to seek it out) between economic and social players in Navarre, leading to a non-systematic series of results.

Iparralde

The industrial situation in Iparralde has been defined most recently by an employment decline, from 18,667 jobs in the industrial sector in 2004 (17.9 percent of the total) to 13,178 jobs in 2009 (10.5 percent of the total). In 2009, forty-two industrial companies had over fifty workers, employing 6,550 people in total. Within the industrial sector, there are several important subsectors. The aeronautical subsector, for example, has close to two thousand jobs and forty subcontracting companies. Indeed, Dassault Aviation is the leading private company in Iparralde. Meanwhile, the food and agricultural subsector has three thousand jobs spread throughout diversified activities. And there are three thousand jobs associated with the metal and metal processing subsector, which is connected to the construction and metalworking sectors. Thus, one might define the industrial sector in Iparralde as composed of two blocs made up of aeronautical, metal, and mechanical equipment companies on the one hand, and agricultural and food concerns on the other.

Innovation and technological change are limited to large companies in the aeronautical and related sectors and the food and agricultural sector. There is, moreover, a degree of innovation in certain subsectors such as defense electronics, medicine, and computer science.

In any case, industrial activity in Iparralde is weak and has significant problems that must be addressed in the future. Most research there is undertaken by university-affiliated or related agencies and research institutions administrated by the state (in other words, it is driven by the public sector). It is worth noting that 57 percent of companies have less than five employees and have very little in the way of innovative policies. Despite all this, however, 219 people work in R&D activities in various types of organizations.

Faced with such unstructured industrial activity, the most pressing needs and activities that need to be developed are divided along the lines of the two previously mentioned blocs. Simulatenously, at the institutional level there is a pressing need for a department or similar institution to implement a general planning strategy. Such a department must have sufficient resources and the authority to allocate resources and establish communal networks among the public sector, universities, and private industry. It should also be able to commit resources to developing a specific technological and R&D developmental policy for Iparralde: the minimum starting point in any restructuring of the current dynamic.

This kind of developmental logic would necessarily involve the creation of a "development and innovation agency" with decision-making authority that could foster the promotion, stimulation, and management of entrepreneurial and socioeconomic initiatives in Iparralde. This agency should also seek to be as independent of central government in Paris as possible and form part of Iparralde's institutional framework.

Based on this approach and within the dynamic of a developing technology and innovation policy, significant changes in the productive structure would be possible and, in the medium-term, the industrial network could be strengthened.

The CAPV/EAE

In 2007, the manufacturing industry in the CAPV/EAE accounted for 29.4 percent of overall wealth and 25.5 percent of employment (257,297 jobs). When broken down by sector, the metallurgy and metal product sectors, together with the machinery and transportation equipment sectors, continued to be the most important areas of the economy in the CAPV/EAE in terms of production and employment.

Metallurgy and metal products includes metalworking, nonferrous metallurgy, foundries, metal construction, forging and stamping, mechanical engineering, and metal products; it represents 30.73 percent of the industrial value added base (VAB), 34.64 percent of employment, 28.01 percent of investment, and 30.1 percent of net sales.

Machinery includes machine tools, domestic appliances, and other machinery; it accounts for 1.56 percent of the industrial VAB, 13.21 percent of employment, 9.1 percent of investment, and 10.7 percent of net sales.

Transportation equipment includes automobiles and auto parts, shipbuilding, and other transportation equipment; this sector accounts for 8.06 percent of the industrial VAB, 8.03 percent of employment, 6.46 percent of investment, and 8.87 percent of net sales.

According to the classification of technological content by the Organisation for Economic Co-operation and Development (OECD), which is also used by Eustat (the Basque Statistics Institute), high-tech industry includes aircraft and spacecraft, pharmaceuticals, office and computer equipment, electronic products, and medical-surgical and precision equipment and instruments.

Medium-high tech industry includes electrical machinery and equipment, motor vehicles, chemical products (not including pharmaceuticals), other transportation equipment, and mechanical machinery and equipment. Meanwhile, medium-low tech industry includes ships, rubber and plastic products, ferrous and nonferrous metals, metal products, and nonmetallic mineral products.

Finally, low-tech industry includes miscellaneous articles and recycling, wood-pulp paper and paper products, food commodities, drinks and tobacco, textiles, clothing, leather products, and shoes. In 2005, based on Eustat data, in the CAPV/EAE there was a decline in high and medium-high tech sectors compared to low and medium-low tech sectors in personnel, added value, and sales. Significantly, the value of the wealth generated by high and medium-high tech level activity represented 28.8 percent in 2005, while medium-low and low-tech activities represented 61.8 percent in the same year. This shows that high and medium-high tech sectors are losing more jobs and generating less added value and less sales than their medium-low and low-tech counterparts.

The technological level of industry in the CAPV/EAE demonstrates an alarming vulnerability when it comes to the challenge of a changing international dynamic, yet other factors should be taken into account. For example, sectors such as the iron and steel industry (that has been traditionally economically significant in the CAPV/EAE) represent medium-low tech activity that is also high in energy consumption. Sectors like chemicals and cement are also very high energy consumers. More than 50 percent of industry in the CAPV/EAE is energy intensive. Although in mid-2009 oil was inexpensive, by May 2011, the price of a barrel of oil had risen to $111. It is more than likely that this price will not stabilize in the medium-term.

Furthermore, the dynamic of business investment is worrying. Between 1993 and 2008, and in the middle of an economic boom, foreign investment by Basque capital amounted to €51 billion, while it only invested €12 billion in the Basque Country itself. Clearly, then, Basque capital is not interested in investing in the Basque Country—yet another dimension of this general vulnerability. It is true that many Basque industries have an international dimension, therefore investment in overseas subsidiaries is necessary, yet the bottom line is that Basque capital funds foreign companies because they are more profitable.

Below, I will examine issues related to research, technology, development, and innovation. A European Union (EU) development plan, the Lisbon Strategy (2000), proposed that by the year 2010 EU member states would achieve a spending of 3 percent of GDP on RDI.

In 2004, CAPV/EAE spending amounted to 1.43 percent of its GDP. In 2007, it rose to 1.67 percent of the GDP (accounting for 29.4 percent of the industrial sector economy), yet remained far below the EU average (1.9 percent). Furthermore, in terms of innovation, the CAPV/EAE was ranked 55th out of 203 European regions in 2006.

As regards *innovation*, the following factors are worth bearing in mind: An innovation is the introduction of a new or significantly improved product (asset or service) or process, a new method of marketing, or a new organizational method for the internal practices of a company, organizing the workplace or foreign relations. In turn, *innovative actions* include all scientific, technological, organizational, financial, and commercial operations that effectively lead to, or have the objective of leading to, the introduction of innovations. Some of these actions are innovative in and of themselves; others are not new but are necessary for the introduction of innovations to occur. Innovative actions also include R&D activities that are not linked to the introduction of a particular innovation. Furthermore, a characteristic common in all types of innovation is a process of introduction. A new (or improved) product is said to have been introduced after its market launch. A marketing or organizational method is said to have been introduced when it has been effectively used within the framework of a company's operations.

In the 2000–2005 period, according to Eustat (which includes industrial sectors and services, including education) about 17 percent of CAPV/EAE companies could be considered innovators. Looking specifically at process and product innovations for the same time period, according to the Spanish Instituto Nacional de Estadística (INE, National Statistics Institute), approximately 29 percent of companies in the CAPV/EAE (with more than nine employees) were innovators. For the same period, close to 42 percent of companies in the EU-27 (the twenty-seven member states of the EU) were innovators. It should be pointed out here that one of the weak points in the innovation system of the CAPV/EAE and for the Basque Country as a whole is the number of patents registered.

European Innovation Index

The Summary Innovation Index (SII) measures the level at which a country's economy performs and develops innovative activity. It is made up of five dimensions: three are estimates of those elements conducive to innovation or input (innovation drivers, knowledge creation, and innovation and entrepreneurship); the other two evaluate results or output (applications of innovations and intellectual property).

The SII uses twenty-five indicators to capture, in a summary index, the scores for the dimensions listed. According to data compiled by Eustat, the CAPV/EAE ranked thirteenth in the EU-27, with an index value of 0.35 (out of a maximum of 1.00), while the EU-27 average was valued at 0.45 in 2006. Therefore, the CAPV/EAE falls short of the European average. This is significant given that the CAPV/EAE is an industrialized European region with higher income levels than the European average. As such, it should be comparable to other similar European regions rather than ranking around the European average. Let us now take a more detailed look at these SII dimensions.

Dimension 1: Innovation drivers; this refers to the structural conditions required so that innovative potential can be developed, and is made up of a series of indicators that are related to human capital. The CAPV/EAE scored high in this area, above the EU-27 average. In analyzing the indicators that comprise this dimension, the CAPV/EAE showed a significant advantage in its number of science and technology graduates, yet a weakness as regards participation in continuous training.

Possessing a higher number of degrees, while being a valuable piece of data, must be put into context: a 14 percent migration of Basque graduates is a concerning figure, and for example, 20 percent of new engineers and doctors work outside of the CAPV/EAE. In Bizkaia, for the past ten years, close to two thousand graduates (especially engineers, economists, physicists, and doctors, among others) have been working outside of the CAPV/EAE. Ninety percent would like to return but only with a similar labor status and salary to that they currently hold. There is, then, a relationship between the technology level of our industrial network (primarily low- and medium-level) and the "excess" of extra graduates. The CAPV/EAE scored poorly on the indicator for continuous training. In addition to less hours devoted to continuous training when compared to other countries, the CAPV/EAE also suffers from a lack of strategic training focus.

Dimension 2: Knowledge creation; this refers to investment made in input, both in terms of human capital and R&D activities. The CAPV/EAE was especially weak in this area in the fields of "public R&D expenditures" and "share of medium-high and high-tech R&D," with the latter the result of the aforementioned modest presence of these sectors in the productive network.

Dimension 3: Innovation and entrepreneurship; this attempts to measures a country's efforts toward innovation at a macroeconomic level. In this dimension, scores were below the EU-25 (the twenty-five member EU) average. The main weaknesses were in two indicators: "SMEs co-operating with each other" and "SMEs innovating in non-technology areas." This demonstrates that these fields have not been sufficiently developed.

Dimension 4: Applications of knowledge; this attempts to identify the performance of a European region or state and the results obtained from innovative activity in terms of labor or business activities. Here, the CAPV/EAE's data were, once again, below the European average.

The strength of the CAPV/EAE on the indicator for employment (out of the total workforce) in medium-high and high technology is significant. However, its weakness on three other indicators—"Sales of new-to-market products," "Exports of high-technology products," and "Sales of new-to-firm products"—is disconcerting because these are critical variables when it comes to the system as a whole.

Dimension 5: Intellectual property rights; this measures the results achieved by the innovation sector in terms of "know-how." The CAPV/EAE was especially weak as regards the number of patents registered in the European, American, and Triad registries. For European patents, the registration level in the CAPV/EAE was half that of the European average (124 per million residents); and only a fifth of the American rate, if patents processed at American patent offices were included. Regarding the numbers of trademarks and designs, scores approximated the EU-25 average.

Figure 6.1. European innovation index, 2006

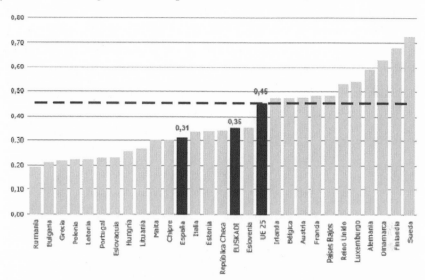

Source: Eustat and European Innovation Scoreboard.

The SII uses cluster analysis techniques to classify European states into four different groups: (1) *Innovation leaders* Countries like Sweden, Finland, Denmark, and Germany received scores well above average for the EU-27; (2) *Innovation followers* Countries like Austria and the Netherlands received scores above the EU-27 average; (3) *Moderate innovators* Countries like Estonia, Norway, the Czech Republic, Spain, Slovakia, and Italy performed below the EU-27 average; (4) *Catching-up countries* Countries like Lithuania, Hungary, Greece, and Portugal scored well below the EU-27 average.

The CAPV/EAE is ranked in the middle range of moderate innovators, with scores slightly higher than those achieved by the Spanish economy. However, there is some concern for the situation in the CAPV/EAE when looked at from the perspective of making improvements and moving up to a new group like "innovation followers."

According to Cotec, the foundation for technological innovation (2008), using a linear approach to examine the time of convergence between clusters of countries, it will take almost forty years for the group of countries that are *moderate innovators* (where both the Spanish and the CAPV/EAE economies are situated) to achieve performance levels in line with *innovation followers*. Although this approach must be looked at in relative terms, the CAPV/EAE is a long way off reaching high-ranking innovation levels within the EU if the dynamic that has existed up until now in the Basque innovation system continues.

Other analysts (Navarro et al. 2008, 14–15) have created a typology of seven groups of innovation systems in European regions. They rank the CAPV/EAE in the G3 group, "regions with average economic and techno-logical performance" (that includes forty-five regions in Italy, Austria, and Ireland, among others). The G4 group is described as "advanced regions, with a certain industrial specialization" (and includes thirty-three regions in Germany, the United Kingdom, Italy, and the Netherlands, among other countries).

According to these authors, the G3 regions—and therefore the CAPV/EAE—must "boost their absorptive and knowledge creation capa-bilities" and "articulate harmoniously their RIS (regional innovation sys-tem), incrementing the quality and quantity of the relationships between their agents" (Navarro et al. 2008, 19). This same study cites the case of the Baden-Württenberg region in Germany, which is ranked in the G4 and resembles the CAPV/EAE as regards sector specialization, yet which has a much higher level of technological development, productivity, and profitability per capita.

The previous analyses can be used as instruments to examine the con-vergence strategies included in the competitiveness plan and the science, technology, and innovation plan (*Plan de Ciencia, Tecnología e Inno-vación*, PCTI 2010). We must determine if they are properly focused and if they establish foundations that will provide improved quality and quan-tity in respect to the conditions, resources, and personnel in the CAPV/EAE innovation system.

The Science, Technology, and Innovation Plan 2010

By 2010, the Basque government planned to achieve RDI spending of 2.25 percent of the GDP in the CAPV/EAE. Over the course of the decade, it approved a competitiveness plan 2006–2009 in 2006, and the science, technology, and innovation plan (hereinafter PCTI 2010), in 2007. Both plans aspired to boost technology development, business competitiveness, and innovation.

It is no coincidence that from CAPV/EAE public funds, 52 percent (€781 million) of what was provided for in the competitiveness plan was marked for innovation-related activities. In both the competitiveness plan and the PCTI 2010, important issues in the area of innovation were addressed. The PCTI 2010 has a €6,714 million budget, with public financing of €2,718 million and private financing of €4,634 million. Based on a diagnostic report of the current situation, it proposes ten basic strategic rules, including the following key points: (1) competitiveness of the current business base, (2) diversification toward emergent sectors, (3) university leadership in knowledge creation, and (4) sustainable development and social innovation.

To achieve the objectives provided for in the PCTI 2010, various programs were created: Innova Cooperación, wherein Innobasque (the Basque Innovation Agency) intervenes to coordinate activities related to sector-wide observatories; Innova Empresas follows the previous guidelines but at the individual business level; action plans for sectoral diversification; action plans for scientific policy, and with various initiatives, including (among others) Basque Excellence Research Centres (BERC).

Other programs and activities are mentioned but they have a different range and no clear budget specification. Regarding the PCTI 2010, some considerations must be taken into account (see Borja 2008, 345–59). Despite the reorganization of several agencies and promoting Innobasque and Ikerbasque (the Basque Foundation for Science), the influence of economic and social agents remains limited.

For example, there has been no effort to integrate ConfeBask (the Basque Business Confederation) or the Basque labor unions into the plan. Likewise, it is worrying that there is no direct link between the Basque university system's 2010 University Plan and the PCTI 2010.

Sustainable Development

The PCTI 2010 (2010, 43) states that "environmental balance through eco-innovation is a key focus in this new scenario." This guideline does not propose providing a systemic horizontal focus, as proposed by the EU, but only the development of an additional sector.

One might also criticize the fact that there is no clear proposal for a public or semi-public service providing technology monitoring and economic intelligence for SMEs. In Bizkaia, these kinds of services are provided by a public agency, Zaintek, but no such bodies exist in the two remaining provinces of the CAPV/EAE: Gipuzkoa and Araba. Clearly, then, there is a need for an agency of this type in the CAPV/EAE as a whole, similar to those introduced in various European countries in the last fifteen years.

Training

Measures to update knowledge for technical personnel and researchers must be considered. Yet continuous training for labor collectives must be looked at strategically and should therefore include strategic innovation parameters. This would require a significant reorientation of the plan.

Specific activity-oriented measures designed around four central elements must be adopted and strengthened in the plan: planning and the powers of the Basque administration, a knowledge generating system, a knowledge exploitation system, and an interface system. Without them, there is no interaction among the component parts of the plan. As a result, the Basque innovation system lacks coherence and makes it difficult to make even partial improvements in certain fields.

Without such modifications, the overall perspective envisaged by the action plans cannot be achieved, nor can the financial classification of resources that the PCTI 2010 anticipates allocating these plans be effective. It has not been made clear that in a budget of €6.714 million, private funding accounts for 54 percent and public funding contributes €2.718 million. It also remains unclear up to what point private contributions in the PCTI 2010 are to be obligatory or negotiated.

For this reason, it is important to establish specific monitoring and evaluation mechanisms for the PCTI 2010 that specify the desired objectives, a timeframe in which to fulfill these objectives, and performance levels.

Cooperatives and Innovation

When analyzing the cooperative dynamic, there are major differences among the Basque territories. In Iparralde, with the exception of several agricultural cooperatives, there are very few cooperatives in the industrial and service sectors, although there are artisan collectives in the latter two sectors. Therefore, innovation has no significant influence in the cooperative field.

In 2009, there were 219 cooperatives in Navarre with 6,293 employees. Thirty-six of these (with 470 employees) were in the agricultural sector. However, the Unión de Cooperativas Agrarias de Navarra (UCAN,

Union of Agricultural Cooperatives of Navarre) has 188 first- and second-order agricultural cooperatives with over twenty thousand members.

AN Coop (Agropecuaria de Navarra, Agriculture and Fishing of Navarre) is among the workers' self-managed cooperatives in Navarre. It is a second-order agricultural cooperative with 140 associated cooperatives in Navarre and other autonomous communities. The AN group sells agricultural products and provides processing companies for subsectors like preserves, fruit, and so on. UCAN's sales revenue for 2009 was €744 million.

In the industrial sector, Navarre has fifty-five cooperatives (2,310 employees). With the exception of the construction sector (556 cooperatives), the service sector is the most significant in this area, with 2,957 employees. Innovation is not especially important in Navarrese cooperatives, except in some agro-industrial companies and several cooperatives that are part of the MCC.

In the CAPV/EAE there were 1,478 cooperatives in 2009 with 55,121 employees. After the agricultural sector (150 employees) and the construction sector (1,616 employees), the industrial sector (21,126 employees) and service sector (22,152 employees) are the most significant areas of cooperative organization.

It is worth considering the Mondragon Group (MCC) in more detail. In 2006, according to Eustat, there were close to 50,400 jobs in CAPV/EAE cooperatives, and MCC accounted for 36,697 of these. That same year, MCC employed a total of 83,601 people in its cooperatives and subsidiaries. Furthermore, an also in 2006, MCC generated 4.1 percent of the total GDP in the CAPV/EAE, with this figure rising to 8.5 percent in the industrial sector alone. Industrial investments made by the MCC group reached €465 million in 2005, representing 16.8 percent of all industrial investments in the CAPV/EAE.

In 2007, total employment in MCC was made up of 103,761 employees distributed in the following manner: 38,380 in the CAPV/EAE (37 percent); 48,755 in the rest of Spain (47 percent); and 16,546 outside of Spain (16 percent). The distribution of this workforce by sector was as follows: in the industrial sector, 43,440 employees; in the financial sector, 2,752 employees; in the distribution sector, 56,523 employees; and in the knowledge sector, 2,006 employees.

While in 2007 profits reached €711 million, in 2008, earnings were only €71 million. International industrial sales account for 58 percent of

MCC's total industrial sales. In 2008, there were seventy-three foreign production plants, providing employment for 13,759 employees, or 34 percent of MCC's industrial workforce.

MCC's global investments in 2007 totaled €2,787 million and later fell drastically to €1.324 million as a result of the economic crisis. MCC's 2005–2008 strategic plan aimed at achieving total sales of €17 billion, creating twenty-four thousand jobs (thereby increasing its workforce to ninety-five thousand people), opening twenty foreign plants, and making global investments totaling €4 million.

In fact, evaluating these objectives in 2009, we can see that MCC was able to achieve investments for the proposed amount and also achieve the predetermined sales figures. However, it did not achieve the figure of ninety-five thousand employees, given that the total at the end of 2008 was 92,773 employees. The economic crisis that began in the last trimester of 2008 has made it difficult to achieve this objective.

R&D spending in technology research and development in the CAPV/EAE rose from €40.34 million in 1993 to €147.44 million in 2007. This indicates that the data regarding Basque cooperatives in the CAPV/EAE encompasses more cooperatives than just those included in MCC.

It is worth noting that growth in spending on R&D in the service sector is higher than in the industrial sector. Therefore, the final amount was greater in the service sector in 2006 and 2007. Additionally, in the industrial sector, the number of cooperatives varied from forty-one to sixty-seven in 2007, with 1,057 total workers' self-managed cooperatives in the same year. Meanwhile, in the service sector for 2007, thirty-five out of seventy-six cooperatives devoted resources to R&D, which is a very large proportion.

Based on an in-depth analysis of service cooperatives for the period 2004–2007, one might make the following observations:

With one exception, all cooperatives that undertook research activities in 2004 continued to do so in 2007. It is precisely these cooperatives that significantly increased their investments in R&D, especially in grounds, buildings, and software designed specifically for R&D.

The cooperatives that included R&D tasks for the first time in 2007 had the following as their primary activities: technical engineering services, technical business services (business consulting and management), IT activities, trade, and non-university education (distance education).

Given the importance of the MCC (the top Basque business group), one should also asses its R&D dimension. MCC's 2005–2008 science and technology plan sought to develop objectives consistent with the previously mentioned strategic plan. It aimed to incorporate new technological learning for MCC that would have a high-impact for its companies and business dealings.

The plan included five strategic projects: information and communications technology (ICT); energy; health and biotechnology; manufacturing materials and systems; and cooperative business management (with sixty-five thousand research hours proposed in total for these different areas). Each of these five areas addressed a complex project with several ramifications. The plan promoted collaboration with other technology centers and universities.

The initial budget was €40 million over four years, with MCC contributing €8 million from its corporate funds (20 percent of the total); 50 percent contributed by the public administrations through participation in Basque government programs (Etortek, and so on); and the remaining 30 percent to be contributed by companies participating in creating major projects.

The major participants in the MCC science and technology plan were MCC's own companies, which in 2005 numbered twenty-three (in 2007, there were thirty-eight cooperatives). Also participating, however, were Mondragon Unibertsitatea (MU, Mondragon University), the Universidad dela País Vasco/Euskal Herriko Unibertsitatea (UPV/EHU, University of the Basque Country), and several technology centers, in addition to MCC subsidiaries including external centers (Inasme and Gaiker, among others). It is worth noting that in 2007, in addition to participation in various projects in Basque, Spanish, and European sectors, these participants also applied for ten patents.

The Garaia Innovation Park was another important initiative. Its purpose is to promote long-term research and bring together universities, technology centers, and the R&D departments of different companies. In 2004, €46.3 million was invested into this project. At the end of 2008, direct and indirect investments in this project surpassed €80 million. Currently, the project employs two hundred professionals working with companies like Ederteck, Ikerlan, the LKS group, an MU research center, Innovación en Servicios Empresariales Avanzados (ISEA, Innovation in Advanced Business Services), the Microsoft Innovation Center, Infonomia, and others.

In order to tackle problem areas in R&D, we must examine the fundamentals of R&D performed within industrial cooperatives and the research associated with the technology centers integrated into MCC.

The amount devoted to R&D by MCC industrial cooperatives and technology centers in the last few years has been the following:

- 2005: €93 million; 5.5 percent of the industrial added value
- 2006: €105 million; 5.3 percent of the industrial added value
- 2007: €101 million; 4.6 percent of the industrial added value

We can also break down this overall figure by the amount allocated toward technology centers. In 2006, the twelve technology centers had an overall budget of €45.8 million and 645 employees (to which forty-six trainees should be added). Ikerlan, the most important technology center, had a budget of €17.6 million. In MU's research section, there are in total 640 researchers working at MCC. In 2007, the twelve centers had a budget of €49.6 million and 723 employees, while Ikerlan had a budget of €18.6 million. From these figures, we can see that €6.25 million was devoted to generic research and €11.1 million to contracted R&D. They also completed four of their own patents and another four in conjunction with customers. Also worth mentioning is the fact that also in 2007, among other MCC companies, Edertek allocated €5.8 million and €10 million for the construction of their own buildings and equipment, respectively.

This manner of allotting resources explains, at least in part, the growth in R&D spending in the service sector of CAPV/EAE cooperatives in the last few years. In addition, as regards R&D spending in relation to the wealth generated (industrial added value), it fell from 5.5 percent in 2005 to 4.6 percent in 2007. This indicates a step back in the process of technological transfer in these companies and fell quite short of the figure of 6.5 percent that the index outlined for 2008.

One should also highlight the importance MU attaches to research. In its 2000–2008 strategic project, for example, it prioritized relaunching research in an attempt to reach a figure of 50 percent of all university activity. And in the academic year 2006–2007, 34 percent of all MU activity was linked to research. Due to this focus, in recent years, MU has participated in various projects in conjunction with the Basque and Spanish administrations and European research programs. This collaborative research model expanded during 2007 and 2008 to include more than fifteen MCC companies.

Continuous training has also increased in the last few years, with more than 3,500 employees taking classes at MU to complete masters degrees, specialist classes, and so on. In the field of education, it is significant that in 2007 there were 695 participants in the area of management development and 749 participants in various cooperative development training programs.

Final Considerations

When addressing the general Basque panorama in the field of research and technology development, we see that the dynamics and starting points for the CAPV/EAE are very different compared to those in Navarre and Iparralde. The potential convergence of an R&D policy and a technology policy for the three regions would involve compiling a series of short- and medium-term measures for various institutional sectors and encompassing diverse economic and social agents.

Excluding Iparralde due to the weakness of its industrial network, one might analyze the situation and outlook for the CAPV/EAE and Navarre in detail. In general, we can see that the greatest weaknesses center on: a predominance of low- and medium-level technologies for Basque companies, little investment in R&D (in both public resources and business resources), low levels of continuous training, lower sales for new products, low levels of high-tech product exports, limited collaboration among SMEs, very limited innovation by SMEs in non-tech areas, very low numbers of patents produced, weaknesses in institutional coordination, and deficiencies in institutional actions as related to SMEs (technology monitoring).

According to the SII European indicators, the CAPV/EAE and Navarre regions rank among those European countries classified as "moderate innovators." If the current dynamic continues, it will take close to thirty years to move into the next European group, that of "innovation followers." I believe the PCTI 2010 does not address problem areas in such a way that would allow the CAPV/EAE to improve its innovation system, make the Basque productive network more efficient, and assume better positioning within the European framework. The PCTI 2010, although offering some positive elements, will not have effective systemic results for the industrial and service sectors.

Instead, ideas emerging in this field must be reworked, not only in regards to R&D funding (which should be much higher than it is currently, prioritizing a commitment of public resources), but also as regards taking action in terms of the Basque productive base. Such action is necessary to modify the technological level and impact of many of the traditional industrial subsectors, and begin to create new key activities based on emerging sectors in line with the latest scientific and technological changes (nanotechnology, biotechnology, and so on).

And if private initiatives cannot address these issues, it will have to come from the public sector, through public investment or Basque public enterprises. They could strengthen these subsectors by either making use of different funding combinations and relying solely on public capital, or in conjunction with private capital, according to different levels of investment. Naturally, the development of Basque public enterprises cannot be addressed if they do not first enjoy strong foundations and public agencies that support technology research and development. All of the above must work in conjunction with other economic policy measures, such as investment by savings banks, financing agreements, and so on.

This does not diminish the importance of initiatives adopted in the last few years that are focused on improving technology centers, creating more R&D centers, and promoting collaboration between companies, universities, and technology centers. However, with the current economic crisis, the public sector should also play an invigorating role in the productive base. Otherwise, as indicated in the *Cotec Report* regarding the Spanish economy, and which for the most part is relevant as regards the Basque economy as well, it will take us close to thirty years to become a country with good technological and scientific development and to be able to maintain a per capita profitability accordingly.

Regarding Basque cooperatives in general and MCC in particular, I would conclude the following: given that MCC's industrial activities are in general medium-tech (although it does have a few minor high-tech productive activities), the productive model must be changed so that higher-tech products are prioritized and new products in areas such as nanotechnology and biotechnology promoted.

Growth at MCC's industrial plants in different countries around the world is significant, but R&D development is not a part of these affiliates' activity, whereas other multinationals are performing scientific and technological developments at their affiliates. In addition, as noted here, R&D

spending at cooperative companies is important, but the relationship of R&D spending compared to industrial added value fell to 4.5 percent in 2007, which is cause for some concern.

I have also described here efforts to develop research projects and scientific-technological centers. Such efforts are necessary and timely, but it remains unclear whether the amount of knowledge "stored" at different times has a direct effect on cooperative companies' products. This is due, in part, to the fact that medium-level technology companies absorb certain types of knowledge and technology.

Furthermore, it is important to have intermediaries (engineers, technicians) that know how to "translate" scientific discoveries into new or better products by implementing those discoveries. This barrier still exists in the current production process but could be overcome by initiating new productive activities based on the new scientific-technological fields mentioned above and by creating new markets and responding to new social needs.

Moreover, MCC's scientific-technological development up until now has been directed toward development in technology and its application in cooperative companies. As noted, MCC has only worked on a few specific patents. This is problematic, considering the growing influence of science in production. That said, various MCC publications make reference to supported projects in health, home automation, and so forth, which is positive.

Yet the speed of these global changes implies increasing investment in new activities. As Jesús Catania, president of MCC in 2005, stated, "Our objective in 2008 is that 25 percent of our sales revenue is generated from activities that didn't exist in 2005" (Catania 2006, 28). I do not think that this has not been achieved. Indeed, according to all indicators, it is impossible to make such changes without first undertaking productive investment in the new sectors. However, faced with the current economic crisis, there is a lot of pressure to maintain current production and staffing levels.

The most paradoxical issue is that right now and in the immediate future, in order to maintain existing employment, new markets with more innovative products must be opened. Clearly, the economic crisis is not affecting all European and Western countries equally, and the influence of these countries is significant in terms of their various production networks, their technological-scientific levels of production, their existing human capital, and their dominant business strategies.

These are some of the most significant challenges facing the MCC. Maintaining current employment must be done with a logic of anticipating productive and social needs and must also include the tools and measures required by various fields. Clearly, this is a major challenge.

References

Borja, Antón. 2008. "Plan de Ciencia, Tecnologia e Innovación 2010. Una visión crítica." In *El Pais Vasco en sus encrucijadas*, edited by Ramón Zallo. Donostia: Ttarttalo.

Catania, Jesús. 2006. "Hay que impulsar la cultura del debate." Interview by Javier Marcos. *Trabajo y Unión* 509 (February): 26–29.

Consejo Económico y Social (CES) del País Vasco. 2007. *Memoria socioeconómica 2006*. Bilbao: CES del País Vasco.

Cotec. 2008. *Cotec Report: Technology and Innovation in Spain, 2007*. Madrid: Cotec.

Gobierno Vasco. *Plan de Ciencia, Tecnología e Innovación (PCTI) 2010*. 2010. At www.euskadinnova.net/Documentos/9.aspx.

Navarro, Mikel, Juan José Gibaja, Ricardo Aguado, and Beñat Bilbao. 2008. "Patterns of Innovation in the EU-25 Regions: A Typology and Policy Recommendations." Orkestra Working Papers Series in Territorial Competitiveness No. 2008–04. Donostia–San Sebastián: Orkestra, Instituto Vasco de Competividad-Fundación Deusto. http://orkestra.deusto.es/images/publicaciones/archivos/000283_WPS2008-04_English_version.pdf.

Orkestra. *II Informe de Competitividad del País Vasco: Hacia el estadio competitivo de la innovación*. Deusto: Fundación Deusto.

7

Sources of Competitive Advantage in the Mondragon Cooperative Group

Imanol Basterretxea Markaida

Translated by Jennifer Martin

The Size of the Mondragon Cooperative Corporation

In 1956, five students from the Arrasate-Mondragón Vocational School established the enterprise ULGOR,[1] dedicated to the production of electrical household appliances, giving it the legal form of a cooperative in 1959. Fifty years after the creation of this first cooperative, the Mondragon experience has grown to establish itself as the seventh largest Spanish business group. It had 92,773 employees at the end of 2008, divided among 260 companies, half of which were cooperatives. The corporation had a turnover of €16,770 million in 2008, and has seventy-three production plants in eighteen foreign countries, as well as branches in another six.

Mondragon is a highly diversified business group, comprised of four areas: finance, industry, distribution, and knowledge.

The Caja Laboral Cooperative Credit Union stands out in the financial sector, with deposits of €13,988 million in 2008 and 401 bank branches in different regions of Spain.

---

1. The acronym ULGOR came from the last names of those five founders: Usatorre, Larrañaga, Gorroñogoitia, Ormaechea, and Ortubay. That enterprise, which is now called FAGOR, is still one of the most important Mondragon groups in 2011.

The bulk of the distribution group's sales correspond to the super-stores and supermarkets of the Eroski group. This group's consolidated sales reached €9,013 million in 2008 and it employed 52,711 people in Spain and France, mainly in superstores and supermarkets, although the group is diversifying into new businesses such as gas stations, sporting goods stores, perfumeries, real estate companies, optical centers, travel agencies, and entertainment and cultural centers.

The industrial group is comprised of 170 companies, divided into five subsectors (consumer goods, capital goods, industrial components, construction, and enterprise services). The value of its sales amounted to €6,511 million in 2008, with more than half of these (3,791) coming from international markets, and it employed 40,822 people.

Along with these areas, Mondragon has a knowledge sector that includes fourteen technological centers, a university, two vocational education or professional training centers, and a management-training center. Although the knowledge sector is smaller than the others in terms of revenue and employment (1,022 jobs, or 1.1 percent of all Mondragon jobs), it has been and will most likely continue to be an important area for the training and recruitment of personnel for the rest of the cooperatives and for driving innovation in the corporation.

These facts lead authors such as Katherine Gibson and Julie Graham to describe Mondragon as "the most successful and well-recognized complex of worker-owned industrial, retail, service, and support cooperatives in the world" (Gibson-Graham 2006, 102). This cooperative success has been studied from different angles by numerous researchers. Here, I intend to summarize this work that analyzes the existence of competitive advantages at Mondragon and the sources of these competitive advantages. This consolidated work can act as a guide and aid for all those researchers that wish to study the Mondragon experience in depth.

Do the Mondragon Cooperatives Obtain Better Results than the Capitalist Companies in Their Environment?

In spite of there being numerous references to Mondragon's economic success and the achievement of sustained competitive advantages over capitalist businesses in its environment, one must stress the existence of certain methodological difficulties in verifying Mondragon's achievement, or lack thereof.

The first difficulty in studying Mondragon's success is finding similar corporations or business groups with which to compare its development. Mondragon is a corporation that includes enterprises of quite different sizes, is highly diversified with varied businesses and sectors that range from banking and insurance to retail distribution, and spans across a multitude of industrial sectors. This has resulted in the literature on Mondragon to abound in analyses that compare the corporation's development with that of the Basque economy in general.

Another approach to analyzing the corporation's development seeks to compare it according on the basis of economic sector it is involved in. In this case however, the particular federal structure of Mondragon makes completing and validating such comparison highly difficult. New cooperatives have freely entered and formed part of Mondragon in different fiscal years, and in some cases, cooperatives have also left the corporation. For this reason, inter-annual comparisons with other companies that use indicators such as sales figures, employees, exports, and market share, do not exclusively reflect increased or decreased efficiency of the corporation. These indicators are biased by the entrance or exit of different cooperatives. It is necessary to stress that this bias is not taken into account in many of the analyses on the Mondragon experience.

In spite of these methodological difficulties in measuring the corporation's economic success, the bulk of the literature on the Mondragon experience coincides with stressing its success and in pointing out that the economic development of its cooperatives has been greater than that of the companies in its capitalist environment.

A large portion of the empirical evidence concentrates on the better relative performance of the Mondragon cooperatives during times of crisis.[2] Along with this better crisis response, another well-documented criterion is the lower failure rate of businesses in the group, during times of crisis as well as in normal periods (Ellerman 1984; Logan 1988; Smith 2001; Arando et al. 2010).

Another widely used argument, mainly for comparing the development of Mondragon's cooperatives with that of Basque and Spanish capitalist companies, is that of the cooperatives' greater exposure to international markets. For decades, Mondragon has had a greater percentage

---

2. See Bradley and Gelb (1983, 1987); Gorroño (1988); Logan (1988); Morris (1992); Albizu and Basterretxea (1988); MCC (2000a); Basterretxea (2008); Arando et al. (2010); Basterretxea and Albizu (2010).

of exports than the companies in its environment (Bradley and Gelb 1983; Logan 1988; Thomas and Logan 1982; MCC 2000a) and continues to do so today. Thus, in 2008, Mondragon's industrial division contributed 8.5 percent to the Basque Country's industrial GDP and 12.6 percent to industrial exports. Chris Logan (1988, 112) sees this greater international presence as an indicator of international competitiveness, an objective measure of the cooperatives' comparative strength, and better management, as well as a key factor in providing security to the group, all the result of a broader client base.

Similarly, authors such as Logan (1988); Christine A. Clamp (2000, 2003); Stephen C. Smith (2001); and Jon Charterina, Eneka Albizu, and Jon Landeta (2007) emphasize that Mondragon's cooperatives have had more success in the implementation of advanced management practices, mainly those related to total quality. All the same, these studies do not analyze the degree to which greater use of advanced management tools influences greater productivity in the cooperatives.

In a comparative study of cooperatives and Basque public limited companies highly innovative in technology and management, Sara Fernández de Bobadilla and Eva Velasco (2008 and chapter 5 of the present work) find that the ratio of Mondragon cooperatives among the most innovative companies is almost 50 percent, much higher than its economic weight. Based on a survey of sixty-six Mondragon human resources managers, Imanol Basterretxea (2008) finds that they perceived their cooperatives as having competitive advantages in attracting, developing, and retaining valuable personnel, along with advantages in knowledge management and in innovation areas. Again, these studies do not measure whether such advantages in attracting and keeping personnel, knowledge management, and innovation reflect greater productivity.

In order to confirm if a better economic performance by the Mondragon cooperatives over their rival capitalist companies really exists, it would be necessary to compare their productivity, but such studies are scarce and are not based on current data. Therefore, Keith Bradley and Alan Gelb analyze the productivity of the cooperatives in the 1970s and early 1980s, and come to a favorable conclusion on their performance: "The ratio of surplus to gross value added has exceeded that in the local industry by a considerable margin. . . . Overall, Mondragon has been profitable and appears to have outperformed its capitalist environment by a considerable margin" (1983, 16).

Henk Thomas and Chris Logan arrive at similar conclusions after comparing the group's cooperatives to Spanish industry during the 1970s. Using indicators such as value added per person, value added per fixed asset, net surplus per person, and a productivity index developed by Caja Laboral, they conclude that cooperatives have been more profitable than capitalist enterprises.

The major influence of these authors' work, along with a certain optimistic or favorable bias toward the cooperative experience found in much of scholarly literature on Mondragon, has caused many subsequent studies to continue to treat the higher productivity of the group's cooperatives as a proven fact, without conducting new empirical comparisons.

An exception to this optimistically biased literature can be seen in David Morris's study, where he points out that cooperatives were concerned about their productivity indexes in comparison to those of their international competitors: "There is some worry that Mondragon's enterprises have a lower productivity compared to international competitors and this could hurt them in a foreign competition." Moreover, "Ormaechea has observed that their productivity ratios, measured by value added, are lower than those achieved by German, Italian, French by each industrial job, and considerably behind Japan"(Morris 1992, 53).

The development of the productivity indicator used by Mondragon, the value added per person, is analyzed by Basterretxea (2008, 177–79) based on employee data and the value added shown in Mondragon's annual reports between 1991 and 2003. Comparing the value added per Mondragon employee, in the Mondragon Industrial Group cooperatives and in the manufacturing industry of twenty-seven European countries, Basterretxea concludes that one cannot justifiably continue to affirm significantly greater productivity at Mondragon when compared to capitalist enterprises, in line with Bradley and Gelb (1983), Thomas and Logan (1982), and all the authors that subsequently follow their work.

In any case, as Thomas and Logan (1982, 106) state, it is not possible to measure the efficiency of the Mondragon cooperative experience by simply looking at productivity or profitability indicators used in capitalist companies as a whole. According to these authors, the objectives of self-management companies such as the Mondragon cooperatives are much more complex than those of other companies, which means that any evaluation of efficiency should be done according to the group's endogenous objectives and rules.

Following this reasoning, much of the literature on Mondragon, as well as the Mondragon annual reports and the group's internal documentation, used indicators such as sales growth, investments, and employment as success factors.[3] Employment creation, the group's own survival, and its growth are endogenous objectives of the corporation, while profitability and business competitiveness are seen more as necessary conditions for the ability to grow. Therefore, good results in these growth indicators and employment could justify overall rates of return that are not very high, due to the fact that they seek to reduce risks through the diversification of markets and business. Likewise, lower productivity rates (especially in time of crisis) are justified by the corporation's efforts to maintain and create jobs. In this regard, asked whether Mondragon is more or less profitable than the capitalist enterprises in its environment, Mondragon's President of the General Council, Jesús Catania, declared:

> We are in so many sectors that it is difficult to make a comparison in standard terms, since there is no company equivalent to Mondragon in the Spanish state. Even so, one could say that, broadly speaking, we are within the average. You have to keep in mind that we have a very important objective and that is the creation of employment, and at times we maintain, circumstantially at least, some jobs that other companies with a more capitalist motive would do away with at once. And this is a factor that hurts us from a profitability standpoint, but that pleases us as being consistent with our reason for being (Jesús Catania, interviewed in Marcos 2003, 22).

Possible Sources of Competitive Advantage at Mondragon

The bibliography that seeks reasons for Mondragon's success is more extensive than the literature containing evidence of specific success. Hereafter, I will analyze the nine most-cited factors explaining Mondragon's competitive advantage:

---

3. See Bradley and Gelb (1983); Logan (1988); Thomas and Logan (1982); Lutz (1997); Albizu and Basterretxea (1998); and Arando et al. (2010).

People and Training

Cooperative members' dual condition of worker and owner—in other words, as members that participate in management, in the ownership, and in the company's results—make the human factor even more key in cooperative enterprises than in capitalist companies.

That dual condition of worker and owner, which does not exist in the most capitalist enterprises, constitutes a distinctive element that could generate sustainable competitive advantages resulting from this kind of participation. In this respect, scholars of the Mondragon experience as well as Dionisio Aranzadi (2003, 69) declare its workers to be at the core of the cooperative group. Mondragon's former president, Jesús Catania (2002, 16), asserted, "The essential and most natural strength of cooperativism lies in the people and their participation." Catania's predecessor in the Mondragon presidency, Antonio Cancelo, used similar terms to explain the cooperatives' success: "Cooperativism has its roots in the leadership of the people, which gives it an advantage to just be consistent in the business organization with this principle. In organizations in which the contribution of all is key, no other model has the initial advantages of the cooperatives" (Cancelo 2000, 16). According to Cancelo, workers' participation in cooperatives' management and decision-making facilitates their subsequent involvement in policy-making, as well as the quick implementation of new policies.

Given that many of Mondragon's industrial cooperatives do business in products and markets that face growing competition from countries with cheaper labor like China, the cooperative group is convinced that the only way to maintain and create jobs in its parent companies in the Basque Country is to manage the knowledge and innovative capacity of its people through their participation and involvement in the cooperatives. The group believes that there are competitive advantages to this participation, which it tries to fuel with appropriate tools and management structures. This participatory advantage is strengthened within Mondragon by the convergence of objectives between capital and labor, both concepts coinciding in the figure of the cooperative member:

> The people of Mondragon are the only guarantee of the success of our cooperative project and of our enterprises. We rely on their commitment to participation and integration, since what is essential to Mondragon's socio-business model and at the same time its differentiating element, is the participation of its members in the capital, the results, and the man-

agement. . . . Participation allows the channeling of people's potential, using it for the common interest and enhancing satisfaction and a sense of ownership on the part of the people. . . . Participation of the members and the people who work with us, along with the convergence of the final objectives allows a greater permeability of entrepreneurial initiatives in the whole organization, which should constitute a permanent competitive advantage (MCC 2000a, 40).[4]

Believing in the cooperative member as a source of competitive advantage requires cultivating and nourishing that source, because capitalist society and the conventional educational institutions that surround the cooperative companies do not typically produce "cooperative people" or provide people with cooperative principles and values. This has been understood as such since the beginnings of the Mondragon group. Mondragon's founder, José María Arizmendiarreta, believed that "one is not born a cooperator, one becomes a cooperator through education and the practice of virtue," which is explained through the following metaphor: "People do not normally become co-operators spontaneously, they have to be taught—the soil may be fertile but it has to be cultivated"(Arizmendiarreta, in Morris 1992, 13).

Based on the belief that cooperative members can be sources of competitive advantage, that one is not born a co-operator, and that the capitalist society and its education system do not help "make co-operators," the Mondragon group has, since its origins, developed an education system that includes a university (Mondragon Unibertsitatea), two vocational schools or professional training centers, and a managerial and cooperative training center, among other institutions. These corporate training centers, along with the training in technology and in cooperative and corporate culture that they provide, are considered an important source of competitive advantage by several authors.[5]

---

4. This text appeared in an almost identical form in the Compendio de Normas en Vigor del Congreso de Mondragón Corporación Cooperativa, updated on February 11, 2005 (MCC 2005, 16, 17).

5. Ellerman (1984); Bradley and Gelb (1983); Asua (1988); Meek and Woodworth (1990); J.M Ormaechea (1991, 1995); F. Ormaetxea (1991); Arrieta and Ormaechea (1991); Thomas and Logan (1982); Leibar and Ormaechea (1991); Hoover (1992); Morris (1992); Cantón (1995); MCC (2000b); Agirre (2001); Chaves (2003); Aranzadi (2003); Basterretxea (2008); and Basterretxea and Albizu (2010, 2011).

Better Management, Better Managers, Self-management Tools

Many researchers who have analyzed the reasons for Mondragon's economic success point to the existence of better managers than those of its competitors and to the development of specific management tools for the cooperative group.[6] Most of these studies stress that the Mondragon cooperatives have been pioneers and have been particularly successful at implementing advanced management practices, especially in quality-related practices. According to these authors, the culture of participation in decision-making and in the self-management of the cooperatives gives them competitive advantages in the application of quality tools, the adoption of organizational models, and the means of management associated with these quality tools.

Corporate and Cooperative Culture

The key role of cooperative culture did not escape the analysis of the corporation itself, which believes that "Mondragon's history would have been impossible without a way of being, of performing, of doing specific and differentiated things, that is, a self-culture" (MCC 2000a, 34).

Mondragon's ten basic principles are the best embodiment of this self-culture;[7] principles that, according to the corporation, constitute "the cornerstone, the starting point" of the cooperative group's ideological construction (MCC 2000a, 15). According to Roy Morrison (1991), Smith (2001), and Gibson-Graham (2006), the Mondragon cooperatives have adhered to these principles since their origins, understanding this adhesion as an exogenous factor that involves distinctive economic management and that makes the cooperatives' adaptations subject to the market's changing conditions. The fact that Mondragon's cooperatives have proven themselves in successive market adjustments leads Smith (2001) to assert that the cooperatives have built competitive advantages on the basis of those ten basic principles.

The creation of a solid cooperative and corporate culture on which Mondragon's structure, organization, and policies rests is also empha-

---

6. Thomas and Logan (1982); Logan (1988); Whyte and Whyte (1988); Albizu and Basterretxea (1998); Cheney (1999); Bakaikoa et al. (1999); Clamp (2000, 2003); Smith (2001); Jakobsen (2001); Irizar (2005); Charterina, Albizu, and Landeta (2007); Basterretxea (2008); and Basterretxea and Albizu (2011).

7. 1. Open admission; 2. Democratic organization; 3. Sovereignty of labor; 4. Subordinate and practical nature of capital; 5. Participatory management; 6. Payment solidarity; 7. Inter-cooperation; 8. Social transformation; 9. Universality; and 10. Education.

sized as having contributed to a sociocultural homogeneity (Bradley and Gelb 1983; Ormaechea 1991; Meek and Woodworth 1990; Smith 2001), a homogeneity that can facilitate democratic decision-making within the cooperatives.

A large portion of the literature on Mondragon stresses the shared culture as the main glue that holds the cooperatives together inside a corporation with a "federal" or "inverted pyramid" organizational structure.

> Mondragon is held together by a set of shared principles. This is reinforced with the provision of real services and other organizational safeguards. . . By [the inverted-pyramid nature of Mondragon] it was meant that while the official corporate chart of Mondragon might resemble that of an ordinary holding company, in reality all the authority was held by the individual co-ops, so that the apparent 'base' of the pyramid was really its (functional) apex. The Mondragon directors are a committee of the co-op directors; and any co-op that does not find that the Mondragon corporate offices are adding value to their operations may secede at any time (Smith 2001, 13, 46).

The freedom of each individual cooperative to leave the group means that the center has to somehow justify the added value to the cooperatives by means of its technical, educational, financial, and strategic services. Otherwise, the constituent companies might leave, as has been the case on occasion.[8] The fact that the bulk of its cooperatives has not left Mondragon is a clear sign that the corporation's incentives to add value are working (Smith 2001, 28) and that the shared mission, culture, and values among the Mondragon cooperatives are an effective unifying link.

Supporting Institutions (Caja Laboral, Training Centers, and Corporate R&D)

The Mondragon cooperative group has developed many support institutions throughout its history, such as a credit union (Caja Laboral), corporate training centers (like Mondragon Unibertsitatea), fourteen corporate R&D centers (like Ikerlan and Ideko), and a voluntary insurance company (Lagun Aro).

Many researchers of the Mondragon phenomenon believe that these support institutions have bestowed important competitive advantages

---

8. During the 2008 General Meeting, members of the Ampo and Irizar cooperatives decided to leave the Mondragon Corporation.

on the cooperatives.[9] In particular, these support institutions help to resolve some of the cooperatives' typical deficiencies by providing personnel familiar with cooperativism (corporate education centers), financial resources (Caja Laboral), insurance services (Lagun Aro), and research (Ikerlan, Ideko, and so on) to meet their needs.

Among all these support institutions, the literature emphasizes the credit union cooperative, Caja Laboral (created in 1959), as a key source of MCC's competitive advantage. The cooperatives often faced financial problems that greatly limited their growth, since neither members' contributions nor accessible external financing was enough to sustain investment projects that required large amounts of capital. Consequently, having a cooperative credit union has allowed the channeling of domestic savings into the cooperatives in need of financing under preferential conditions. In certain times of crisis, Caja Laboral has allowed financing with reduced or no interest rates for certain cooperatives experiencing difficulties (Gorroño 1988, 92) and has waived repayment in extreme cases (Gorroñogoita 1988, 297). In the current crisis, which has been marked by strong credit recession, Caja Laboral has returned to being an important factor in financing the cooperatives. The corporation has also created other organizations that have joined Caja Laboral in this purpose.[10]

In sum, the credit union, as well as the training centers, and the corporate research centers, and the corporation's insurance company, not only contribute competitive advantages individually, but are also interconnected with the rest of the organizations. The "interrelationship of these support institutions" (Cantón 1995, 187) might constitute a competitive advantage base, and also function as a barrier to imitation.

Although a competitor might try to imitate one of Mondragon's four pillars (the financial, educational, social welfare, and R&D foundations), and invest in a similar way to that of the cooperative group, such investment

---

9. See Ellerman (1984); Asua (1988); Gorroño (1988); Gorroñogoita (1988); Whyte and Whyte (1988); Gutiérrez Johnson and Whyte (1977); Thomas and Logan (1982); Leibar and Ormaechea (1991); Arrieta and Ormaechea (1991); Hoover (1992); Morris (1992); Ormaechea (1994, 1995, 1998); Cantón (1995); Cancelo (1997); Bakaikoa et al. (1999); Cheney (1999); Smith (2001); Chaves (2003); Aranzadi (2003); Bakaikoa et al. (2004); Basterretxea (2008); Iriziar and MacLeod (2008, 2010); and Basterretxea and Albizu (2010, 2011).

10. The Mondragon foundation allocates part of its central Inter-cooperation funds to financing cooperatives that have exhausted their debt capacity, contributing the resources needed to support a rollover through loans or capital increases.

would lead to worse results for the company attempting to copy the MCC system because it would not involve the other three cooperative pillars.

In their analysis on Mondragon and the possibility of reproducing a similar experience in the United States, Ana Gutiérrez Johnson and William F. Whyte (1977), warn that in addition to industrial cooperatives, the imitator would have to create teaching, banking, and research organizations to support each other. Begoña Asua (1988) and Basterretxea (2008) also arrive at similar conclusions.

Employment Policy and Job Flexibility

Various researchers of the Mondragon phenomenon stress that the cooperative group has an employment policy that gives it competitive advantages over conventional capitalist companies.[11] This employment policy is characterized by the use of flexible work schedules, a high flexibility in salaries, flexibility of job duties performed by the members of each cooperative, as well as the relocation of members from cooperatives in crisis to those cooperatives in need of manpower. Thanks to those measures, the Mondragon cooperatives have been able to overcome different economic crises by retaining more capital, enjoying a lower failure rate, and closing down less of their interests than their competitors.

Business Creation Know-How

Shortage conditions and the value of human resource as a source of competitive advantage are especially relevant when we speak of a human resource typology that is smaller than others—that of people who start businesses successfully (Penrose 1959; Lado and Wilson 1994; Mahoney and Michael 2004).

If there is a shortage of successful entrepreneurs, those entrepreneurs that start up businesses under the legal form of a cooperative will be even more scarce: "If one has the talent to organize a co-op, one could probably also organize a conventional firm, and become not only the manager, but the residual claimant on the net income of the firm as well. As a result,

---

11. See Bradley and Gelb (1983, 1987); Gorroño (1988); Logan (1988); Whyte and Whyte (1988); Hoover (1992); Morris (1992); Ormaechea (1994, 1998); Goienetxe (1996); Cancelo (1997); Albizu and Basterretxea (1998); Bakaikoa (1996); Bakaikoa et al. (1999); MCC (2000a, 2000b); Smith (2001); Clamp (2003); Basterretxea (2008); Arando et al (2010); and Basterretxea and Albizu (2010).

there is a severe incentive problem for co-op entrepreneurship" (Smith 2001, 27).

To cope with these limitations, Mondragon has created different organizations and divisions that boost cooperative entrepreneurship. In its early days, this impetus came from the corporate training centers. In the 1970s and 1980s, backing for the formation of new cooperatives rested in the business division of the Caja Laboral credit union. Presently, the creation of new businesses is boosted by different departments and companies within the corporation, such as the business incubators Saiolan and Azaro, or the promotions department of Mondragon's new businesses. Throughout this process, Mondragon generates valuable knowledge of cooperative business creation, according to authors like David P. Ellerman (1984); José Mª Ormaechea (1998); Gurli Jakobsen (2001); Isabel Uribe and Iñazio Irizar (2005); and Basterretxea (2008).

Inter-cooperation

As Smith (2001) contends, even though a cooperative overcomes various entry barriers and establishes itself in a certain sector, it is still possible that it might not survive. This is not because of intrinsic inefficiencies, but simply because of the absence of other cooperatives to work with in its sector or area. Using the metaphor "a single rose may not bloom alone: it may need to be part of an ecosystem in which other roses are present, and in which supporting actors and structures (e.g. bees, soil conditions, rainfall) are present," Smith (2001, 29) suggests that co-ops may only survive if there are other co-ops to cooperate with in their region, in their sector, or in their supply chain.

In Mondragon, inter-cooperation and the solidarity between cooperatives constitute the rank of basic principle. According to the Mondragon inter-cooperation principle, individual cooperatives must work in a joint and controlled manner. This results in the establishment of a homogenous social and occupational system, the shared restructuring of profits, regulation of the transference of worker members, and the search for potential synergies.

Until 1991, the restructuring of profits was done at the level of territorial groupings, thus cooperatives with profits transferred part of these gains to other co-ops with losses in their region. From 1991 to the present, this profit restructuring has been performed at the level of the corporation's sectoral divisions.

Together with the profit restructuring in each division, Mondragon also restructures profits at the corporate level through its central inter-cooperation fund (CIF). This fund is annually endowed by the cooperatives with an outlay equivalent to 10 percent of the gross surpluses from the previous financial year (20 percent in the case of Caja Laboral). Part of the CIF resources are intended for the funding of cooperatives that have exhausted their debt capacity, contributing the resources needed to support their rollover plan through guarantees, loans, or compensation of losses. In 2003, a corporate solidarity fund was also created to supplement the loss compensation system of the cooperatives in the industrial area.

Various authors underscore this profit restructuring inter-cooperation among cooperatives with both gains and losses as one of the pillars of survival and success within the Mondragon experience.[12]

Capitalization of Profits

One key to Mondragon's success, according to various analyses,[13] is its systematic reinvestment of the cooperatives' profits. Part of these profits come from the cooperatives as interest on capital and monetized dividends.[14] However, the bulk of earnings are used to capitalize the cooperatives in the form of capitalized returns on investment and reserve funds.[15] This continuous practice of profit capitalization throughout Mondragon's history has permitted a strengthening of the cooperatives' own resources and led to the sustained growth of the cooperatives. Its own resources have also been strengthened in times of crisis by means of capital increases (through the capitalization of overtime, capitalization of extra payments, and so forth), helping to improve the response of the Mondragon cooperatives to successive economic crises.

---

12. See Gorroño (1988); Gorroñogoita (1988); Cantón (1995); Cancelo (1997); Ormaechea (1998); Bakaikoa et al. (1999); Agirre (2001); Errasti et al. (2003); Chaves (2003); Aranzadi (2003); and Arando et al. (2010).

13. Bradley and Gelb (1983); Gorroño (1988); Gorroñogoita (1988, 1995); MCC (2000a); Irizar and MacLeod (2010).

14. A full 23.6 percent of the 2007 economic performance was distributed among the cooperative members in this way.

15. Of the 2007 earnings, 67.6 percent was used to capitalize the cooperatives and the corporation.

Structure and Control Systems

Several authors point to the Mondragon Corporation's organizational structure and cooperative control systems in order to explain the success of this cooperative experience.

Shann Turnbull (1985) compares the custom-designed control and incentive architecture of Mondragon with Japanese Keiretsus. He considers the control architecture within and among Mondragon co-ops as far more complex than that of ordinary firms. And in his opinion, this complexity creates operational and competitive advantages.

According to Smith (2001), the co-op is designed to be a small organization, which facilitates democratic decision-making. By grouping individual co-ops within a larger corporate structure, Mondragon co-ops still maintain the advantages of participation, while they take more systematic advantage of economies of scale and scope.

Christina A. Clamp (2003, 26–27) also underscores the fact that each cooperative remains self-sufficient and retains its own autonomy in several administrative aspects, but at the same time, the corporation gives individual cooperatives much more visibility in global markets, enhancing their ability to take advantage of market opportunities, exploiting the synergistic potential of the cooperatives, and enabling them to be an aggressive and able competitor.

Conclusions

The consolidated findings of the studies that emphasize the existence of competitive advantages in the Mondragon group prove the existence of continuing evidence of a greater international competitiveness from the Mondragon cooperatives than from capitalist companies in their geographical environment, a higher growth in sales and employment, greater gains in quality, less failure rates, better response to crises, and a greater innovation capacity. That said, there are few studies and little evidence to demonstrate that cooperatives are more productive, and what studies there are date back to the 1970s and the 1980s. Much of the literature on Mondragon continues to validate this premise of greater productivity without providing recent empirical evidence. Given the academic interest in the Mondragon experience, it would be interesting to see more complete and recent comparative analyses to see whether the Mondragon cooperatives have been, and are currently, more or less productive than competing public limited companies operating in their sectors.

Here, I have also summarized the explanations given by scholarly literature for Mondragon's achievements. A large part of Mondragon's sources of competitive advantage come from its human resource policies. Therefore, among the most emphasized sources of competitive advantage, it is the people who shape Mondragon and its training, the existence of better management and management tools, the corporate and cooperative culture, and the group's employment policy and labor flexibility. Along with these reasons, another important set of explanations for Mondragon's success focuses on its organizational structure, on the corporate organizations that support the cooperatives, and on the inter-cooperation tools between cooperatives.

I believe that this summary of the literature analyzing the success of the Mondragon experience can be a starting and a focus point for those scholars who wish to know and continue studying this experience in more depth.

References

Agirre, Amaia. 2001. "Los principios cooperativos atractores de la gestión eficiente: Su medición: Aplicación al caso de Mondragón Corporación Cooperativa." *CIRIEC-España*, 39: 93–113.

Albizu, Eneka, and Imanol Basterretxea. 1998. "Flexibilidad laboral y generación de empleo en tiempos de crisis: El caso de Mondragón Corporación Cooperativa." *Revista Europea de Dirección y Economía de la Empresa* 7, no. 3: 83–98.

Arando, Saioa, Fred Freundlich, Mónica Gago, Derek C. Jones, and Takao Kato. 2010. "Assessing Mondragon: Stability & Managed Change in the Face of Globalization." William Davidson Institute Working Paper 1003 (November). University of Michigan.

Aranzadi, Dionisio. 2003. "El significado de la Experiencia Cooperativa de Mondragón." *Estudios Empresariales* 112: 58–69.

Arrieta, Juan José, and José Mª Ormaechea. 1991. *Caja Laboral Popular*. Textos básicos de Otalora. Capítulo IX. Aretxabaleta: Otalora.

Asua, Begoña. 1988. "Educación y trabajo en la sociedad industrial del País Vasco: La 'Eskola Politécnica José María Arizmendiarreta' en el Grupo Cooperativo Mondragón." Ph.D. Diss. University of the Basque Country .

Bakaikoa, Baleren. 1996. "La solidaridad intercooperativa y la política de empleo en Mondragón Corporación Cooperativa (MCC)." *CIRIEC-España* 22: 81–94.

Bakaikoa, Baleren, Agurtzane Begiristain, Anjel Mari Errasti, and Gorka Goikoetxea. 2004. "Redes e innovación cooperativa." *CIRIEC-España* 49: 263–94.

Bakaikoa, Baleren, José Mª de Uralde, Javier Erdocia, Iñigo Nagore, and Javier Salaberria. 1999. "Mondragón Corporación Cooperativa-MCC." In *Grupos Empresariales de Economía Social en España*, edited by José Barea, Juan Francsico Juliá, and José Luís Monzón. Valencia: CIRIEC y Ministerio de Trabajo y Asuntos Sociales.

Basterretxea, Imanol. 2008. "La política de formación como fuente de ventaja competitiva en la experiencia Mondragon: Un análisis desde la visión basada en los recursos." Ph.D. Diss. University of the Basque Country.

Basterretxea, Imanol, and Eneka Albizu. 2010. "¿Es posible resistir a la crisis?: Un análisis desde la gestión de las políticas de formación y empleo en Mondragón." *CIRIEC España* 67: 75–96.

———. 2011. "Management Training as a Source of Perceived Competitive Advantage: The Mondragon Cooperative Group Case." *Economic and Industrial Democracy* 32, no. 2: 199–222.

Bradley, Keith, and Alan Gelb. 1983. *Cooperation at Work: The Mondragón Experience*. London: Heinemann Educational.

———. 1987. "Cooperative Labour Relations: Mondragon's Response to Recession." *British Journal of Industrial Relations* 25, no. 1: 77–97.

Cancelo, Antonio. 1997. "Cultura social y cooperativismo." In *Cuadernos de cooperativismo: Cooperativismo y nuevo milenio*. Bilbao: Fundación Sabino Arana.

———. 2000. "Entrevista con Antonio Cancelo, Presidente de MCC." *Koop* 2 (January): 13–16.

Cantón, Julio. 1995. "La gestión social y de recursos humanos en las cooperativas de trabajo asociado." *Actas Oficiales de la IV Conferencia Mundial del CICOPA:* 183–88.

Catania, Jesús. 2002. "Entrevista con Jesús Catania: Presidente del Consejo General de Mondragón Corporación Cooperativa." *Koop* 12 (July): 13–16.

Charterina, Jon, Eneka Albizu, and Jon Landeta. 2007. "The Quality of Management in Basque Companies: Differences Existing between

Cooperative and Non-cooperative Companies." In *Cooperative Firms in Global Markets: Incidence, Viability and Economic Performance*, edited by Sonja Novkovic and Vania Sena. Vol. 10 of *Advances in Economic Analysis of Participatory and Labor-Managed Firms*. London and Amsterdam: Elsevier JAI.

Chaves, Rafael. 2003. "El modelo cooperativo de Mondragón: El desarrollo económico basado en el cooperativismo." In *Elementos de economía social: Teoría y realidad*, edited by Rafael Chaves, José Luis Monzón, and Antonia Sajardo Moreno. Valencia: Dpto. de Economía Aplicada, Universidad de Valencia.

Cheney, George. 1999. *Values at Work: Employee Participation Meets Market Pressure at Mondragón*. Ithaca, NY: ILR Press.

Clamp, Christina A. 2003. "The Evolution of Management in the Mondragon Cooperatives." Paper presented at the conference *Mapping Co-operative Studies in the New Millennium*, May 28–31. University of Victoria, Victoria, British Columbia, Canada.

———. 2000. "The Internationalization of Mondragon." *Annals of Public and Cooperative Economics* 71, no. 4: 557–77.

Ellerman, David P. 1984. "Entrepreneurship in the Mondragon Cooperatives." *Review of Social Economy* 42, no. 3: 272–94.

Errasti, Anjel Mari, Iñaki Heras, Baleren Bakaikoa, and Pilar Elgoibar. 2003. "The Internationalisation of Cooperatives: The Case of the Mondragon Cooperative Corporation." *Annals of Public and Cooperative Economics* 74, no. 4: 553–84.

Fernández de Bobadilla, Sara, and Eva Velasco. 2008. "¿Gestionan mejor la innovación las empresas de economía social que las sociedades anónimas?: Estudio comparativo de empresas innovadoras vascas." *CIRIEC-España* 63: 5–37.

Gibson-Graham, J.K. [Pseud. Katherine Gibson and Julie Graham]. 2006. *A Postcapitalist Politics*. Minneapolis: University of Minnesota Press.

Goienentxe, Jesús. 1996. "La experiencia de la gestión del empleo en MCC." *Ekonomiaz* 34: 155–61.

Gorroño, Iñaki. 1988. "El cooperativismo industrial de Mondragón: Respuesta ante la crisis económica." In *Congreso sobre el cooperativismo y la economía social en el mundo: II Congreso Mundial Vasco*. Vitoria-Gasteiz: Servicio Central de Publicaciones del Gobierno Vasco.

Gorroñogoitia, Alfonso. 1988. "El grupo asociado a Caja Laboral Popular (Mondragón) como fenómeno típico mundial." In *Congreso sobre el cooperativismo y la economía social en el mundo: II Congreso Mundial Vasco*. Vitoria-Gasteiz: Servicio Central de Publicaciones del Gobierno Vasco.

——. 1995. "Mondragón." *Actas Oficiales de la IV Conferencia Mundial del CICOPA*: 47–54.

Gutiérrez Johnson, Ana, and William F. Whyte. 1977. "The Mondragon System of Worker Production Cooperatives." *Industrial and Labor Relations Review* 31, no. 1: 18–30.

Hoover, Kenneth R. 1992. "Mondragon's Answers to Utopia's Problems." *Utopian Studies* 3, no. 2: 1–19.

Irizar, Iñazio, and Greg MacLeod. 2008. "Innovación emprendedora en el grupo Mondragón: El caso de sus centros tecnológicos." *CIRIEC-España* 60: 41–72.

——. 2010. *32 claves empresariales de Mondragon*. Arrasate: ACD.

Jakobsen, Gurli. 2001. "Cooperative and Training Dimensions in Entrepreneurship: A Study of the Methodology of the Saiolan Centre in Mondragon." *INUSSUK. Arctic Research Journal* 1: 137–46.

Lado, Augustine, and Mary Wilson. 1994. "Human Resource Systems and Sustained Competitive Advantage: A Competency-based Perspective." *Academy of Management Review* 19, no. 4: 699–727.

Leibar, Juan, and José Mª Ormaechea. 1991. *Dn. José María Arizmendiarreta y sus colaboradores*. Textos Básicos de Otalora: Capítulo II. Aretxabaleta: Otalora.

Logan, Chris G. 1988. "An Experiment that Continues: The Mondragon Co-operatives." In *Congreso sobre el cooperativismo y la economía social en el mundo: II Congreso Mundial Vasco*. Vitoria-Gasteiz: Servicio Central de Publicaciones del Gobierno Vasco.

Lutz, Mark A. 1997. "The Mondragon Co-operative Complex: An Application of Kantian Ethics to Social Economics." *International Journal of Social Economics* 24, no. 12: 1404–21.

Mahoney, Joseph, and Steven Michael. 2004. "A Subjectivist Theory of Entrepreneurship." University of Illinois, College of Business Working Papers 04–0104.

Marcos, Javier. 2003. "Entrevista con Jesús Catania. Presidente del Consejo General de MCC." *TU Lankide* 476 (February): 22–25.

MCC. 2000a. *Mondragón Corporación Cooperativa: Historia de una experiencia.* Arrasate-Mondragón: MCC.

———. 2000b. *Política y gestión de empleo en Mondragón Corporación Cooperativa.* Mondragón: MCC.

———. 2005. *Compendio de normas en vigor del congreso de Mondragón Corporación Cooperativa, Actualizado al 11 de febrero de 2005.* Mondragón: MCC.

Meek, Christopher B., and Warner P. Woodworth. 1990. "Technical Training and Enterprise: Mondragon's Educational System and its Implications for Other Cooperatives." *Economic and Industrial Democracy* 11: 508–28.

Morris, David. 1992. *The Mondragon System: Cooperation at Work.* Washington, DC: Institute for Local Self-Reliance.

Morrison, Roy. 1991. *We Build the Road as We Travel: Mondragon's Cooperative Society.* Philadelphia: New Society Publishers.

Ormaechea, José Mª. 1991. *Los principios cooperativos de la experiencia.* Textos Básicos de Otalora. Capítulo V. Aretxabaleta: Otalora.

———. 1994. "Las crisis en empresas personalistas: Caso aplicado a Mondragón Corporación Cooperativa (1974–1985)." *Información Comercial Española* 729: 73–84.

———. 1995. "La eficacia económica y la democracia cooperativa." In *Actas Oficiales de la IV Conferencia Mundial del CICOPA:* 245–53.

———. 1998. *Orígenes y claves del cooperativismo de Mondragón.* Arrasate-Mondragón: Caja Laboral Popular.

Ormaetxea, Felix. 1991. *Eskola Politeknikoa Jose Maria Arizmendiarreta: Sdad: Coop.* Textos básicos de Otalora. Capítulo XII. Aretxabaleta: Otalora.

Penrose, Edith. 1959. *The Theory of the Growth of the Firm.* New York: John Wiley.

Smith, Stephen C. 2001. "Blooming Together or Wilting Alone? Network Externalities and the Mondragon and La Lega Cooperative Networks." United Nations University/WIDER Discussion Paper No. 2001/27. Helsinki: UNU-WIDER.

Thomas, Henk, and Chris Logan. 1982. *Mondragon: An Economic Analysis.* London: Allen & Unwin; The Hague: Institute of Social Studies.

Turnbull, Shann. 1995. "Innovations in Corporate Governance: The

Mondragon Experience." *Corporate Governance: An International Review* 3, no. 3: 167–80.

Uribe, Isabel, and Iñazio Irizar. 2005. "Challenges and Opportunities for MCC Co-operative Companies in the Face of Globalization." In *The Mondragon Co-operative Research Conference 2005, Proceedings of the Conference*, edited by Mikel Cid and Marienella López. Oñati: School of Management, Mondragon University.

Whyte, William F., and Kathleen K. Whyte. 1988. *Making Mondragon: The Growth and Dynamics of the Worker Cooperative Complex.* Ithaca, NY: ILR Press.

8

Basque Cooperatives and the Crisis: The Case of Mondragon

ITZIAR VILLAFAÑEZ PÉREZ

In a context of a global economic recession in which the capitalist economic system and traditional forms of business organization are being questioned for their role in generating the crisis and offering few solutions to it, it is interesting to analyze the consequences of this crisis in other forms of enterprise as well as their responses, particularly in regard to cooperatives, the principal exponent of the social economy. In this sense, cooperative societies, based on democracy and centered on people rather than capital, have traditionally shown greater resilience when faced with economic adversity, precisely due to the principles and values on which they are based.

The Basque cooperative movement, especially the Mondragon experience, the largest business group in the Basque Country and seventh biggest in the Spanish state, has been and continues to be a major point of reference in the cooperative world. The cooperatives in this group, following a catalogue of management-approved recommendations to confront the crisis, in addition to showing greater strength in the face of the economic downturn than other types of entrepreneurs, have demonstrated a

* Revision of "People before Profit: The Response of Co-operatives to the Global Financial Crisis and Economic Recession." Paper presented at the ICA (International Co-operative Alliance) Research Conference, Queens College, Oxford University, Oxford, September 2–4, 2009.

significant capacity to react to the new situation. They have done this by by adopting measures that, leaving aside the search for short-term profit, are grounded in cooperative principles such as solidarity and concern for the environment. Thus they have come to agreements with workers over relinquishing bonuses, freezing salaries, capitalizing their interests as a means of safeguarding employment, filling positions with workers from other cooperatives in the group, applying funds to other cooperatives with major problems, and so on.

Taking Basque cooperatives as a field of study, especially members of the Mondragon Corporation (MCC), the aim of this study is to identify the consequences of the economic crisis for these societies and to analyze the measures they are taking to overcome it.

The Basque Cooperative Movement: A Brief Overview

Without wanting to offer a detailed study of the history, individuals, and other aspects of Basque cooperativism, which have been addressed thoroughly by many studies (mainly as a result of the well-known Mondragon phenomenon), it is worth emphasizing certain elements of this story to contextualize the present chapter.

Basque cooperativism emerged at the end of the nineteenth century and mainly adopted the form of consumer cooperatives in a more general environment of large industrial businesses. With time this model extended to new sectors, and in 1920 the first associative work cooperative was born, Alfa. Yet the key date in the history of cooperatives in the Basque Country is 1956: the year the by now well-known Mondragon experience began. Indeed, some authors regard it as the most important cooperative movement in the world. From their creation at this time, the Mondragon cooperatives have grown to become the largest Basque business group. These cooperatives currently employ 92,000 people—this, despite job cuts as a result of the global financial crisis—and are made up of over 250 companies (cooperatives, subsidiaries, mutual aid societies, foundations, insurance companies, and international services). Specifically, these include Caja Laboral, Fagor, Maier, Batz, and other important industrial businesses, including Eroski and Mondragon Unibertsitatea (MU, Mondragon University).

However, Basque cooperativism is not limited to Mondragon, since at present there are around 1,700 such cooperatives.[1] Worth mentioning among these other experiences is that of the Ikastolas (Basque-language schools), which are united in the Ikastolen Elkartea confederation and which have recently formed the first Basque European Cooperative Society, as well as the cooperative experience of Hemen and Herrikoa in the French Basque Country (Urteaga 2008).[2]

In this way, we can clearly see that Basque cooperativism has deep and extensive roots in Basque society, and is the result of long-held forms of cooperation in the community (for example, *auzolana* or the traditional practice of helping one's neighbors), associationism, the industrial tradition, religious sentiment, or even Basque nationalism (Altuna 2008), throughout the whole Basque Country. One should point out, however, that this pattern is uneven. Most cooperatives and the most important of these companies are located in the Comunidad Autónoma del País Vasco-Euskal Autonomia Erkidegoa (CAPV/EAE, Autonomous Community of the Basque Country), and it is here I will focus my study.

The Influence of the Global Economic Crisis on Cooperatives: An Example of Strength

In the current context of global economic crisis, social economy companies, and particularly cooperatives, have become a focus of study for politicians and workers' organizations of workers. This is because they offer an alternative possible solution to confronting the disastrous consequences of the downturn, as demonstrated by their greater resilience. Likewise, in other periods of recession they have also proved to be a viable and successful option and even a source of employment creation. This has led to the contention that cooperatives experience anti-cyclical behavior.

It is probably too much to say that cooperatives are immune to the current crisis. Insofar as these companies are integrated in the market and they depend on its development, they suffer the consequences of its cycles just like other enterprises. They thus have to face decreasing demand and difficulties when trying to raise capital or financing because of a general

---

1. According to the data of www.ine.es (Instituto Nacional de Estadística, the Spanish National Statistics Institute) and www.creesaquitaine.org (Chambre Regionale de l'Economie Sociale et Solidaire d'Aquitaine, the Aquitaine Regional Office for Social Economy and Solidarity).

2. See www.hemen-herrikoa.org/ and www.herrikoa.com/.

reduction in their profits and employment, and even the possibility of suffering insolvency or starting bankruptcy procedures.

Nevertheless, despite such risks, the data do confirm the greater strength of cooperative companies when confronting periods of economic difficulties compared to other types of enterprises. For example, statistics regarding bankruptcy procedures clearly reflect this greater residual strength. In the period 2005–2009, the number of debtors facing insolvency in the Spanish state—whether individuals or legal entities, businessmen or not—multiplied considerably.[3] According to INE data, bankruptcy procedures increased from a number of between 900 and 1,000 in 2005, 2006, and 2007 to 2,902 in 2008, reaching 1,558 already by the first quarter of 2009 in the Spanish state. In the CAPV/EAE there were 83 bankruptcies in 2007, 171 in 2008, and 93 during the first quarter of 2009, while in the same period there were 12, 44, and 20 bankruptcies respectively in Navarre. However, scarcely any cooperatives were involved in these bankruptcy procedures, according to both INE data and the Official State Bulletin (*Boletin Oficial del Estado*, BOE).[4]

What Are the Main Factors of this Strength?

There are various explanations for why cooperative companies are better placed to confront the present crisis.

In this regard, the principles and values that characterize these kinds of companies (solidarity, financial participation in the business on the part of the workforce, autonomy, cooperation among cooperatives, and so forth) are crucial. Such factors translate, among others things, into a greater predisposition on the part of cooperative members to accept certain necessary measures—such as wage freezes, giving up bonus, and so on—for the economic viability of their business and maintaining jobs.

Of course, because of this, it is essential to have a legal framework that allows such measures to be taken. The fact that Spanish legislation does

---

3. To this we should add an important increase in redundancy dismissal procedures and unemployment rates. The unemployment rate was around 5–6 percent in the CAPV/EAE before the economic crisis, and rose to 12.23 percent in the second quarter of 2009, and rose in the same period in Navarre from 4.5 percent to 12.23 percent.

4. For example, of the 2,902 bankruptcies in 2008, 2,876 were in relation to individuals, limited companies, and public limited companies; in other words, more than 99.1 percent. The remaining 26 cases (less than 0.9 percent of the total) were in regard to cooperatives, agricultural collectives (*sociedades agrarias de transformación*), community properties (*comunidades de bienes*), and so on.

not consider cooperative worker members to be employees, but rather members in the full sense, makes the system more flexible and allows for measures to be taken that would not be possible within the framework the basic Spanish employment law. In this way, although legally the status of a cooperative member is quite similar to that of an employee,[5] to the extent that there is debate about the very nature of a cooperative member and it is generally acknowledged to be a borderline status, there are still marked differences.

Thus, the law indicates that, according to cooperative legislation,[6] if a cooperative business suffers losses, cooperative members do not necessarily have the right to collect advances on their wages.[7] And it is accepted that in case of such financial difficulties, payment of these advances can be postponed,[8] or even reduced.[9] Moreover, the Central Labor Court (Tribunal Central de Trabajo) has stated that "in light of the special nature of cooperatives, in which collective interest takes priority over members' individual interests . . . agreements of this kind are legal that, reducing provisionally the imbursement of 10 advance payments to which members have the right, contribute to overcoming an economic crisis."[10] As regards Basque cooperative legislation, the High Court of Justice of the Basque Country indicates that the minimum established in article 99.6 of the Basque law on cooperatives (the right to receive periodically, within a

---

5. Thus, worker members have the right to collect periodically at intervals of no more than one month "*anticipos laborales*" (wage advances), which should not be lower than the minimum wage, and which are considered as regular wages for fiscal purposes; they enjoy the same regulations on safety and hygiene at work; the same limitations on underage work established by the labor legislation are applied; and, for the purposes of state healthcare and benefits programs, they are considered in the same category as regular employees and self-employed workers.

6. One should bear in mind that there are different laws on cooperatives in the Spanish state, according to the particular powers that the different autonomous regions have to legislate on this matter. This in effect results in very different solutions depending on the autonomous region's law. Specifically, this case is resolved according to article 80.4 of the general Spanish state law on cooperatives, which says that such advances will be made in relation to the surplus made by a cooperative business.

7. Sentence of the High Court of Justice of the Canary Islands (Santa Cruz de Tenerife), labor division, 145/2008, February 27.

8. Sentence of the High Court of Justice of Catalonia, labor division, 7665/1999, October 29; Sentence of the High Court of Justice of Andalusia (Málaga), labor, 1975/2000, November 17.

9. Sentence of the High Court of Justice of Andalusia (Granada), labor division, 1st section, 1956/2003, June 24; Sentence of the High Court of Justice of Asturias, labor division, 1st section, 1053/2006, March 31; Sentence of the High Court of Justice of Navarre, labor division, 126/1999, March 24.

10. Sentence of the Central Labor Court of January 17, 1989.

time limit of no more than one month, advanced payment that does not fall below the minimum wage, calculated on annual basis) is not available in parts.[11]

In this sense, cooperative legislation also has specific provisions for situations of economic difficulty (based on "organizational, technical, economic, production or force majeure reasons"), and in such cases the temporary suspension or compulsory leave of workers' self-managed cooperative members is allowed when such measures are necessary to maintain the economic viability of the cooperative. This decision should be adopted by a general assembly of the cooperative in question, with members maintaining their remaining rights and obligations not connected with work (in case of temporary suspension) and the preferential right of re-entry into the workforce (in the case of compulsory leave).[12]

Of course, this does not at all mean that employees' rights are reduced. The basis of this system is ownership of the cooperative by its workers. They are in this sense their own employers, and they have the authority to make any such decisions—with some limits—within the framework of the cooperative's general assembly.

Clearly, in order to face up to periods of economic difficulty, any business must have a solid financial structure. In many private companies there is an exaggerated tendency to seek short-term profit, thereby often resulting in under-capitalization and a consequent financial weakness when it comes to confronting an economic crisis. In contrast, those companies operating according to cooperative principles have traditionally rejected the search for a short-term profit value, and have instead prioritized the strengthening and stability of the business, which can leave them in an advantageous situation should such a downturn take place.

In a similar way to that noted above, cooperative members tend to feel more implicated and involved in their company than workers in other kinds of businesses. As such, they assume objectives that go beyond mere financial gain, seeking the consolidation and growth of the company because they are organizations that, among other things, generate quality employment in their local environment, leading them to allow a policy of capitalization of profits.

---

11. Sentence of the High Court of Justice of the Basque Country, labor division, 158/2001, January 23.

12. Article 103 of the Basque law on cooperatives (hereafter referred to as BLC). This provision does not exist in other cooperative laws, such as that, for example, in Navarre.

Of course, as indicated previously, the legal regulation of these companies is also important here. Such regulation should be aimed at strengthening cooperatives financially, attracting resources, and promoting the capitalization of the company.[13]

In the case of the BLC, a minimum capital amount of €3,000 is required to constitute a cooperative,[14] the same amount required to set up a limited company (*sociedad limitada*)—the most typical kind of trading company. One of the main features of a cooperative's capital—a result of the first cooperative principle (open and voluntary membership or its open-door policy)—is its variability. For example, members are free to leave the cooperative, in the event of which their contributions will be returned to them, thereby reducing the cooperative's capital. This instability of the cooperatives' capital, which can be very damaging for these kinds of companies when it comes to operating in the market and obtaining new resources, is alleviated to a certain extent by cooperative legislation. Specifically, this legislation allows cooperatives to establish a period of minimum continuance in the company according to their statutes for a member (which can at most be five years, according to the article 26.3 BLC), a time limit for legal notice to be given when a member wishes to leave the cooperative (article 26.1 BLC), a period of time to refund members' contributions, and the obligation to set a minimum capital amount in the cooperatives' statutes.[15]

In this regard, there was an important modification of the BLC by Basque parliamentary law 8/2006, of December 1, which introduced a new classification of the contributions to the cooperatives' capital. They can now be catalogued as contributions with the right to reimbursement in case of leaving and contributions whose reimbursement can be unconditionally refused by the general assembly or executive council of the cooperative.[16] With the adoption of international account standard

---

13. On the financial status of cooperatives in the BLC, see Gadea (1999, 197–227).

14. Depending on the activity of the cooperative, the minimum capital amount required can be greater by virtue of the regulation of the activity, as is the case with credit or transport cooperatives.

15. As Carlos Vargas points out (2008, 285–88), in this way at least a part of this capital would not therefore be variable, and if the capital were to go below this minimum amount, the company should be dissolved. See also Gómez and Miranda (2006, 41).

16. Thus according to the new article 57.1 bis BLC, "the statutes will be able to foresee that, when in a financial year the amount of the refund of the contributions surpasses the percentage of capital established in them, the new reimbursements will be conditioned to the favorable agreement of the executive council." This classification was also introduced by the new Law

(IAS) 32 by Council Regulation no. 2237/2004, members' contributions to a cooperative's capital would be considered liabilities, because of the right of these members to receive their reimbursement in the event of them leaving the company or, in the words of the introductory paragraph 18 of the IAS 32, because of the right of the holder (member) to collect the financial instrument from the transmitter (cooperative). The existence of contributions whose reimbursement can be unconditionally refused is actually an important measure for the protection and stability of the cooperatives' capital. It also guarantees them greater financial strength because they can now consider these types of contributions as their own funds.

Moreover, cooperative legislation has introduced (especially as a result of the latest reforms) different instruments designed to endow the cooperatives with greater financing possibilities. As such, they are now allowed to obtain nonmembers' investment by means of a wide variety of financing formulae that permit them, in principle, to assure control of the company by cooperative members (Pastor 2002, 392). Because of these new regulations, then, mixed cooperatives have emerged that are more traditionally capitalist in nature. Their main feature is that they have minority members, whose right to vote is determined on the basis of their contribution to the overall capital of the cooperative. These minority members' contributions are thus treated like shares in subsidiary limited companies. Likewise, they are permitted entry into the cooperative or periodic quotas, subordinate financing (which can be part of the capital), obligations, and participatory titles or joint ownership agreements. However, although they might strengthen the cooperative financially, one could question some of these measures because they usually imply moving away from cooperative principles and criteria.

In the search to strengthen cooperatives financially and increase their resources, the importance of reserve funds cannot be overlooked. In general, cooperatives must have an obligatory reserve fund (*Fondo de Reserva Obligatorio*, FRO), comparable to the legal or statutory reserve fund of typical trading companies, and designed to "consolidate, develop, and guarantee the cooperative" (article 68.1 BLC).[17] The duty of setting

---

14/2006 on Cooperatives in Navarre, as well as in other laws on cooperatives, such as the Spanish state law on cooperatives (by means of the fourth additional provision of Law 16/2007).

17. Law 6/2008 clarifies that the cooperative education and promotion fund (Fondo de Educación y Promoción Cooperativa, FEPC, now renamed "contribution to cooperative education

up this fund is considerably greater than that of other trading companies, because according to the BLC at least 30 percent[18] of the company's available annual surplus must go into the FRO and the former FEPC for the entire lifespan of the cooperative—aside from the economic regulations for members, entry quotas, and deductions on the contributions in the event of members leaving—against 10 percent of all profits, up to 20 percent of the capital, which all other trading companies must allocate to their legal reserve. It should be added that, according to the third cooperative principle, these funds cannot be distributed among the members (even in the event of a company winding up). Together with the high percentage of profits destined for this fund, one could say that this explains the greater strength of cooperatives when confronting an economic crisis.[19] Additionally, as regards the tax treatment this fund receives, because 50 percent of it is destined for the FRO (by legal or statutory obligation)—as well as the contribution to cooperative education and promotion and other activities in the public interest—it is considered as deductible expenses when calculating the base tax rate of corporation tax.

Lastly, another crucial factor explaining greater cooperative strength during the current financial crisis is the development of complementary structures among different cooperatives. As the sixth cooperative principle states, cooperation among cooperatives serves their members most effectively and strengthens the cooperative movement by working together through local, national, regional, and international structures. One of the best examples of this was the creation of the International Cooperative Alliance in 1895.

---

and promotion and other goals in the public interest") characteristic of this type of company, which is destined to aid the training and education of cooperative members or labor matters, the promotion of the relations among cooperatives, and the promotion of cooperativism and the social environment, is not really a cooperative fund, because it has to be channeled through contributions to other nonprofit or intercooperation entities.

18. At least 20 percent of the available surplus must be allocated to the FRO, and at least 10 percent to the (formerly termed) FEPC, although if the amount of the FRO does not reach half the capital, the percentage can be reduced by half in the case of the former FEPC, applying the amount to the FRO (Gadea 2008, 172). The duty of establishing these reserves varies depending on the law of cooperatives applicable. In the law on cooperatives in Navarre, for example, the minimum percentage of the surplus that must be allocated to these reserves oscillates between 20 and 30 percent. Likewise, the total noncooperative profits must be allocated to the company's reserves.

19. Thus Gadea (2008, 222) argues that the FRO, because of its very stability, is extremely important to a company with variable capital as in the case of a cooperative, because it "favors maintaining and developing the cooperative's business activities."

There is a well-known high level of cooperative development in the Basque Country, and within this context, the birthplace and headquarters of the Mondragon group and most of the more than 250 companies that comprise it occupies a prestigious place, although the birth of the cooperative associativism predates the founding of the Mondragon Corporation.[20] Basque cooperativism is not, then, limited to the Mondragon experience, as already noted in the example of Herrikoa in Iparralde (the Northern Basque Country). Nevertheless, the development of cooperativism is undoubtedly greater in Hegoalde (the Southern Basque Country), and especially in the CAPV/EAE. This is reflected in legislation on these kinds of companies and in the development of the intercooperative structures intended to promote and defend cooperativism.

Cooperation among cooperatives goes further than the just the establishment of second-level cooperatives, business groups, or groups of cooperative corporations, all of them modalities of integration and cooperative association recognized and protected by the law.[21] This is because all forms of cooperative associativism aimed at supporting and promoting the interests of these companies are promoted by the law. In this way, the BLC explicitly regulates unions, federations, and confederations of cooperatives, as well as the Higher Cooperative Council of the Basque Country (Euskadiko Kooperatiben Goren-Kontseilua/Consejo Superior de Cooperativas de Euskadi),[22] with all of these constituting an important network integrated into the cooperative movement. They are also, of course, integrated inside state and international networks,[23] as can be seen in figure 8.1.

---

20. The antecedents and historical evolution of the Basque cooperative movement and the important role played by associativism in this movement are explained in Salaberria (2008).

21. For example, article 138.3 BLC offers cooperatives that concentrate their businesses "all the benefits offered in the legislation on groups and concentration of businesses." There are also a number of public administration financial grants available for intercooperation among businesses; and in a similar way to the funds, contributions to cooperation institutions among cooperatives are deductible expenses when determining the base tax rate of corporation tax.

22. This is the main body that promotes and diffuses cooperativism in the CAPV/EAE, with the Basque public administrations having a consultative and advisory role in all matters referring to the cooperativism. There is even a cooperative arbitration service, Bitartu.

23. Besides the EKGK-CSCE, there is also Konfekoop (the Confederation of Cooperatives in the Basque Country), Erkide (the Federation of Workers' Self-Managed, Teaching, and Credit Cooperatives in the Basque Country, the Federation of Agricultural Cooperatives in the Basque Country, the Federation of Consumer Cooperatives in the Basque Country, and the Federation of Transport Carriers in the Basque Country. As noted, such structures are not so well developed in the rest of the Basque Country. Exceptions to this are the Union of Agricultural Cooperatives

Figure 8.1. Basque network of cooperative associativism in the international network

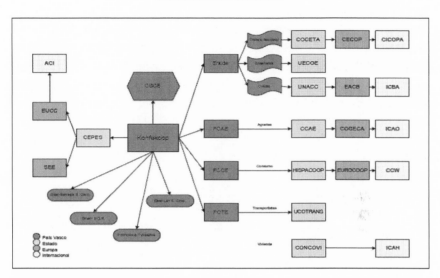

Source: Konfekoop.

The Case of Mondragon

This brief analysis of Basque cooperatives during this time of economic crisis cannot be concluded without referring to the Mondragon cooperatives, because they are a point of reference in the cooperative world.

The Mondragon Group has not been immune to the economic crisis, and when at the end of May 2009 it announced its latest results, it was revealed that in 2008 its profits had fallen by 91 percent compared to the last fiscal period, though MCC still had profits of €71 million. Its own resources fell by 16.1 percent, and the jobs fell from 93,841 to 92,773. However, its revenues and total sales increased by 2.4 percent and 3.5 percent respectively.[24]

As a result of the economic downturn, MCC's industrial sector has been affected by a major fall in demand for, among other things, electrical appliances, furniture, property (in general, goods connected with real

---

in Navarre and the Cooperative Council of Navarre (although the latter is much less active than the EKGK-CSCE), and Hemen. There are also institutions like Oinarri, a reciprocal guarantee company for companies involved in the social economy, and one must not leave out the long cooperative experience of the Ikastolas.

24. Data from the MCC 2008 financial year report, available in www.mcc.es.

estate and construction, where there has been an especially major crisis in the Spanish state), and transport. Nevertheless, at the same time sales have increased, for example, in capital equipment and business services. Its financial sector has also been severely hit by the crisis due to the general increase in the default rate and because Caja Laboral had invested €162 million in Lehman Brothers, although it has maintained its solidity having increased its resources from clients, as well as its own funds and the credit granted. For its part, MCC's distribution sector has actually expanded, with increasing sales and the employment in the sector, while at the same time the knowledge sector has intensified its activity and increased the number of students involved in training programs.

Although it has been affected by the crisis, the Mondragon group is confronting and surpassing it relatively well because, despite a significant reduction in profits and demand in some strategic sectors, its profits have remained stable as a result of increasing revenues. Indeed, none of the businesses that are part of MCC has been declared insolvent.

There are several reasons why MCC has been able to resist the economic downturn, as noted previously. Clearly, being such a major cooperative (with more than one hundred subsidiary cooperatives being part of the corporation), as well as its policy of cooperation with other cooperative groups, give it a solid basis. Yet one should also note the variety of its activities and sectors. Such activities are often strategically important within the industrial sector as whole. And in the financial sector, Caja Laboral (created in 1959) has been essential for the collecting and managing of the necessary capital and financial resources to advance the cooperatives in the group and its general growth and development (Altuna 2008, 16). Meanwhile, the knowledge sector continues to flourish, with thirteen research centers and several important training centers, such as Mondragon Unibertsitatea. Indeed, training was always an important part of the MCC philosophy, from its very inception. Finally, one should not forget the important business network and umbrella organizations that have also emerged around these cooperatives.

Of course, one should also mention a key characteristic of the Mondragon group: its proven capacity to adapt to different contexts (Altuna 2008, 33n67).[25] Likewise, to understand its strength it is also necessary to keep in mind the principle of cooperation among cooperatives, under-

---

25. At the same time, one should also note that many of the measures adopted by both MCC and other cooperatives in recent years in order to adapt to changing market conditions have been criticized for emphasizing efficiency and profit—and thereby resembling more traditional

stood, according to the First Cooperative Congress of the Mondragon cooperatives held in 1987, as the concrete application of solidarity and the requirement of business efficiency. Such principles have been evident in, among other examples, the pooling of profits, transfers of worker-members among different companies within the cooperative, and the search for potential collaborations (Altuna 2008, 68).

An important group policy has been the capitalization of profits instead of distributing them among the group's members. Thus, from a long-term perspective, the cooperative return—a quantity the member collects from the annual surpluses—increases the member's capital in the cooperative (Fernández 2001, 90).[26] The evident consequence of this measure is a greater financial strength of the group's cooperatives in contrast to the under-capitalization of businesses that have traditionally pursued short-term profits for their associates.

Further, cooperatives set aside part of their surpluses for redistribution, which constitutes a "genuine expression of solidarity within the MCC environment" (Fernández 2001, 91). In this regard, the Intercooperation Funds—provided financially by Caja Laboral and the rest of cooperatives—are especially important, being "one of the clearest demonstrations of adjusting the principle of intercooperation and support to the social and business development of the MCC corporation," and created with the purpose of "assuring secure and sufficient financing for all the cooperatives" (Fernández 2001, 91). In this way, MCC Investments and the MCC Foundation administer and allocate the central intercooperation fund,[27] the intercooperative education and promotion fund, and the corporate solidarity fund. Thus, the Mondragon cooperatives must allocate a percentage of their profits to a common box, one of the purposes of which is the partial compensation of losses on the part of the cooperatives (up to 20 percent). This, together with "the pooling of profits permitted to maintain businesses in an activity that otherwise would have been closed," constitutes an important mechanism for the group's cooperatives to reduce "the negative effects of economic cycles or those affecting their activities" (Altuna 2008, 81).

---

capitalist goals—to the detriment of cooperative values and principles. See, for example, among many others, Azkarraga (2007) and Paz Canalejo (2002).

26. Azkarraga (2007, 256) underlines the importance of this to the general success of the Mondragon cooperatives.

27. Whose goal is "the financing of business projects that by their importance or risk surpass the possibilities of the cooperatives or groups implied" (Fernández 2001, 91).

As an example of this ability to react to such changes, when it became obvious there was a global financial crisis, the group adopted a series of tough recommendations for its cooperatives. These contained measures such as the adjustment of both activities and workforce, increased working hours, the elimination or relinquishing of bonuses, the closing down of non-profitable affiliates or subsidiaries, outsourcings, the creation of joint platforms of purchase, a reduction in provisioning before other kinds of costs, renting instead of purchasing premises, encouraging an increased presence in emerging markets, and so on.[28] Although MCC has been forced to lay off some of its workforce, there is still a clear sense of solidarity and collective effort when it comes to confronting the crisis. While some workers have been dismissed, others (including both members and employees) have been relocated in other cooperatives or enterprises within the group, such as the supermarket chain Eroski. Meanwhile, the preretirement age has been lowered to fifty-five. And in companies like Fagor Electric, worker-members have decided to renounce their bonuses, a measure that does not affect the regular employees (nonmembers), as a means of maintaining the business's viability and, among others things, to finance the costs of pre-retirements. Some cooperatives have also decided to freeze wage levels or close down their operations for one or more days a week in order to reduce costs. Another example is the reduction in the interest members collect, a measure adopted during the 2008 Cooperative Congress.[29]

Conclusion

Although not immune from the financial crisis and its negative effects, cooperatives do appear to have demonstrated a greater resilience to it. Such resilience is the result of the very cooperative principles and values they are based on, especially those concerning solidarity and cooperation among cooperatives. It is, however, essential that legislation for these kinds of companies contains provisions in order to guarantee this solidity, especially when it comes to the cooperatives being able to protect their own resources.

Such strength is clearly evident in the remarkable Mondragon experience. Its mechanisms for intercooperation and cooperative solidarity, its

---

28. See Lezana (2008b).

29. See Artea and Vadillo (2008), Aranguren (2008), Gara (2008), Lezana (2008 a, 2008c), and *Noticias de Gipuzkoa* (2010). Such measures are not new and have been adopted during previous moments of economic crisis. On this see Larrañaga (1994).

policy of capitalizing profit, its flexibility and capacity to react, as well as sacrifices on the part of its associates all explain, among other reasons, the relatively successful response of its constituent cooperatives to the financial crisis relatively well. It thus serves as a good example for both other cooperative companies and other kinds of businesses of how to operate not just at this time of economic downturn, but also in times of prosperity.

References

Altuna, Rafa. 2008. "Bases culturales e institucionales del desarrollo empresarial cooperativo de Mondragón." In *El fenómeno cooperativo en el mundo: Casos de Argentina, Brasil, Italia, País Vasco y Paises Nórdicos*, edited by Rafa Altuna, Hervé Grellier, and Eguzki Urteaga. Arrasate-Mondragon: Mondragon Unibertsitateko Zerbitzu Editoriala.

Aranguren, Pilar. 2008. "El grupo Mondragón contempla adelantar la edad de las prejubilaciones a los 55 años." *Diario Vasco* (digital edition), September 1. At www.diariovasco.com/20080901/economia/grupo-mondragon-contempla-adelantar-20080901.html.

Artea, K., and J. Vadillo. 2008. "Fagor sacrifica la paga extra para pagar prejubilaciones." *Cincodias* (digital edition), November 5. At www.cincodias.com/articulo/empresas/fagor-sacrifica-paga-extra-pagar-prejubilaciones/20081105cdscdiemp_15/.

Azkarraga, Joseba. 2007. *Nor bere patroi: Arrasateko kooperatibistak aro globalaren aurrean*. Vitoria-Gasteiz: Eusko Jaurlaritza-Gobierno Vasco.

Fernández, Jose Ramón. 2001. *1956–2000: La Experiencia Cooperativa de Mondragón: Mondragon Esperientzia Kooperatiboa: The Mondragón Co-operative Experience*. Arrasate-Mondragón: Mondragón Corporación Cooperativa.

Gadea, Enrique. 1999. *Derecho de las cooperativas: Análisis de la Ley 4/1993, de 24 de junio, de cooperativas de País Vasco*. Bilbao: Universidad de Deusto.

———. 2008. "Régimen económico: Otras financiaciones." In *Manual de Derecho de Sociedades Cooperativas*. Vitoria-Gasteiz: CSCE-EKGK, Gezki.

Gara. 2008. "Mondragón plantea la prejubilación a los 55 años para cooperativas en crisis." *Gara* (digital edition), August 3. At www.gara.net/

paperezkoa/20080803/89768/es/Mondragon-plantea-prejubilacion-55-anos-para-cooperativas-crisis.

Gómez, Pilar, and Marta Miranda. 2006. "Sobre el régimen económico y financiero particular de las sociedades cooperativas." *Revesco* 90: 28–46.

Larrañaga, Jesús. 1994. "Las cooperativas en la crisis industrial." *Ekonomiaz: Revista Vasca de Economía* 30: 230–33.

Lezana, Carlos. 2008a. "Fagor Ederlan paraliza siete plantas diez días por la crisis del automóvil." *El Correo* (digital edition), November 12. At www.elcorreo.com/alava/20081112/economia/fagor-ederlan-paraliza-siete-20081112.html.

———. 2008b. "Mondragón pide a sus 260 cooperativas que contemplen cierres y ajustes de plantilla." *El Correo* (digital edition), December 11. At www.elcorreo.com/vizcaya/20081211/economia/mondragon-pide-cooperativas-contemplen-20081211.html.

———. 2008c. "Todo el grupo Mondragón se congelará el sueldo en 2009." *El Correo* (digital edition), December 4. At www.elcorreo.com/vizcaya/20081204/economia/todo-grupo-mondragon-congelara-20081204.html.

Noticias de Gipuzkoa. 2010. "Mondragón limita las retribuciones de los socios sobre los beneficios." *Noticias de Gipuzkoa* (digital edition), April 15. At www.noticiasdegipuzkoa.com/2010/04/15/economia/mondragon-limita-las-retribuciones-de-los-socios-sobre-los-beneficios.

Pastor, Carmen. 2002. *Los recursos propios de las cooperativas.* Madrid: Editoriales de Derecho Reunidas.

Paz Canalejo, Narciso. 2002. *La sociedad cooperativa ante el reto de los mercados actuales: Un análisis no sólo jurídico.* Madrid: MTAS.

Salaberria, Javier. 2008. "El asociacionismo cooperativo." In *Manual de Derecho de Sociedades Cooperativas,* edited by Santiago Merino Hernández. Vitoria-Gasteiz: CSCE-EKGK, Gezki.

Urteaga, Eguzki. 2008. "El fenómeno cooperativo en el País Vasco Francés: La experiencia de Herrikoa." In *El fenómeno cooperativo en el mundo: Casos de Argentina, Brasil, Italia, País Vasco y Paises Nórdicos,* edited by Rafa Altuna, Hervé Grellier, and Eguzki Urteaga. Arrasate-Mondragon: Mondragon Unibertsitateko Zerbitzu Editoriala.

Vargas, Carlos. 2008. "La solvencia y garantías de las cooperativas en el tráfico: Algunas peculiaridades de su concurso." *Revista de Derecho Concursal y Paraconcursal* 8: 281–94.

9

Characteristics of Human Resource Management in Basque Cooperatives and Their Response to New International Contexts

AITZIBER LERTXUNDI

Translated by Julie Waddington

More and more companies are establishing themselves abroad as a way of reducing costs and expanding their markets. As an indication of this, and in line with global trends, total Spanish gross investment abroad registered in the first half of 2010 rose to €9,247 million.[1] Basque cooperatives have been no exception in this trend. The fabric of Basque business culture is characterized by a significant presence of cooperativism. Thus, for example, at the beginning of 2010, 1,262 cooperatives were registered in the Comunidad Autónoma del País Vasco-Euskal Autonomia Erkidegoa (CAPV/EAE, Autonomous Community of the Basque Country), employing 45,756 people;[2] this, out of a total of 73,037 businesses and 646,211 employees.[3] Moreover, out of the 131 Basque companies that have production plants abroad, 25 were Basque cooperatives.[4] Having a physical

---

1. Source: *Inversiones españolas en el exterior (Spanish investment abroad)*, Dirección General de Comercio e Inversiones (Ministerio de Industria, Turismo y Comercio) General Directorate for Commerce and Investment (Ministry of Industry, Tourism and Commerce), www.comercio. es.

2. Eustat (Basque Statistics Institute): www.eustat.es.

3. Without considering public entities or individuals.

4. Civex (Eusko Jaurlaritza – Basque Government), www.civex.net.

presence in other countries generates, among other things, a very important question about the way in which the people who work at these sites are managed. In terms of human resources (HR), businesses have to make a difficult and strategic decision regarding whether to continue with what they already know and to implement the same practices that are applied in the parent company, or, by contrast, whether it is more appropriate to adapt to the values that prevail in the new context. This question becomes even more relevant when these businesses are located in environments which are socioculturally different. It is a well-known fact that, among other things, the work ethic (cultural values and attitudes to work) is not the same in all countries and that human resource management (HRM) is a functional area in which this question takes on particular significance. Accordingly, literature on this subject includes different research studies that indicate that ignoring these considerations may result in conflicts and inefficiencies and that also demonstrate the dysfunctions produced by the mismatch between specific characteristics of HR practices and the national context in which they are applied.[5] Within this framework, the specificity of cooperatives is a factor that introduces an additional element of analysis, in the sense that many practices derived from cooperative principles form part of what some authors refer to as "best practices" in HR (Morales 1998). In terms of implementing HRM strategies, the competitiveness and efficiency attributed to these kinds of practices can encourage a managerial team to transmit them to foreign plants as a way of propagating their competitive potential (Bae, Chen, and Lawler 1998; Dickmann 2003; Gamble 2003; Gooderham and Nordhaug 2003; Taylor, Beechler, and Napier 1996). In short, multinational enterprises (MNEs) are faced with two competing requirements: the need to adapt to the new national context and an interest in transmitting its domestic management systems that they deem to be competitive. Consequently, the general strategy of MNEs, and therefore of multinational cooperatives in particular, should be adopted on the basis of social and economic rationality. But in the case of cooperatives, this decision is even more difficult given the nature of the way they are managed, which is supposedly more efficient. To give an example, although one might consider participation —one of the basic principles in the management of cooperatives—to be a "universal" practice that all workers in all countries expect and with

---

5. Adler (1997); Bae, Chen, and Lawler (1998); Gómez-Mejía and Palich (1997); Newman and Nollen (1996); Tayeb (2005); Yuen and Kee (1993).

which they feel comfortable, there is evidence to suggest that this is not always the case (Adler 1997). This, along with other examples, makes the already difficult decision that Basque cooperatives have to take in terms of their position on the configuration of HR systems in foreign plants even harder.

In order to analyze the behavior of a sample of Basque cooperatives in the face of this issue, and with the hope that these case studies may serve as an additional element in the analysis of other MNEs, this exploratory work has a dual aim. On the one hand, and as a contribution to the literature on the specificity of these aspects, I wish to gauge the extent to which HR management practices in Basque cooperatives are in line with HR categories such as "best practices," and to what degree their use is significantly more or less in comparison with other noncooperative businesses. Likewise, on the basis of the characteristic principles of HR management in the aforementioned cooperatives, my aim is to reveal the nature of their general attitude in the design of HR practices at their foreign plants in view of the new institutional-cultural contents of the countries where they are located and, in this sense, to carry out a comparative analysis with other noncooperative businesses.

Distinguishing Features in the Human Resource Management of Basque Cooperatives

The cooperative principles that define the specific nature of modern cooperatives originated in 1844 with the Rochdale Pioneers in England and thus came to be known as the "Rochdale Principles." Thereafter, different interpretations of these principles led to a reworking of the cooperative idea, culminating in our times with a formal definition of seven principles by the International Co-operative Alliance (ICA): voluntary and open membership; democratic member control; member economic participation; autonomy and independence; education, training, and information; cooperation among cooperatives; and concern for the community. This same body also defines the values that underlie these principles: self-help, self-responsibility, democracy, equality, equity, and solidarity. And likewise, cooperative members take on board the ethical values of honesty, openness, social responsibility, and caring for others. Because of their adherence to these principles, cooperatives acquire certain features that are different in relation to other capitalist enterprises (García-Gutiérrez 1994). In particular, the main distinguishing features that impact management systems are the principle of democratic management, the principle of education, and the principle of cooperation among cooperatives (Agirre 2001).

HR systems in cooperatives have an even more important role than in other companies. The fact that many of the practices stemming from the aforementioned principles encompass the features of what many authors call "best practices" is a clear indication of this. Among these, it is worth mentioning participation, teamwork, contingent payment, and training (Morales 1998). More specifically, research carried out in the CAPV/EAE on the quality of management concludes that the level of quality is higher in cooperatives and that the most significant differences are linked to the social commitment of the company (Charterina, Albizu, and Landeta 2007).

With regards to HRM "best practices," different studies offer different perspectives. A universalist perspective indicates that their competitive potential is not determined by the existence of elements that are internal and external to the organization. This view is based on the premise that whoever employs such practices will always report better results (Arthur 1994; Guthrie 2001; Huselid 1995; Pfeffer 1994; Walton 1985). Among these practices we find (among others) security of employment, rigorousness in the selection of employees, the existence of working teams, contingent retribution, communication, and extensive training and participation. By contrast, the contingent focus advocates "adjustment" and points out that the efficiency of these practices is determined by the way efficiency fits with a number of different factors. This view is based on the theory of contingency in the sense that the basic premise taken is that the validity and effective application of practices cannot be generalized to all circumstances. This is because in relations with business profits there are variables involved that alter the original effects and that should be consistent with these (Boselie, Paauwe, and Jansen 2001; Ichniowski, Shaw, and Prennushi 1997; Wright, Smart, and McMahan 1995; Youndt et al. 1996).

At an international level, these practices are the object of controversy in a debate that remains open with regard to convergence or divergence in management practices. Given the potential attributed to such practices, from a universalist perspective their diffusion could be fostered in other countries. Yet from the point of view of different national contexts, the driving forces that aim to maintain specific kinds of management are also relevant.

The International Human Resource Strategy: The Importance of the Cultural and Institutional Context

The review and analysis of the work carried out in the area of HR international strategy show the importance given to the institutional-cultural factor.[6] Sully Taylor, Schon Beechler, and Nancy Napier (1996) present one of the typologies that is most frequently cited in the literature on international strategies in the design of HR systems: leaning toward adaptation, exportation, or integration.

The adaptation strategy aims for as much alignment as possible with the specific local characteristics of the subsidiaries and therefore it is they who develop their own system. In the search for this differentiation, there is practically no transmission of ethics, policies, or practices between the parent company and the foreign establishments, nor among the latter. This approach is underpinned by the view that companies do not consider the HR system to be a key field. The main reason for this approach is to make HR management systems fit the local context perfectly. Among its disadvantages, there are potential inconsistencies within MNEs, such as discrepancies in terms of the criteria for appraising employees or in selection processes (among other issues). The exportation or transfer strategy, on the other hand, consists in transferring HRM systems from the parent company directly to its foreign establishments. In contrast to the previous approach, this strategy aims to achieve greater levels of internal consistency, although it may entail a certain degree of inflexibility given that it ignores potential local differences that may have repercussions in terms of the organization's potential for learning in general. Furthermore, it also runs the risk of causing feelings of rejection in the other units. Head office assumes that the way of managing its central headquarters is better or more appropriate than other systems, which is to say that it is based on the belief that the domestic system is a key field that offers a competitive advantage regardless of where it is applied. Finally, the inclusive strategy aims to harness and use HR "best practices" in the creation of a global system. The key lies in achieving a considerable level of integration that, at the same time, allows for an acceptable level of local differentiation.

It is worth highlighting that adaption is not a monolithic concept but rather one of the alternatives of the two poles of a continuum (Evans

---

6. See Adler and Ghadar (1990); Evans and Lorange (1989); Milliman, Von Glinow, and Nathan (1991); Schuler, Dowling, and De Cieri (1993); Taylor, Beechler, and Napier (1996).

and Lorange 1989). On this, Chris Brewster (2002) adds that, in practice, there is always interaction between the two sides and that both tend to be applied up to a certain point. Ken Kamoche (1996) agrees with this when he indicates that exportation and adaptation are not mutually exclusive.

The Cultural and Institutional Context and Its Influence on HRM

Typically, there are two ways of examining the influence of the national framework on the interaction of an organization with its environment: an institutional and a cultural perspective. Despite different approaches, all of them emphasize the role of the environment as a conditioning factor in the configuration of the internal structures of an organization.

Institutional Theory (DiMaggio and Powell 1983; Meyer and Rowan 1977; Scott 1995) is based on the premise that organizations are social phenomena and that their structures and processes are not shaped solely by criteria related to economic rationality. Institutionalism studies the social context and focuses on isomorphism within the institutional environment whereby organizations adopt guidelines that the external agent defines as appropriate for their environment and that are strengthened through interaction with the latter. The key institutions in question are the state, the legal system, the financial system, and the family. Legitimacy is a key concept in this theoretical line of thought. The most socially predominant and institutionalized organizational concepts of workplace rationality encourage organizations to incorporate them, thereby increasing their legitimacy and the possibility of their survival, regardless of the immediate efficiency of the practices and procedures involved (Meyer and Rowan 1977).

The second approach, the *Cultural Focus* (Adler 1997; Hofstede 1984; Laurent 1986; Schwartz 1994; Trompenaars 1994), is based on culture as the origin of differences in the configuration of management systems and the structure of organizations. From this perspective, national cultures determine, to a large extent, the level of bureaucracy found in an organization, the concentration of power, the flow and direction of communication, the manner of participating, the way of approaching and managing conflicts and their resolution, the level of control exercised by management, and in general, the formal structuring of an organization and its management processes (Gómez-Mejía, Balkin, and Cardy 1998; Hofstede 1998; Laurent 1986). There is some consensus that organizational behavior reflects and reproduces the cultural characteristics of the country in which it is located.

In terms of functional areas, it appears that HRM practices are particularly susceptible to cultural diversity (Hofstede 1984; Laurent 1986). Various studies discuss the influence of national cultures on HRM policies and practices.[7]

Motivational and leadership techniques are intrinsically linked to the design of HRM practices because these are considered to be two factors that have an impact on business efficiency and that also reflect the implications of a country's culture[8] (House et al. 2004; Mead 1998).

Although institutional and cultural approaches appear to involve different theoretical inclinations, the proximity of their theoretical foundations makes it difficult to differentiate them. Even in the specific literature on HRM, some authors include some institutional elements in the cultural perspective. In other words, they understand the former to be an integral part of a wider perspective, the latter (Child 2002; Greif 1994; Westney 1993).

Research Methodology and Analysis of Results

For the purposes of this study, I have selected Basque industrial cooperatives with more than one hundred employees and that have at least one production plant abroad. In fixing a lower threshold regarding the number of employees, I aim to increase the probability that the participating companies will use relatively formalized HRM systems and that they conform to the size of company upon which the research carried out has tended to be based with regards to "best practices." Furthermore, in selecting the criteria requiring that they have at least one production plant abroad, I aim to homogenize the characteristics of the different units of study (Basque parent company and its plant abroad) as much as possible. This way, I avoid the inclusion of plants that are exclusively

---

7. See for example Bae and Rowley (2001); Gooderham and Nordhaug (2003); Khilji (2003); Myloni, Harzing, and Mirza (2004); Newman and Nollen (1996); Rosenzweig and Nohria (1994); Schuler and Rogovsky (1998); Tayeb (1998); Yuen and Kee (1993).

8. There are those who question the applicability of the main theories formulated in the United States, exposing their relativity or cultural bias (Adler 1997; Hofstede 1984; Mead 1998; Tayeb 2005; Trompenaars 1994). Similarly, there is evidence pointing to a similarity between preferences regarding leadership styles and characteristics attributed to leaders and cultural clusters previously identified in the literature (House et al. 2004).

commercial, or that take the form of an agent or commercial delegation or any other kind of distribution company where the nature of HRM may differ. There are fifteen cooperatives in the CAPV/EAE that meet these requirements.[9] The working sample is made up of eleven of these cooperatives. Interviews were carried out with the managers or with the heads of human resources.

With regards to the level of usage of "best practices" in HR, the practices analyzed include those extracted from the review of the most important empirical and theoretical jobs belonging to this line of research.[10] There are twenty-four items in total. There are different ways of making the usage level of these practices operational, and (among others) I opt for the procedure of assigning practices to different groups on the basis of theoretical precepts, subsequently verifying the reliability of the scales (Guthrie 2001; MacDuffie 1995; Youndt et al. 1996; Way 2002). Furthermore, following Jay B. Barney and Patrick M. Wright (1998), Brian E. Becker et al. (1997), and Brian E. Becker and Mark A. Huselid (1998), who recommend the use of a unit value index that takes into account the use of these practices,[11] I use a single measure for assessing them. The score achieved by each company on this index, referred to as HPWS (High Performance Work Systems),[12] represents the grade of usage made of HR "best practices." Moreover, and following Eileen Appelbaum et al. (2000), John T. Delaney and Mark Huselid (1996), Timothy M. Gardner et al. (2001), and David Guest (1997), I base my study on the theoretical approach of AMO (*Ability, Motivation, Opportunity*) as a basis that allows one to define and structure the set of practices that are integral to HPWS. On the basis of this view, the measuring scale used is configured as a measurement composed of six dimensions that are divided into three indicators. The first indicator, ability, is broken into training and selection; the second, motivation, into communication and retribution; and the third, opportunity, into participation and teamwork.

---

9. Civex - Accessed on April 11, 2010 (Basque Government - Eusko Jaurlaritza), www.civex. net.

10. Arthur (1994); Bae and Lawler (2000); Delery and Doty (1996); Delaney and Huselid (1996); Guthrie (2001); Huselid (1995); Ichniowski, Shaw, and Prennushi (1997); Peck (1994).

11. Other authors also confer on this, such as Appelbaum et al. (2000); Arthur (1994); Chang (2006); Guthrie et al. (2009); Ichniowski, Shaw, and Prennushi (1997); MacDuffie (1995); Park et al. (2003); Youndt et al. (1996).

12. It frequently refers to a level of analysis at group rather than individual level.

The numerical average of the items in its component parts has been calculated for the quantification of each of the indicators. The HPWS Index variable is obtained by adding together the six groups of indicators in line with other studies in this field (Chang 2006; MacDuffie 1995; Park et al. 2003). In order to guarantee the basic aspects when building the scale, I have employed the following procedure (Hair et al. 1998): in the first place, the conceptual definition has been carried out in such a way that it fulfils the validity of its content. For the design of the initial questionnaire and the proposal of the items, I initially based the approach on a comprehensive review of the relevant literature and also by asking different academics and managers of MNEs to review the pilot questionnaire. Secondly, I carried out a reliability analysis based on Cronbach's α coefficients for each of the indicators. This led me to eliminate four of the items initially considered, resulting in a final tally of twenty items. Subsequently, the one-dimensional nature of the index was verified using a factor analysis of the principal components. As expected, a single factor was extracted with its own value that is higher than the unit, thereby demonstrating the one-dimensionality of the index.[13] Finally, the convergent validity of the index was verified by calculating its correlation with an item that the interviewee was asked to score on a scale of 1 to 5 (1 = worse; 5 = much worse): the competitiveness of the HRM system (To what extent would you say that the organizational system of the workplace and the human resource management of your PARENT company is "better or worse" than your competitors in the sense that it offers you a competitive advantage?). The Pearson correlation for these items and the HPWS Index of 0.708 corroborate the convergent validity. I therefore consider the measuring scale designed to be reliable and valid.[14]

---

13. With regards to the cases of application and their relevance, the correlation matrix shows that the total number of correlations is significant and that the value of their determinant factor is near to zero (0.102). Furthermore, Kaiser-Meyer-Olkin's measure of sampling adequacy as well as Bartlett's sphericity test, confirm the relevance of the application: the first with a value (0.849) that easily exceeds the minimum value that is usually fixed (0.50), and the second with a chi-square value that shows an excellent level of significance (0.000). The total variance shown is of almost 56 percent. The value is significantly less than the 60 percent regarded as indicative in the social sciences (Hair et al. 1998). However, the application of this analysis has only been carried out for the purpose of verifying the one-dimensionality of the index compiled and not in order to substitute the original values of their component parts.

14. The statistical procedures involved in the construction and verification of the reliability of the scale have been carried out on a sample of fifty-eight MNEs (both cooperative and non-cooperative) that make up the total number of MNEs analyzed in this study and whose characteristics will be described later.

According to this measurement, Basque cooperatives obtain an average of 6.24 points on the level of usage of HR "best practices" (table 9.1), which indicates that HR management styles in these cooperatives are, to a large extent, in line with the practices considered to be most efficient in the literature on the subject. This result complies with the information on this subject in the relevant literature (Morales 1998).

In order to find out if this outline confirms the specific nature attributed to cooperatives with regards to their competitiveness in terms of managing people, I provide below a comparative analysis of a group of noncooperative companies that nevertheless share the same characteristics.[15] This group comprises forty-seven companies. Consequently, there are a total of fifty-eight Spanish MNEs (eleven Basque cooperatives and forty-seven noncooperatives).[16] Since the size of the companies could affect the use of these practices, they are introduced as co-variable to the size;[17] furthermore, an ANCOVA analysis is carried out.[18] The results obtained (F = 11.983, Sig. = .001) show that, on average, Basque cooperatives make slightly more use of the HR practices that are considered to be the most efficient according to the literature (table 9.1). This result is consistent with that obtained in the research carried out by Jon Charterina, Eneka Albizu, and Jon Landeta (2007).

Table 9.1. Use of best practices in Basque cooperatives and noncooperatives

	HPWS Index	
	Average	Standard deviation
Basque cooperatives	6.24	0.55
Noncooperatives	5.29	0.85
Difference	0.95*	

Note: p < 0.01 (Levene's test: F = 1.825, Sig. = 0.182).

---

15. A multinational company from the industrial sector with more than one hundred employees and with at least one production plant abroad. In this case, I took companies from the Spanish state as a whole into consideration, given the scarcity of these kinds of noncooperative companies in the business culture of the CAPV/EAE.

16. The companies in the sample participated in a larger research program in which, among other things, the question of the influence that cultural-institutional contexts have on HRM strategies was considered. The sample used was composed of companies that meet the requirements set out in the previous note. See Lertxundi (2008).

17. Logarithm of the number of workers.

18. The relevant tests concerning the supposed normality of the data and the homogeneity of variances were carried out beforehand.

In relation to Basque cooperatives' attitudes to the *transfer/adaptation* binomial of their HR systems, in presenting the following questions I attempt to show—as as far as possible—how they face this strategic decision and the principles and general guidelines they follow when designing practices at a foreign plant. The relevance given to the different factors of national context, as well as their behavior and attitude in the face of this challenge, shows, to a certain extent, the international strategy that these cooperatives adopt in relation to the planning of HRM. To this end, the cooperatives were asked in the first instance to select those foreign plants that most resembled the parent company in terms of their size and dimensions in order to analyze the attitude of parent cooperatives with regards to the design of the HR system at these foreign plants. Five of these foreign plants were located in China, four in the Czech Republic, one in France, and another in Mexico.

The questions asked consider the key generic factors of national context that have the most influence on the configuration of HRM (Brewster and Hegeswich 1994). The questions included: the degree to which cultural (customs, social values, etc.), economic (salary costs, competitiveness, etc.), and political and legal factors (labor legislation, union power, etc.) played a role in decisions to apply or modify HRM. They also gauged how much of an attempt was to incorporate or extend Spanish workplace and HRM into foreign start-ups. Finally, respondents were asked to determine, on the Leikert scale (1 = nothing, 7 = totally agree), how much HRM should transfer Spanish cultural characteristics or adapt to local systems.

The results of the V1 variable show that, on average, the cooperatives interviewed consider the cultural values of the country in question to have had a significant influence on the design of the HR practices of their affiliate. More precisely, almost half state that these have had a total influence, while more than a quarter give a significant level of importance to these factors. In general, nine of the eleven cooperatives agree that the cultural framework is an element that has been considered in the configuration of the system. In fact, none of them believe that the national culture of the country is a variable that has had no influence or very little influence on the design of HR practices. Differences at a cultural level are considered very important when a decision needs to be taken to transfer the HRM system of the Spanish parent company or to adapt it to the local context. Some managers believe that cultural differences may play a critical role as they could hinder the direct implementation of certain practices or even their effectiveness, with the negative repercussions that this could have in terms of achieving the desired results. Workers' attitudes and their approach to work in general were, sometimes, not the same as those expected and this caused problems. Furthermore, these difficulties sometimes emerged in subsidiaries of countries supposedly close to the parent companies' own environments, as was the case in various affiliates in France and Argentina. To give an example, one manager commented that in Argentina one had to take things "very calmly" up to the point that "the company could be practically paralyzed due to a game of soccer"; something that would be unthinkable in the home environment of these companies. Furthermore, in some cases, feelings of resentment arose that were linked to the stereotypes of specific countries or geographical areas. To give an example, in the Czech Republic, the turnover of workers was worrying given that "there, labor stability does not have the same meaning as here" and therefore it was, to a certain extent, an inconvenience in the provisions, as one company's head of HR explained. Cultural differences also have to be seriously considered in the case of China, a country experiencing constant economic development that is very different culturally: "you had to learn a lot to be able to work well with them," since their conception of work is completely different to that of the parent company, according to the manager interviewed who worked as an expatriate for several years at the plant in China.

Responses concerning the economic characteristics of the country (V2) were not as conclusive as in the case of cultural features. Although almost half of the Basque cooperatives believe that this variable has an influence on the configuration of the HRM system at the subsidiary, four of them think that its impact has been scarce or even nonexistent. Neither was there any noticeable homogeneity with regards to where the affiliates were located. For example, in the case of China, the responses of those interviewed cover both extremes. In other words, there are those who suggest that economic circumstances have not had any impact at all on the configuration, but at the same time, there are others who place particular importance on its influence.

Responses concerning the legal-political framework (V3) suggest that, although it is a significantly relevant factor, it is not as significant as the cultural context. Specifically, five cooperatives claim to have taken it into account in the design of their practices, while three did not take it into account at all or only very slightly. With regards to where the affiliates are located, there does not appear to be any significant behavioral difference among countries.

It seems that the cooperatives' tendency to transfer (V4) is significant given that, except for one case, the rest state that their efforts to transmit their domestic systems was, on average, very important. Statements such as "we try to transmit the system but adapting it gradually," or "we try to export general policies but, obviously, we try to accommodate ways of carrying this out" are particularly illustrative. However, it was also stated that "we try to replicate the domestic criteria whenever local legislation allows," which suggests the strong will of the parent company to completely standardize practices throughout its foreign subsidiaries. Nevertheless, except in this case, in the rest an attempt was made to export the general way of working while trying to ensure at the same time that, in practice, the procedure or the most suitable method was adapted to fit the way of working and the customs of the country. To a certain extent, managers are conscious that when implementing the general principles of the parent company's HRM, which are assumed to be a strength and that tend to coincide with the principles accepted as important by the academic and business community, in practice and in specific sub-processes of the subsidiaries, it is important to take into consideration the cultural particularities of the national context of the affiliates in question.

As the results obtained in the first question (V1) demonstrate, cooperatives' attempts to adapt to the new cultural values (V5) where they establish themselves is very important. All of them, without exception, clearly reveal a willingness to adapt their way of managing people to the cultural particularities of the new contexts. Four of the cooperatives interviewed explain how they tried to adapt their system significantly to fit the new cultural context, while five consider the attempt to have been very important, and two indicate that they attempted to adapt it completely. In the light of these results, it seems that the strategy of adapting the HRM systems applied in the parent cooperative is the prevailing strategy. This result contrasts with the findings of the previous question. In that question, which discusses the intention to transfer, it seems that in general cooperatives tend toward the transfer of practices to the foreign subsidiary. However, answers to this latter question show that the actual effort they make to adapt to the new cultural context is highly significant. This apparent incongruence between both positions can be explained by the managers' answers themselves, which revealed different attitudes to policies or practices according to the question asked. This is consistent with some of the evidence offered by the literature on the subject. In the case of an intraorganizational transfer, it is typically argued that the results will

very likely differ in terms of the level of transfer according to their stand-
ing or level in the system (Björkman 2006). To be precise, some observers
contend that there is a tendency to transfer general policies and to adapt
practices (Becker and Gerhart 1996; Stroh and Caligiuri 1998). This idea
substantiates those studies that see different levels of abstraction in the
design of global HRM systems (McGaughey and De Cieri 1999; Pudelko
2006; Schuler, Dowling, and De Cieri 1993).

Cooperatives' opinions concerning the strategy they should theo-
retically follow in relation to different countries' cultures (V6) contrasts
with the actual behavior that is reflected in their responses to the previous
question. In general, cooperatives take the middle ground. To understand
the divergence that exists between actual behavior and what the cooperatives themselves believe to be the most desirable conduct, it is important
to take into account that exportation and adaptation strategies should not
be considered as two necessarily exclusive alternatives. The global arena
in which organizations operate is highly complex to the extent that it may
be an over simplification to try to delimit a global strategy to two radically
opposed alternatives. Indeed, some observers warn against this duality
(Brewster 2002; Kamoche 1996). It is precisely this complexity that should
form the basis of any interpretation of this apparent incoherence, as well
as the different levels of abstraction referred to above. The perception that
cooperative managers have of the efficiency of their HR system might
influence their attitude, thereby favoring its transfer to all other units. But
at the same time, the particular circumstances or the specific problems of
each case might force them to adapt their set of practices (even if these are
efficient in the Basque Country) to the customs, values, and work ethic
of the country in question. It seems that competitive practices, or those
often referred to as "best practices," can be found in the architecture of
the management system, to which one might add the many practices that
Jeffrey Pfeffer (1994) suggests belongs to this category, such as (among
others) development, communication, participation, rigorousness in the
selection of employees, or assessment and contingent payment (see also
Becker and Gerhart 1996; Boxall and Purcell 2003). Practices rooted in
cooperative principles, such as participation or contingent remuneration,
support this view that in theory their transfer may be the best option for
cooperatives from the perspective of their competitiveness while, at the
same time, their actual implementation may require them to be adapted
to the singularities of the particular context.

Subsequently, and in order to show if there are significant differences in attitudes to these variables between Basque cooperatives and other multinational companies, I carried out another ANCOVA analysis in which I included as a variable the level of autonomy held by the foreign site, given that this could influence the parent company's foreign strategy (Scullion and Starkey 2000).[19] In the light of the results (table 9.2), with a level of significance of 0.05, Basque cooperatives do not show significantly different attitudes in terms of the variables analyzed compared to the other multinational companies in the same sector.

Table 9.2. Behavior in the configuration of human resources practices in the foreign subsidiaries of Basque cooperative and noncooperatives

	Averages					
	V1	V2	V3	V4	V5	V6
Basque cooperatives	5.91	4.55	4.27	5.82	5.82	3.91
Noncooperatives	5.11	5.23	5.23	4.89	5.33	2.77
Difference	0.8	−0.69	−0.96	0.92	0.49	1.14
F	1.63	0.64	2.179	2.396	1.564	2.331
Levene (sig.)	0.44	0.2	0.11	0.25	0.22	0.54

Conclusions

In light of these results, it seems that HRM in Basque cooperatives adapts to a large extent to the characteristics marked out as "best practices" by the literature on the subject and, in this sense, one can conclude that their style of management is competitive. Furthermore, and bearing in mind the scope of this research, comparative analysis with noncooperative companies indicates that the use of these practices is slightly higher in Basque cooperatives, thereby confirming that they are marked by a certain specificity as has been suggested by the academic world as well as the cooperatives themselves. The competitive potential that the management systems of these kinds of organizations supposedly have makes them, to a certain extent, a reference point for companies in general.

---

19. It was measured on the basis of the question "What level of autonomy does this foreign plant enjoy compared to its Spanish parent company with regards to decisions concerning their operations in the local market?" based on a Likert scale of 7 points. A low score would indicate a global foreign strategy, while a high score would point toward a multi-domestic direction; a tendency toward local adaptation.

With regards to the attitude of Basque cooperatives when they consider the design of HR practices at foreign plants, the national context of these plants seems to play a significant role in their way of operating, particularly in terms of the cultural framework. This way of working is consistent with the permeability attributed to HRM in terms of the values, beliefs, and customs of the society in which it is applied. Although the general tendency is to try to transmit the HRM style of the Basque parent company, at the same time there is an attempt to adapt to the new context of the location. It therefore seems that while the principles and values upon which the predominant practices of cooperatives are based are considered to be highly competitive, they maintain a relatively open and flexible attitude and also try to adapt as far as possible to local particularities. The strategy they adopt appears to be based on the simultaneous conjunction of the transfer of their domestic practices together with the adaptation of particular aspects, linked to situational factors, that help to adapt them to the institutional and cultural framework (and especially the latter).

The fact that these practices, which are considered to be more efficient, are employed more intensively in cooperatives, could make attempts to transmit them to foreign plants even more intense, but, contrary to what may be expected, there are no indications of this. This would suggest that as well as the competitiveness of the domestic management system, there are also other variables that have an impact on organizational behavior in terms of the international HRM strategy and that play a decisive role in the case of cooperatives. Any future analysis that considers these variables will shed more light on this question.

Nevertheless, the previous conclusions should be understood within the framework in which the present study has been carried out. This research has certain limits, the most important of which is the reduced size of the sample. Although the sample is not small in proportion to the number of Basque cooperatives, working with a larger number would be more advantageous in order to increase the force of statistical interpretations. Yet working with a larger sample would also mean studying a group of cooperatives that would exceed the real existing number in the CAPV/EAE; in other words, it would go beyond the geographical limits set. Nevertheless, and taking into account the framework of the Spanish state, this would not in fact increase the current sample considerably given that most of the Spanish multinational cooperatives are located in the Basque Country. The criteria set, which establishes the need to have at least one production plant abroad in order to homogenize the basic characteristics of the parent plant and the subsidiary, considerably limited the target group and, consequently, the sample of the study. At the same time, however, I believe that this has contributed to improving the rigor of the analysis. The opening of new factories in other countries over the coming years will mitigate this limitation.

In the future, as a further development of this research, it would be interesting to combine the data on the transfer and adaptation of HRM practices of the parent company with an analysis of workers' satisfaction levels.

References

Adler, Nancy J. 1997. *International Dimensions of Organizational Behavior.* Boston: Kent.

Adler, Nancy, and Fariborz Ghadar. 1990. "Strategic Human Resource Management: A Global Perspective." In *Human Resource Management: An International Comparison*, edited by Rüdiger Pieper. Berlin: De Gruyter.

Agirre, Amaia. 2001. "Los principios cooperativos atractores de la gestión eficiente: Su medición: Aplicación al caso de Mondragón Corporación Cooperativa." *CIRIEC* 39: 93–113.

Appelbaum, Eileen, Thomas Bailey, Peter Berg, and Arne Kalleberg. 2000. *Manufacturing Advantage: Why High-Performance Work Systems Pay Off.* London: Cornell University Press.

Arthur, Jeffrey. 1994. "Effects of Human Resource Systems on Manufacturing Performance and Turnover." *Academy of Management Journal* 37, no. 3: 670–87.

Bae, Johnseok, Shyh-jer Chen, and John Lawler. 1998. "Variations in Human Resource Management in Asian Countries: MNC Home-country and Host-country Effects." *International Journal of Human Resource Management* 9, no. 4: 653–70.

Bae, Johnseok, and John Lawler. 2000. "Organizational and HRM Strategies in Korea: Impact on Firm Performance in an Emerging Economy." *Academy of Management Journal* 43, no. 3: 502–17.

Bae, Johnseok, and Chris Rowley. 2001. "The Impact of Globalization on HRM: The Case of South Korea." *Journal of World Business* 36, no.4: 402–28.

Barney, Jay B., and Patrick M. Wright. 1998. "On Becoming a Strategic Partner: The Role of Human Resources in Gaining Competitive Advantage." *Human Resource Management* 37, no. 1: 31–46.

Becker, Brian E., and Barry Gerhart. 1996. "The Impact of Human Resource Management on Organizational Performance: Progress and Prospects." *Academy of Management Journal* 39, no. 4: 779–801.

Becker, Brian E., Mark A. Huselid, Peter Pickus, and Michael F. Spratt. 1997. "HR as a Source of Shareholder Value: Research and Recommendations." *Human Resource Management*, 36, no. 1: 39–47.

Becker, Brian E., and Mark A. Huselid. 1998. "High Performance Work Systems and Firm Performance: A Synthesis of Research and Managerial Implications." *Research in Personnel and Human Resources Management* 16: 53–101.

Björkman, Ingmar. 2006. "International Human Resource Management Research and Institutional Theory." In *Handbook of Research in International Human Resource Management*, edited by Gunter Stahl and Ingmar Björkman. Cheltenham, UK: Edward Elgar.

Boselie, Paul, Jaap Paauwe, and Paul Jansen. 2001. "Human Resource Management and Performance: Lessons from the Netherlands." *International Journal of Human Resource Management* 12, no. 7: 1107–25.

Boxall, Peter, and John Purcell. 2003. *Strategy and Human Resource Management*. Basingstoke, UK: Palgrave MacMillan.

Brewster, Chris. 2002. "Human Resource Practices in Multinational Companies." In *The Blackwell Handbook of Cross-Cultural Management*, edited by Martin Gannon and Karen Newman. Oxford: Blackwell.

Brewster, Chris, and Ariane Hegewisch. 1994. *Policy and Practice in European Human Resource Management: The Price Waterhouse Cranfield Survey*. London: Routledge.

Chang, Eunmi. 2006. "Individual Pay for Performance and Commitment HR Practices in South Korea." *Journal of World Business* 41, no. 4: 368–81.

Charterina, Jon, Eneka Albizu, and Jon Landeta. 2007. "The Quality of Management in Basque Companies: Differences Existing between Cooperative and Non-cooperative Companies." In *Cooperative Firms in Global Markets: Incidence, Viability and Economic Performance*, edited by Sonja Novkovic and Vania Sena. Vol. 10 of *Advances in*

Economic Analysis of Participatory and Labor-Managed Firms. London and Amsterdam: Elsevier JAI.

Child, John. 2002. "Theorizing about Organization Cross-nationally: Part 2 – Towards a Synthesis." In *Managing Across Cultures: Issues and Perspectives,* edited by Malcolm Warner and Pat Joynt. London: Thompson.

Delaney, John T., and Mark Huselid. 1996. "The Impact of Human Resource Management Practices on Perceptions of Organizational Performance." *Academy of Management Journal* 39, no. 4: 949–69.

Delery, John E., and Harold D. Doty. 1996. "Modes of Theorizing in Strategic Human Resource Management: Tests of Universalistic, Contingency and Configurational Performance Predictions." *Academy of Management Journal* 39, no. 4: 802–35.

Dickmann, Michael. 2003. "Implementing German HRM Abroad: Desired, Feasible, Successful?" *International Journal of Human Resource Management* 14, no. 2: 265–83.

DiMaggio, Paul, and Walter Powell. 1983. "The Iron Cage Revisited: Institutional Isomorphism and Collective Rationality in Organizational Fields." *American Sociological Review* 48: 147–60.

Evans, Paul, and Peter Lorange. 1989. "The Two Logics behind Human Resource Management." In *Human Resource Management in International Firms: Change, Globalization Innovation,* edited by Paul Evans, Yves Doz, and André Laurent. London: MacMillan.

Gamble, Jos. 2003. "Transferring Human Resource Practices from the United Kingdom to China: The Limits and Potential for Convergence." *The International Journal of Human Resource Management* 14, no. 3: 369–87.

García-Gutiérrez, Carlos. 1994. "La concentración económico-empresarial de sociedades cooperativas." In *Las empresas públicas sociales y cooperativas en la nueva Europa: XIX Congreso Internacional CIRIEC.* Valencia: CIRIEC.

Gardner, Timothy M., Lisa M. Moynihan, Hyeon Jeong Park, and Patrick M. Wright. 2001. "Beginning to Unlock the Black Box in the HR Firm Performance Relationship: The Impact of HR Practices on Employee Attitudes and Employee Outcomes." *Working Paper Series of the Center for Advanced Human Resource Studies* (CAHRS), Cornell University, Working Paper 01-12.

Gómez-Mejía, Luis. R., and Leslie E. Palich. 1997. "Cultural Diversity and the Performance of Multinational Firms." *Journal of International Business Studies* 28, no. 2: 309–35.

Gómez-Mejía, Luis. R., David B. Balkin, and Robert Cardy. 1998. *Human Resources: A Managerial Perspective.* Englewood Cliffs, NJ: Prentice-Hall.

Gooderham, Paul N., and Odd Nordhaug. 2003. *International Management: Cross-boundary Challenges.* Oxford: Blackwell.

Greif, Avner. 1994. "Cultural Beliefs and Organization Society: A Historical and Theoretical Reflection on Collectivist and Individualist Societies." *Journal of Political Economy* 102, no. 5: 912–50.

Guest, David. 1997. "Human Resource Management and Performance: A Review and Research Agenda." *International Journal of Human Resource Management* 8, no. 3: 263–76.

Guthrie, James P. 2001. "High-involvement Work Practices, Turnover, and Productivity: Evidence from New Zealand." *Academy of Management Journal* 44, no. 1: 180–90.

Guthrie, James P., Patrick C. Flood, Wenchuan Liu, and Sarah MacCurtain. 2009. "High Performance Work Systems in Ireland: Human Resource and Organizational Outcomes." *International Journal of Human Resource Management* 20, no. 1: 112–25.

Hair, Joseph, Rolph E. Anderson, Ronald L. Tatham, and William Black. 1998. *Multivariate Data Analysis.* 5th ed. Upper Saddle River, NJ: Prentice Hall.

Hofstede, Geert. 1984. *Culture´s Consequences: International Differences in Work-related Values.* Beverly Hills, CA: Sage.

———. 1998. "Think Locally, Act Globally: Cultural Constraints in Personnel Management." Paper presented at the *Sixth Conference on International Human Resource Management.* June 22–25, University of Paderborn, Germany.

House, Robert, Paul J. Hanges, Mansour Javidan, Peter W. Dorfman, and Vipin Gupta. 2004. *Culture, Leadership, and Organizations: The GLOBE Study of 62 Societies.* Thousand Oaks, CA: Sage.

Huselid, Mark A. 1995. "The Impact of Human Resource Management Practices on Turnover, Productivity, and Corporate Financial Performance." *Academy of Management Journal* 38, no. 3: 635–72.

Ichniowski, Casey, Kathryn Shaw, and Giovanna Prennushi. 1997. "The Effects of Human Resource Management Practices on Productivity:

A Study of Steel Finishing Lines." *The American Economic Review* 87, no. 3: 291–313.

Kamoche, Ken. 1996. "The Integration-Differentiation Puzzle: A Resource-Capability Perspective in International Human Resource Management." *International Journal of Human Resource Management* 7, no.1: 230–44.

Khilji, Shaista E. 2003. "To Adapt or Not to Adapt, Exploring the Role of National Culture in HRM – A Study of Pakistan." *International Journal of Cross Cultural Management* 3, no.1: 109–32.

Laurent, André. 1986. "The Cross-cultural Puzzle of International Human Resource Management." *Human Resource Management* 25, no.1: 91–102.

Lertxundi, Aitziber. 2008. "La influencia de los Sistemas de Trabajo de Alto Rendimiento y del entorno cultural en la estrategia de Dirección Internacional de Recursos Humanos." PhD Diss. University of the Basque Country.

MacDuffie, John Paul. 1995. "Human Resource Bundles and Manufacturing Performance: Organizational Logic and Flexible Production Systems in the World Auto Industry." *Industrial and Labor Relations Review* 48, no. 2: 197–221.

McGaughney, Sara, and Helen De Cieri. 1999. "Reassessment of Convergence and Divergence Dynamics: Implications for International HRM." *The International Journal of Human Resource Management* 10, no. 2: 235–50.

Mead, Richard. 1998. *International Management: Cross Cultural Dimensions.* Oxford: Blackwell.

Meyer, John W., and Brian Rowan. 1977. "Institutionalized Organizations: Formal Structure as Myth and Ceremony." *American Journal of Sociology* 83, no. 2: 340–63.

Milliman, John, Mary Ann Von Glinow, and Maria Nathan. 1991. "Organizational Life Cycles and Strategic International Human Resource Management in Multinational Companies: Implications for Congruence Theory." *Academy of Management Review* 16, no. 2: 318–39.

Morales, Alfonso Carlos. 1998. *Competencias y valores en las empresas de trabajo asociado.* Valencia: CIRIEC-España.

Myloni, Barbara, Ann-Wil Harzing, and Hafiz Mirza. 2004. "Human Resource Management in Greece: Have the Colours of Culture

Faded Away?" *International Journal of Cross Cultural Management* 4, no.1: 59–76.

Newman, Karen, and Stanley Nollen. 1996. "Culture and Congruence: The Fit between Management Practices and National Culture." *Journal of International Business Studies* 27, no. 4: 753–79.

Park, Hyeon Jeong, Hitoshi Mitsuhashi, Carl F. Fey, and Ingmar Björkman. 2003. "The Effect of Human Resource Management Practices on Japanese MNC Subsidiary Performance: A Partial Mediating Model." *International Journal of Human Resource Management* 14, no. 8: 1391–1406.

Peck, Sharon R. 1994. "Exploring the Link between Organizational Strategy and the Employment Relationship: The Role of Human Resources Policies." *Journal of Management Studies* 31, no. 5: 715–36.

Pfeffer, Jeffrey. 1994. *Competitive Advantage through People: Unleashing the Power of the Work Force.* Boston: Harvard Business School Press.

Pudelko, Markus. 2006. "A Comparison of the HRM Systems in the USA, Japan and Germany in their Socio-economic Context." *Human Resource Management Journal* 16, no. 2: 123–53.

Rosenzweig, Philip M., and Nitin Nohria. 1994. "Influences on HRM Practices in Multinational Corporations." *Journal of International Business Studies* 25, no. 2: 229–51.

Schuler, Randall, Peter J. Dowling, and Helen De Cieri. 1993. "An Integrative Framework of Strategic International Human Resource Management." *International Journal of Human Resource Management* 4, no. 4: 717–64.

Schuler, Randall, and Nikolai Rogovsky. 1998. "Understanding Compensation Practice Variations across Firms: The Impact of National Culture." *Journal of International Business Studies* 29, no. 1: 159–77.

Schwartz, Shalom H. 1994. "Beyond Individualism/Collectivism: New Cultural Dimensions of Values." In *Individualism and Collectivism: Theory, Method and Applications*, edited by Uichol Kim, Harri C. Triandis, Cigdom Kagitçibasi, San-Chin Choi, and Gene Yoon. Thousand Oaks, CA: Sage.

Scott, W. Richard. 1995. *Institutions and Organizations.* Thousand Oaks, CA: Sage.

Scullion, Hugh, and Ken Starkey. 2000. "In Search of the Changing Role of the Corporate Human Resource Function in the International

Firm." *The International Journal of Human Resource Management* 11, no. 6: 1061–81.

Stroh, Linda, and Paula Caligiuri. 1998. "Strategic Human Resources: A New Source for Competitive Advantage in the Global Arena." *International Journal of Human Resource Management* 9, no. 1: 1–17.

Tayeb, Monir H. 1998. "Transfer of HRM Practices Across Cultures: An American Company in Scotland." *International Journal of Human Resource Management* 9, no. 2: 332–58.

———. 2005. *International Human Resource Management: A Multinational Company Perspective.* Oxford: Oxford University Press.

Taylor, Sully, Schon Beechler, and Nancy Napier. 1996. "Toward an Integrative Model of Strategic International Human Resource Management." *Academy of Management Review* 21, no. 4: 959–85.

Trompenaars, Fons. 1994. *Riding the Waves of Culture: Understanding Cultural Diversity in Business.* London: Nicholas Brealey.

Walton, Richard. 1985. "From Control to Commitment in the Workplace." *Harvard Business Review* 63, no. 2: 77–84.

Way, Sean A. 2002. "High Performance Work Systems and Intermediate Indicators of Firm Performance within the US Small Business Sector." *Journal of Management* 28, no. 6: 765–85.

Westney, Eleanor. 1993. "Institutionalization Theory and the Multinational Corporation." In *Organization Theory and the Multinational Corporation,* edited by Sumantra Ghoshal and Eleanor Westney. London: MacMillan Press.

Wright, Patrick M., Dennis L. Smart, and Gary McMahan. 1995. "Matches between Human Resources and Strategy among NCAA Basketball Teams." *Academy of Management Journal* 38, no. 4: 1052–74.

Youndt, Mark A., Scott A. Snell, James W. Dean Jr., and David P. Lepak. 1996. "Human Resource Management, Manufacturing Strategy and Firm Performance." *Academy of Management Journal* 39, no. 4: 836–66.

Yuen, Edith C., and Hui Tak Kee. 1993. "Headquarters, Host-culture and Organizational Influences on HRM Policies and Practices." *Management International Review* 33, no. 4: 361–80.

10

Globalization and Knowledge Management in the Industrial Cooperatives of the Mondragon Corporation

ANTXON MENDIZÁBAL

Translated by Jennifer Martin

The new technologies in microelectronics and biotechnology derived from current globalization have shaped the knowledge society. In a sense, knowledge redesigns and transforms the classical concept of capital. Knowledge management becomes a strategic and central axis here for the durability and development of current production processes.

Thus, in the new business literature, knowledge management appears as a system that articulates and drives ideas, strategic thinking, teamwork, shared experience, and new values.

In its strictest sense, the primary aim of knowledge management is to manage outside knowledge. It is also a matter of developing intercommunication among different companies and among various departments within each company. Finally, it also aims to achieve an organization that is capable of improving teamwork procedures.

In its broadest sense, it is important to consider those transformations and variables that structure knowledge management today in the face of the vagaries of globalization. This applies to the whole business world in general as well as to industrial cooperatives in particular. This is even more the case when these businesses are pioneers in introducing many socio-organizational changes into the Spanish state.

This is the objective of the present study. It essentially presents the results of an empirical observation of knowledge management and transformations in Basque industrial cooperatives.[1] I will, therefore, refer to transformations in labor organization, flexibility, customer-focused business, the new management system, a sense of ownership, the business innovation system, the local productive system, new business values, and the business internationalization processes.

Since these transformations are not specific to Basque industrial cooperatives, I will analyze them in the light of the changes in industrialized societies as a whole.

The Scientific Management of Labor: Traditional Knowledge Management

It is commonly agreed that the scientific management of labor explicitly reflected knowledge management in industrialized societies up until the mid-1970s. For this reason, I take this to be a necessary analytical reference. Indeed, the scientific management of labor continues to reposition us today, combined with the new systems of participation, and still shapes the new socio-productive organization model.

In the early twentieth century, Taylorism divided up the labor process and established the bases for the scientific management of labor,[2] thereby eliminating the artisan's control over his working environment and his union negotiating capacity. Taylorism eliminated the downtime that was found inside of a workstation by dividing up the artisan's labor process.

Fordism, in turn, and on the same basis established by Taylorism, eliminated downtime in the workstation, established the assembly line, and socialized the rate of output through its external imposition. Fordism mechanized the Taylorist system by including technological devel-

---

1. The interviews carried out with the general manager of the Ulma Group and the former manager of Maier, Mr. Arrillaga, have provided valuable information on the leading experiences of these two cooperatives; they make up a considerable portion of the developments discussed here. They were supplemented with technical staff interviews and interviews of partners with social responsibilities. The interviews and observations made in the Irizar cooperative complement the empirical basis of this work. As a whole, it is an empirical study based on practical and contextualized observations with the support of a general bibliography.

2. Division of the jobs, management and implementation duties, manual labor, and intellectual labor.

opments within its management system.[3] Thus, the myth of the neutral nature of technology in production processes was once again destroyed. [4]

In this reference to the basic modalities of the scientific management of labor, one should also mention an organizational system that carried this division of labor to its quintessential form: the famous MTM (methods-time management). This system analyzed every movement a worker might make during any production activity, established a system of predetermined times (based on the scientific management of labor), and encoded them into a collection of universal application cards for any type of activity. MTM was then applied in new production facilities and in new production processes, tracking workers' "micro movements" and specifying a precise time for their completion.[5]

Taylorism, Fordism, and MTM made up what essentially came to be called the scientific management of labor, unequivocally reflecting the knowledge management historically established in industrialized societies. The industrial cooperativism of the Mondragon Corporation has never been an exception to this matter and adopted a production management method that contradicted the self-management model for which it claimed responsibility.

In fact, this traditional knowledge management boosted a way of operating in which a few people think, others decide, and the vast majority is limited to carrying out the ideas and decisions of the initial few. Consistent with the logic of the time, the quality of the thinking minority defined economic and technological efficiency, as well as the placement of their respective states in the international market. Consequently, those states with a brilliant thinking minority enjoyed an advanced technological system and efficient production processes. In those states or places where "the thinking minority did not perform well," technological delay together with economic and job instability were the norm. This was, for

---

3. Fordism introduced a new system of accumulation in which productivity gains were distributed regularly between workers and the company. In turn, it established a new regulation method that institutionalized labor unions and brought collective agreements into general use.

4. Fordism introduced its management systems in the design of new machines.

5. The tables (of movement and distance) were produced through a sampling of five thousand workers, controlled by video as well as by specialized personnel. MTM found that any movement that a worker might make in any production activity systematized into twelve basic movements: in turn, each of these subdivided into another one hundred micro movements. Universally valid tables based on a system of predetermined times, breaking down the work into small, basic movements was thus produced.

example, the different ideological representation held for countries such as Germany (in the former case) and Spain (in the latter).

Here, mention should also be made of the knowledge management model implemented in Sweden. In this model, the 1976 Swedish participation law regulated the presence of workers' representatives in companies' different economic and technological procedures. In accordance with this participation law, Swedish companies were obligated to negotiate the social and labor repercussions of their workers' productive investment. This way, increasing productivity was always based on negotiations with workers, and this led to better security, skills, and job conditions. From 1976 to the present, workers in the most efficient Swedish companies have been informed and consulted on the technical and economic aspects of business strategy and planning. These technical relations have served to shape a specific knowledge management model for Sweden in the same time period.

New Technologies: Changes in Work Organization

The introduction of new technologies derived from the microelectronic revolution (new materials, numerically controlled machines, flexible assembly systems, "transfer lines," the industrial robot, programmable controllers, telematics systems, management systems performed by computers, and so on) in production processes transformed those production processes and the management systems. These new technologies allowed small-series and sophisticated production, progressively transforming the structure of the most dynamic demand sectors.

In turn, Taylorist work organization (based on individualized workstations) was progressively transformed, assuming a new structured management based on working groups.[6] The Mondragon Corporation was a pioneer in the application of these new management models. Since the second half of the 1990s, most of its production has come from a system based on "work teams."

We therefore find ourselves in the face of a new reality. The use of production potential driven by new technologies demands the development of "intangible capital." In other words, some aspects of this intangi-

---

6. Traditional Taylorist work organization was based on the relationship between worker and workstation. The new technologies modified this management system by imposing a new relationship between groups of workers and groups of machines.

ble capital such as motivation, initiative, creativity, skills, training, and in particular, identification with the business project, have acquired strategic importance.

Within the logic of capital interests, all of this has rendered obsolete the figure of the worker previously associated with the scientific management of labor. This figure essentially lacked initiative, did not identify with the business project, and was devoid of skills and motivation. Instead, the new situation demands the involvement of human intelligence in the production process and, consequently, a new status and prominent role for workers in a company's knowledge management. In other words, the use of production potential made possible by new technologies has led to a transformation in the socio-technical relationship in the productive process, demanding a new distribution of power within the company.

It should be noted that this redistribution of power has resulted in important consequences for industrial cooperatives, insofar as it touches upon industrial democracy and further develops self-management. Generally, the major challenge of capital in these new circumstances is precisely how to implement a redistribution of corporate power that preserves the historic control of capital over the whole work process, while at the same time bestowing control of particular socio-technical areas to the workers. This concern about capital has also been evident among the technocratic elite of the Mondragon Corporation's industrial business cooperatives.

In both systems, variety in work organization and in knowledge management systems is established in practice, contradictorily supporting a human relations strategy and systems based on the scientific management of labor.[7]

In any case, we are generally witness to the progressive development of the participation strategy in comanagement experiences, quality circles, group technology, and participatory management by objectives, which demands a new cohesion with the business project and a new involvement of human intelligence in the production process, more in line with the potential of the new technological paradigm.

---

7. Here we have the fundamental contradiction of the modern enterprise: on one hand, establishing a human relations strategy that boosts workers' motivation and skills, while on the other hand, maintaining traditional work organization systems that are demotivating and deskilling.

As a consequence of technological advances[8] and class struggles,[9] labor legislation has been consolidated differently according to the particular states that have institutionalized the workers' participation within companies. This includes European Union (EU) labor laws that regulate workers' participatory rights on supervisory boards and on administration boards of different businesses.[10]

Consequently, countries like Sweden, Norway, Germany, Holland, France, and Luxembourg have by law institutionalized workers' participation in business management. This has not been the case in the Spanish state, although the new situation has encouraged Mondragon Corporation policies that promote and boost worker participation.

In general, the modern expression of this present-day reality is called Toyotism. Shaped by specific historical and cultural reasons, Japanese Toyotism established a system of work organization based on flexible production, socio-professional multitasking, job rotation, worker communication, and corporate cohesion that progressively and irreversibly marginalized traditional Taylorism and Fordism in the most dynamic areas of the production process.[11]

Flexibility

The new technologies associated with the microelectronic revolution allow the structure of work processes to be modified, changing all the equipment in short periods of time and diversifying production. In this way, the large standardized series of the Fordist time period progressively became smaller and more sophisticated series that meet the more specific demands of the customer.

---

8. Together with the implementation of new technologies, we are also witnessing the development of participation-based management systems everywhere.

9. Although divided in their positions on self-management and co-determination, labor unions have always looked favorably on workers' control. This workers' control defends workers' rights to information about the company's socioeconomic evolution and their consultative and negotiating authority on those business decisions that would affect their skills and socio-labor conditions.

10. Mention should be made of the Vredeling proposal (after Henk Vredeling) in the EU context, which introduced the right of workers to be informed and consulted on investment and management decisions within multinational businesses.

11. Toyotism eliminated downtime in the whole manufacturing process. It also introduced flexibility in production through "just-in-time," which requires the manufacturing of the appropriate product at the right moment—all of this on the basis of a management system established on working groups and quality self-control.

We can see, then, a trend to increase flexibility in manufacturing workshops in order to be able to better diversify products. Here, the old production system based on large factories designed in order to reduce unit costs in large series manufacturing has been replaced by the construction of flexible workshops manufacturing small series, with electronic controls that allow the programming of rapid changes in both product range and production times.

This production flexibility system is known as "just-in-time." It calls for the production of the product required by the customer and no other at the opportune moment and not any other. The merger of this productive flexibility with the new computer and communication systems created three significant consequences in most of the Mondragon Corporation's industrial cooperatives and in the running of modern business in general.[12]

The first consequence has been a tendency to progressively increase the information intensity in the production of goods and services. This involves the construction of factories that use computer-aided manufacturing techniques and the replacement of certain products for services. The second consequence has been a new information design that affects the whole enterprise, integrating all of the business activities. Here, thanks to computing, a new business can merge designing, producing, marketing, and coordinating activities in a network where all the elements are interrelated on the basis of an influx of multidirectional information. The third consequence has been a trend to internationalize the information system itself through the consolidation of an "Intranet" system that coordinates the communication of a set of internationalized company activities.

Productive flexibility, then, rests increasingly on a dynamic process of "total quality" that integrates suppliers, workers, technicians, and customers in their own interactive system of production and knowledge management.

Ownership

A sense of ownership has become a decisive instrument for socio-productive involvement and for workers to identify with the business project. New

---

12. The new characteristics of modern business are: increased information intensity in manufacturing; increased production flexibility; and the systematic integration of all business activities.

business management works to advance this sense of ownership by organizing the company into internal "mini companies."

In the Mondragon Corporation's industrial cooperatives, this sense
of ownership was developed in new "worker-member" relations characteristic of these companies. In fact, the worker-owners of these companies
naturally acquired this sense of ownership, due to their condition as such.
Nevertheless, organizational changes that further boosted this sense of
ownership have also been made in these companies.

In order to establish mini companies, a preliminary analysis is made
of the "value chain" (delivery and ordering processes, manufacturing process of something concrete, and so on) that identifies the key processes on
which the mini companies are created.

The first structuring of mini companies is based on the product-client
relationship, in which attention is paid to the process from the start of the
raw material being formed up until the moment the product is delivered
to the final customer. Generally speaking, the structuring of productivity
in mini companies depends on the floor layout to better handle production flow, since production efficiency depends in large part on this flow.

The second method of organizing mini companies concentrates on
a fraction of the production process. These are mini companies inside
of complex productive structures, and that operate with the concept of
internal customer and internal supplier. Within this new context, the
mini company in question has to know precisely who their suppliers and
clients are. And regulating these relationships is tremendously important
for their success.

In general, the ideal size varies between fifteen and forty people. The
staff could be increased if there were shifts, so if there were twenty people in each mini company's shift and there were three shifts, up to sixty
people could be involved. These mini companies must determine their
components, their physical spaces, and their floor layout, paying attention
in each case to the respective flow of information and production. The
operational framework of each mini company defines the relationship
of customer-supplier, with appropriate quality guarantees, cost, delivery
times, safety, and so on.

Management of these mini companies is different for each organizational experience, but they generally establish their own operating income
account and integrate their own engineering and sales department services. These mini companies establish a form of management and knowl-

edge production supported by groups of workers who are very closely linked with the business activity, which stimulates a sense of ownership.

The New Management System

The new business management system shapes many aspects of today's knowledge management. Modern business tries to shape a new management system by means of the so-called "core knowledge." In the Mondragon Corporation's industrial cooperatives this core knowledge concerns matters related to communication, the social framework, strategic planning, audits, the information system, and the customer-market area. "Forums" are set up around each one of these knowledge cores with people from different businesses, and all this represents a key dynamic for a broad sense of knowledge management.

An intensive internal training process in questions of continuous improvement takes place in these industrial cooperatives for the components of these forums. Training is also developed on the basic concepts of continuous improvement for three management areas: deployment of objectives, process management, and the daily management of mini companies. This training process thus leads to a "common language" among all forum participants regarding new business issues (the mini companies, standard work procedures, and so forth).

Along with all this, a universal model—the European Foundation for Quality Management or EFQM model—was established in 1989 that involves the whole company.[13] The model's goal is to achieve "excellence," which is defined as having a shared vision, systematic action or a systematic approach, and a common language. Finally, a quality system has also been developed based on teamwork that had enormous potential.

The acceptance of a charter of values by all has been the fundamental step forward. Reflection on the new style of management has been systematized in such a way in these industrial cooperatives that it serves as a reference for each business or mini company. The process begins with a reflection group in which a significant part of the staff takes part in discussing what changes needed to be made in order to improve management. After comments are made, the manager or the leader responsible

---

13. Quality model and quality systems are two different things. The quality model sets out what must be done, and the quality system establishes guidelines on how to do this or the best way to do it.

for guiding and coordinating the discussion takes note of the comments that he/she considers the most appropriate.[14]

Later, the necessary steps for proceeding and transforming these reflections into action are discussed. At the end of the process these reflections are systematized, ideas documented, and values formulated for a new style of management. In this way, a charter of internalized and agreed upon values is established that becomes the backbone of the new management system.[15]

Three different themes are basically addressed in these new styles of management. In the first place, the company as an entity in a permanent state of unstable equilibrium is considered. The aim is to bring a "non-alarmist" concern to the whole group about the company being subject to numerous problems and the fact that it needs to address these problems.[16]

In contrast to this consideration that causes concern for the company's uneven stability, there are two other important considerations that do provide some balance. On one hand, the notion that all people are considered capable of generating value is promoted. While on the other, the concept of the participatory system as creating a greater competitive edge is encouraged. A series of guideline values has been implemented on the basis of these three concepts to help each business or mini company later develop their objectives.

However, the application of this new management system raises difficulties. Specifically, the socio-productive involvement of human intelligence and the collective identification of the company's objectives do not always take root. Empirical experience shows that if a sufficient critical mass does not exist at the corporate management level and is not achieved thereafter at the workers' collective level, such a strategy is impossible.

Successful experiences in this field suggest that a critical mass at the corporate management level must be rather high (always higher than 50 percent), while a lower critical mass at the worker's collective level (always higher than 20 percent) would still make an important implementation process feasible.

---

14. Nevertheless, it must pointed out that it is normally a "manager" who takes the notes and selects the thoughts and comments that he/she believes to be the most appropriate.

15. For example: trust in co-workers, priority given to customer satisfaction, participatory management by objectives, and so on.

16. It should be remembered that if we begin to analyze the lifespan of a business, few exist longer than twenty or thirty years. And almost all of them go through critical situations.

Customer-Focused Company

Transformations in flexibility and work organization clarify the new character of the industrial cooperatives. Now, "customer-focused companies" incorporate the new management model, the improvement groups, and the mini companies.

The new management system is the essence of new knowledge management, and mini companies are the more flexible and appropriate structures for the involvement of human intelligence in productive processes. Since I have already discussed the new management model and the mini companies, I will now move on to these "improvement groups."

These are groups of people that manage knowledge or, in effect, the real players or "subjects" of knowledge management. They meet to deal with certain issues or with the aim of finding a solution to particular problems, and they can come from several different mini companies. It is clear that beyond the limits of the Mondragon Corporation's industrial cooperatives, the changes mentioned thus far really do clarify the new character of the modern company.

They may come in the form of an improvement group for a particular function. If a problem should emerge while making a part, if information arrives badly, or the productive process is interrupted, this type of problem is solved appropriately by the precise functional improvement group. The improvement group ceases to exist after solving the problem. There can also be project improvement groups (for the construction of a new plant for example). These groups always have a more strategic intent and therefore they are likely to be more permanent in nature. There are also improvement groups that seek to change work processes. These improvement groups that transform "the way to do" work processes more specifically manage internal company knowledge. They are the genuine improvement systems of any company.

The "Business" System of Innovation

Another standard in business knowledge management is its innovation system. The first source of business innovation consists of acquiring existing innovation from outside of the company. Here, innovation emerges from a technological and/or organizational leap that takes place outside and that affects processes within companies. This requires a connection with the sociological and technical business environment in order to gain admission to the dynamic of external trade shows, new machines, and new patents.

Another decisive source of business innovation is not exactly innovation in its own right, but rather the application of innovation. Effective innovation application occurs as the result of organizational changes, in such a way that use of the same innovation might have substantially distinct results for two different companies depending on the application system implemented.[17]

Generally speaking, such innovation application takes two distinct forms: The first is "continuous improvement." This might be understood as the "sum of a many small parts" or the result of many small improvements that often go noticed. This is the most common kind of innovation application within the Mondragon Corporation's industrial cooperatives. The second kind of application may be termed "engineering." In other words, this implies thinking about the whole process and business strategy, and then introducing (via technological innovations) "qualitative leaps" in the process.[18] It is the lesser-used application of the two, although still a qualitative feature of these cooperatives.

A third innovation source stems from a collaboration with the customer's project; in other words, jointly participating with the customer in the development of the product. This new approach is used when companies seek a partnership with clients in their projects. This is a feature of the pre-production rather than the production phase; in other words, in the product development phase of a client. This is very common, for example, in the automotive industry.

The principle aim here of the innovative core is to develop partnerships with automobile companies during the development phase of vehicles. This means of innovation allows the innovative core to join in the design and joint development of a structured vehicle, with value added and significantly higher commercial margins. This in turn encourages a technologically active approach that progressively incorporates new activities and transforms the company in question into a privileged supplier, assuring the client of its value.

This third source of innovation is widely promoted in the Mondragon Corporation's industrial cooperatives. Many technological centers here,

---

17. With respect to the current stock maturity process, the difference can be enormous.
18. The case of the Irizar cooperative was a significant benchmark in this respect.

to some degree at least, are the result of this corporate policy. One particular example of just such a cooperative within the Mondragon Corporation is the Maier Technology Center in the Comunidad Autónoma del País Vasco-Euskal Autonomia Erkidegoa (CAPV/EAE, Autonomous Community of the Basque Country).

The Local Production System

This refers to the integration of a company into its local innovative system. It represents a territorial entity that combines a sociocultural reality, production specialization, certain professional skills and a human capital system, a specific set of institutions, a fixed technological network, and a specific system of teaching. Specifically, the company in question integrates and joins these various bodies into its own production system, thereby boosting the distinct synergies and economies of scale originated by this process.

The local production system represents a knowledge management system through "shared knowledge." Research and innovation are the knowledge supply sources. Shared knowledge becomes the principle development factor in such regions and the principle source of business competitiveness.

Endogenous efforts are made by companies in order to make a qualitative strides with regard to research, from relying on policies of being "technology followers" to designing their own innovation policies that allow them to compete in international markets. Just as important as "knowledge creation" is "knowledge circulation," from which innovation application may result.

This process is especially necessary for small and medium-sized enterprises (SMEs).Their size makes such endogenous development difficult on their own, so they are forced them to develop shared collaboration strategies. This cooperation network in research seeks to coordinate company projects with universities and technology centers, creating a "knowledge circle" where ideas and people can circulate.

The local production system is thus transformed itself into an innovation pole that shares space, infrastructures, and people, recasting itself into an essential instrument for business development. In this way, a company's smaller size is compensated for by the aptitude of important knowledge managing and promoting entities that join the company in innovation and technological development.

Currently, the unidirectional relationship between science, technology, and business has evolved into a circulation network where alliances to generate innovation are made. Thus, a vital factor for strengthening the productive structure of a territory is the network between companies, research centers, and universities that guarantees the continuous innovation of products and processes and the creation of new businesses.

In its strictest sense, the local production system is commonly identified with "scientific parks." These scientific parks or innovation centers were designed to provide a link between science, technology, and business development. Universities and business are closely associated here, sharing physical spaces and establishing innovative networking and mutual collaboration systems.

The recently created Garaia Innovation Center is an attempt to boost and develop the innovative potential of the cooperative group's territorial grid. This technological and scientific park's goal is to create a hub of excellence to permit the strengthening of long-term research within the framework of technological innovation, and coordinating Mondragon Unibertsitatea (MU, Mondragon University) with technological centers and R&D departments within the Mondragon Corporation's companies.

Its main objectives are to strengthen the creation of skilled jobs, monitor new businesses, and diversify the economic fabric. This center promotes R&D projects in sectors such as energy, materials technology, business and management, business organization and administration, electronics, microelectronics, nanotechnology, and machines.

The United States was a pioneer in developing such hubs (for example, Silicon Valley, the Research Triangle Park, and Massachusetts-128/ M.I.T.), and the idea later expanded throughout Europe, Southeast Asia, and Australia. Now, all over the world there are renowned sites such as the Manchester Science Park, the Oxford Science Park, the United Kingdom Science Park Association, Kazusa Academia Park, the Kyoto Research Park, and others.[19]

---

19. There are more than twenty scientific parks in Sweden around the country's most prestigious universities, such as the Mijärdevi Science Park and Kista Science Tower. Although somewhat delayed by comparison, this process has also led to the creation of similar parks in the Spanish state: several technology parks in the Basque Country, the Scientific Park of Catalonia, the Andalusia Technology Park, the Boecillo Technology Park in Valladolid, and so forth.

Internationalization

It is evident that global differences in salaries and social and labor practices have become a condition of business accumulation in the globalized world today. In other words, we are witnessing the spread of business internationalization processes.[20] It is therefore necessary to conclude this reflection on knowledge management in modern business by addressing the distribution of this cognitive management within internationalized companies.

Put another way, there is the issue of to what extent the knowledge management implemented in the parent company is reproduced in the production plants of the periphery. In particular, to what extent is this cognitive management reproduced in those business establishments located in the third world? The empirical experience shows us that the transfer of skills according to companies or regions varies, depending on the policy of the parent company.

- Some of the Mondragon Corporation's industrial cooperatives have internationalized their cognitive system through a retraining system based on direct internships with the parent company.[21]
- Other companies (the majority within the Mondragon Corporation) have instead merely established a salary reduction policy along with the work and knowledge management systems based on Taylorism and Neo-Taylorism.
- As a whole, however, we might speak of a gradual distribution of international cognitive labor marked by a gradual approach to the transfer of skills according to company or region.

Along with the internationalization process, new information technologies allow for the realization of new communication systems that affect the internationalized companies as a whole. This creates an internal telematics network that communicates directly with the different production plants according to new efficacy and global profitability criteria.

---

20. With seven corporate delegations and sixty-one production subsidiaries in 2008, only a third of the workers in the Mondragon Corporation had the status of cooperative members.

21. The Gipuzkoan cooperative, Irizar, is also a significant benchmark in respect to this transfer of "skills" policy.

Conclusions

Based on my study of knowledge management methods in the Basque cooperatives of the Mondragon Corporation, I would conclude the following:

In line with the changes in management and industrial policy that more advanced companies have implemented, the Mondragon Cooperative Group replaced the old Taylorist management system (in which one person was responsible for one task and/or one workstation) with a new relationship in which groups of workers look after one area of activity. In this way, computer-aided group technology has been developed that is particularly adaptive at batch manufacturing and applicable for design as well as for production. Each member of the team is therefore obliged to develop his/her multi-skilling productive abilities. As in other technologically advanced companies, a work organization system has thus been established based on flexible production, socio-professional multi-skilling, job rotation, worker communication, and corporate cohesion.

A key element of the new socio-business structure has been the implementation of a new organization based on mini companies. Its aim was to deepen the sense of belonging and ownership that the cooperative companies, unlike public limited companies, subscribed to. These mini companies are based on the product-client relationship, in which special attention is paid to the process from the start of the raw material being formed up until the end product is delivered to the final customer.

Together with the implementation of new technologies, we have witnessed the development of participation-based management systems everywhere. This required a new cohesion with the business project and a new involvement of human intelligence in the production process, and is more in line with the potential of the new technological paradigm. The Mondragon Corporation's strategic project consequently introduced the new management system based on teamwork, the creation of "knowledge cores," the use of these cores as "forums for discussion" on specific issues, and the implementation of an intensive internal training process for continuous improvement in three areas of management: objectives deployment, process management, and the daily management of mini companies.

Along with all this, a "universal" quality model (the EFQM) was applied that involves the whole corporation. This universal quality model implies the involvement of all agents that participate in the economic process of product and process improvement. The aim is to develop a quality model based on teamwork in which "excellence" is identified with having a shared vision, a systematic approach, and a common language.

The acceptance of a charter of values by all was the fundamental step forward. Reflection on the new style of management has thus been systematized in such a way in these new cooperatives that it has served as a reference for each business or mini company. In this way, a charter of internalized and agreed upon values has been established that became the backbone of the new management system. A series of guideline values was also introduced so that each business or mini company could later develop them.

A new company focused on the customer has been stablished that integrates the new management model, the improvement groups, and the mini companies. A fundamental element in the application of this business model in the cooperative group is the creation of "improvement groups." These are groups of people that manage knowledge. They meet to deal with a certain issue or with the aim of finding a solution to a particular problem, and they might come from several different mini companies. They may be established as an improvement group for a particular function, to complete a project, or to change work processes.

The innovation systems of the Mondragon Group's cooperatives moved on from the phase of innovation acquisition outside of the company to extending "continuous improvement" and "re-engineering" systems in innovation application. Nevertheless, the most dynamic cooperatives have developed an innovation policy based on collaboration with the client's project; in other words, they jointly participate with the client in product development. In turn, this allows the development of a technologically active approach and requires integrating a system of technology centers that allow these companies to apply their own policies.

The Mondragon Cooperative Group has developed a local production system with the "Garaia Project." Its objective is to strengthen the production structure of the area where the cooperatives are concentrated by means of a network linking companies, research centers, and universities. This guarantees product and process innovation and the creation of new companies. Thus, the Garaia project has been transformed into an innovation center that shares space, infrastructures, and people, recasting itself into an essential instrument for business development.

In this era of globalization we are witnessing the diffusion of corporate internationalization processes and the Mondragon Cooperative Group is immersed in this process. The question arises of knowing to what extent the knowledge management implemented in the parent company is reproduced in the peripheral production plants. Empirical evidence regarding the cooperative group shows us that the transfer of skills according to companies or regions varies, depending on the policy of the parent company. Thus, some of the Mondragon Corporation's industrial cooperatives internationalized their cognitive system through a retraining system based on direct internships with the parent company. Other companies (the majority within the corporation) have instead merely established a salary reduction policy along with the work and knowledge management systems based on Taylorism and Neo-Taylorism.

References

Aglietta, Michel. 1999. "Des mutations du capitalisme: ¿Une societé saláriale schizophrène?" *La Revue de la CFDT* 17 (February): 14–23.

Bueno Eduardo. "Los parques científicos y tecnológicos en la sociedad del conocimiento." At www.madrimasd.org/revista/revista6/transferencia/transferencias3.asp.

Chesnais, François. 2001. "'La nouvelle économie': Une conjoncture propre a la puissance hégémonique dans le cadre de la mondialisation du capital." In *¿Une nouvelle phase du capitalisme?* by François Chenais, Gérard Duménil, Dominique Lévy, and Immanuel Wallerstein. Collection Séminaire marxiste. Paris: Éditions Syllepse.

Davis, Louis E. 1971. "The Coming Crisis for Production Management: Technology and Organisation." *International Journal of Production Research* 9, no. 1: 65–82.

Duménil, Gérard, and Dominique Lèvy. 1998. "Rapports de production et structure de classe du capitalisme: 150 ans après." *Cahiers Marxistes* 210: 131–61.

Escorsa Castells, Pere. 2001. "De la vigilancia tecnológica a la inteligencia competitiva de las empresas." At www.uoc.edu/web/esp/art/uoc/escorsa0202/escorsa0202_imp.html.

Feldman, Maryann P. 2002. "La revolución de Internet y la geografía de la innovación." *Revista Internacional de Ciencias Sociales* 171 (March). At www.oei.es/salactsi/feldman.pdf.

Fosfuri, Andrea. 2001. "Mercados tecnológicos: Evidencia empírica e implicaciones económicas y empresariales." *Revista de Economía Industrial* 339: 105–16.

Foulon, Sandrine. 2000. "La net-economie chamboule le monde du travail." *Liaisons Sociales* 16 (November): 20–33.

Foulon, Sandrine, and Valérie Devillechabrolle. 2000. "Les perdants de l'entreprise light." *Liaisons Sociales* 12 (May): 16–30.

Greenspan, Alan. "Technological Innovation and the US economy." *BIS Review* 31 (April): 1–4.

Lam, Alice. 2002. "Los modelos societales alternativos de aprendizaje e innovación en la economía del conocimiento." *Revista Internacional de Ciencias Sociales* 171 (March). At www.oei.es/salactsi/lam.pdf.

Lorino, Philippe. 1988. "Les systèmes socio-économiques: Une nouvelle micro-économie." *Problèmes Economiques* 2073 (May): 3–11.

Mendizábal, Antxon. 2001. "Mutaciones tecnológicas y nuevo orden social en la empresa moderna." Paper presented at the *V Congreso Vasco de Sociología*, March 1–2, Bilbao, Spain.

———. 2002. "Nueva economía y procesos de acumulación." Paper presented at the *IV Reunión de Economía Mundial*, April 25–26, A Coruña, Spain.

Mendizábal, Antxon, and Antón Borja. 2000. "Nuevos sistemas organizacionales y democracia económica en la empresa." In *Sobre la democracia económica*, edited by Armando Fernández Steinko and Daniel Lacalle. Vol. 2. Barcelona: El Viejo Topo.

Molero, José. 2002. "La internacionalización de la innovación tecnológica." Madrid 9. At www.madrimasd.org/revista/revista9/tribuna/tribunas3.asp.

Nadler, Richard. 1999. "The Rise of Worker Capitalism." *Cato Institute Policy Analysis*, no. 359 (November 1). At www.cato.org/pubs/pas/pa359.pdf.

Petit, Pascal. 1999. "Les aleas de la croissance dans une economie fondee sur le savoir." CEPREMAP Working Papers. At www.cepremap.ens.fr/depot/couv_orange/co9909.pdf.

Steinmueller, W. Edward. 2002. "Las economías basadas en el conocimiento y las tecnologías de la información y de la comunicación." *Revista Internacional de Ciencias Sociales* 171. At www.economicasunp.edu.ar/episteme21/Epistemologia_digital/Unidad_IV/Steinmueller_W. Edward Las_economias_basadas_en_el_conocimiento_y_las_tecnologias_de_la_informacion_y_la_comunicacion.pdf.

Index

Page references followed by *t* and *f* indicate tables and figures, respectively. Page numbers followed by n indicate footnotes.

List of Contributors

For full biographical information about the contributors, links to their projects, and more, visit www.basque.unr.edu/currentresearch/contributors.

Eneka Albizu
Baleren Bakaikoa Azurmendi
Imanol Basterretxea Markaida
Antón Borja Alvarez
Javier Cerrato Allende
Victoria de Elizagarate Gutierrez
Sara Fernández de Bobadilla Güemez
Aitziber Lertxundi
Antxon Mendizábal
Fernando Molina
Jon Morandeira Arca
Eva Velasco Balmaseda
Itziar Villafañez Pérez
Miguel Ángel Zubiaurre Artola

Made in the USA
Charleston, SC
14 October 2012